UP YOUR BUSINESS!

UP YOUR BUSINESS!

7 Steps to Fix, Build, or Stretch Your Organization

Second Edition, Revised and Expanded

Dave Anderson

FOREWORD BY JOHN C. MAXWELL

John Wiley & Sons, Inc.

Contents

CONTENTS

Foreword

I realized Dave Anderson was a communicator the first time I heard him speak at a meeting for my nonprofit organization, EQUIP. He immediately connected with the audience as he talked about his experience leading a $300 million retail organization. Dave has a down-to-earth, no-nonsense approach to getting the job done, which made the ideas he shared that day refreshing and effective. In fact, it was my confidence in Dave's abilities that prompted me to produce a video series with him to adapt my book *The 17 Indisputable Laws of Teamwork* to a specific corporate sector.

Dave now brings that same talent for communicating real-world, "walk-the-talk" strategies to *Up Your Business!* He presents his ideas and principles in a clear and to-the-point way, and provides hundreds of easy-to-adapt strategies you can use to fix, build, or stretch your organization. It doesn't matter if your organization is large or small; these principles can help a leader at any organizational level.

As the head of three organizations, I can relate to the emphasis *Up Your Business!* places on getting the right people on your team. Without the right people to implement vision and strategy, vision and strategy become useless. In this book, Dave not only shows the importance of people, he spells out specifically what you must do to find them, develop them, and retain them. He'll also sell you on the necessity of ridding yourself of the wrong people quickly, professionally, and humanely.

Perhaps the most significant aspect of *Up Your Business!* is that it ignores fads and quick fixes, opting instead to provide timeless leadership and management principles that work when they are applied. As you join Dave in the quest to fix, build, or stretch your organization, I can assure you that you're in good hands. Open your mind, get out your legal pad, and prepare to take action. My best wishes are with you as you begin to set the stage for your best year ever.

—John C. Maxwell
Founder
The INJOY Group

Preface

Up Your Business! is written for leaders or aspiring leaders at all levels in an organization. Regardless of whether your goal is to fix, build, or stretch your organization, the principles herein will help you. They apply equally to the CEO of a Fortune 500 company and to the home-based-business owner wanting to take his or her enterprise to a higher level. The strategies are presented in a step-by-step sequence and in easy-to-understand terms, and are ready for immediate application. You will be able to use the book as a blueprint to fix, build, or stretch your business. I've included numerous real-life examples that support the book's key points. You'll find the style nonacademic and politically incorrect. In fact, I'd rather offend you by being direct than affront you with fluff. I believe you'll find the lack of sugarcoating and rationalizing refreshing.

Up Your Business! eschews fads and the latest business buzzwords. It offers sound, tried-in-the-trenches leadership and management principles that work if you work them. The chapters proceed in blueprint fashion.

Chapter 1, "Always Remember, 'It's the People, Stupid!'" leaves no doubt that without the right people your vision and strategy are worthless. But it doesn't leave you there. It provides numerous tips on recruiting and interviewing the right people as well as strategies for removing the wrong ones.

Chapter 2, "Abolish Corporate Welfare: Create a Culture of Merit," defines the difference between a culture of entitlement and one of merit and teaches you how to develop the latter. It explains how to produce a positive pressure to perform and how to differentiate your best people so you leverage the organization's strengths.

Chapter 3, "Develop Your Human Capital: How to Train, Coach, Mentor, and Retain Eagles," provides step-by-step instructions on how to develop the right people once you get them. Training, coaching, and mentoring are covered extensively, and after reading this chapter you'll have the tools you need to retain and develop the eagles you bring on board.

Chapter 4, "It's All Right to Aim High if You Have Plenty of Ammo," presents a case for thinking bigger and going for unreasonable gains. After all, if you've brought the right people on board, removed the wrong ones, created the right environment, and are training the great people you've assembled you've earned the right to swing for the fences rather than bunting your way through business.

Chapter 5, "Look in the Mirror: Executing Your Leadership Twelve-Pack," explains why you, as a leader, must look in the mirror and take responsibility for your organization's vitality. It provides a Leadership Twelve-Pack: a list of nonnegotiable tasks you are responsible for executing day in and day out in order to fix, build, or stretch your organization.

Chapter 6, "Survive Success: How to Overcome the Six Temptations of Successful Organizations," explains how to survive success. There are six temptations of successful organizations that cause you to plateau or lose ground. This section creates great awareness of these temptations and offers remedies to overcome them.

Chapter 7, "Build Long-Term Vitality: Steps for Execution and Follow-Through," is the most important in the book because it lays out how you must take what you've learned and implement it. Knowing what to do is not enough — you have to *do* it. This chapter provides step-by-step change principles that guide you to get the job done.

Chapter 8, "Close the Gap between Knowing and Doing!" is a new chapter that reinforces and expands on the principles in Chapter 7 and provides new strategies and inspiration to help you to become more committed to changing your organization and leading it to a higher level by taking the right and consistent action necessary to optimize your results.

At the conclusion of each of the first seven chapters I have added a "Further Up Your Business" section that will isolate a key strategy in the chapter and provide you more insight and support in your efforts to implement the information presented. Throughout the book I intersperse the text with "Up Your Business! Bullets." These short strategies will help refine your thinking on the points being made in a chapter and provide motivation for action.

I believe we are living in unforgiving times for business and its leaders. There is less margin for error than in the past. This should excite you, because I am confident that *Up Your Business!* will lead you to create an unlevel playing field, angled substantially to your advantage. As you compete in times that are both challenging and pregnant with possibility, my belief is that as you execute the strategies in these eight chapters you will earn more than your fair share of the market — and that you will, in fact, dominate it.

Author's Note

I'm excited about the revised edition of *Up Your Business!* Much has changed since I wrote the first edition of this book. At that time, I sounded an alarm that political correctness in society and complacency in business were diminishing corporate cultures at an accelerated rate of destruction and planting the seeds for the rapid descent of many enterprises. I also provided hands-on tools to fix, build, or stretch your organization and rise above the demise that would affect so many. Some listened the first time around. Many more did not. For the readers who perused the first edition and have chosen to invest your time and dollars in the revised work, you won't be disappointed. First, I think you'll be surprised how much you missed the first time through the book and will be delighted with the "Further Up Your Business" sections I've placed at the conclusion of each chapter that expand on the original strategies. You'll also enjoy the new closing chapter and will probably wish it had been there for you the first time you went through *Up Your Business!* Oh well, better late than never.

First-time readers will get the benefit of a full dosage of *Up Your Business!* strategies the first time through. Although the first group will have a head start on you in implementing many of the ideas in this book, with commitment and discipline you can be up to speed in no time. And make no mistake about it: Moving fast with these strategies will be essential to your very business survival. I'm trying to be an alarmist, so please stay with me here and consider the following:

The clock is ticking but many business leaders can't hear it. The sound of their own boasts, slaps on the back, and soliloquies of celebration have drowned it out. Business has been good for a while now. Yes, people still whine about a weak economy, but they need to get a grip, gain some perspective, and understand the difference between a down economy and a bad one. Many of us have gotten so spoiled we can't remember what a truly bad economy is: 21 percent interest rates, 13.5 percent inflation, 7 percent unemployment, and the like. Some of you remember those numbers, but many leaders today can't imagine them because they never led through such times. In fact, anyone who has been in a leadership position for under a dozen years has never had to lead through sustained down economic times, and if you've been in leadership for less than twenty-five years you've never had to function through the economic disaster on a national scale found during the Carter presidency or its immediate aftermath.

You may think the good times will last forever. Perhaps with the success you've enjoyed you've even made the error of mistaking a bull market for brains. You may be tempted to use the great years you've had as a license to stay the same — write it down, build the manual, and document the formula. If so, you'll also be authoring your own business obituary.

Just as it did on Cinderella's enchanted night, the clock will strike midnight for many of you. Business still travels in cycles, and so do economies. A day of reckoning will come — probably not suddenly but gradually, so as to catch many of the unaware napping. The time to prepare for "midnight" is before the bottom falls out.

You have two choices after reading the strategies in this book: You can dismiss them as being too dramatic, negative, or irrelevant. Or you can decide to return to the basic disciplines they espouse that will fuel your business to greater success in good or bad times. To help you make the right choice, I should remind you that choosing to live in denial concerning business cycles and embracing the "we'll never see another poor day" mantra of manure is a catalyst to a future of longing for yesteryear and boring your friends with pathetic reminiscences about the good old days and the big one that got away.

Few people would deny that the points presented in the upcoming pages would improve one's enterprise substantially and quickly. Thus, the only question is *when* you should get serious about putting them to work. You can either fix the roof while the sun is shining or wait for it to leak and cave in. Choose well.

Introduction

The world has become too politically correct, and quite frankly, it's sickening. The "rationalize, sugarcoat, and don't offend" mind-set of society has carried over into business and is perverting the performance-based psyche you must have to fix, build, or stretch your organization. Business leaders are not facing the tough issues. They're seeking harmony over truth, and it's creating a morass of mediocrity. Everywhere you look you see that marginal and moronic business leaders and philosophies have reached critical mass.

Business is simple. Not easy; simple. (Intellectuals try to complicate it.) It still boils down to having the right people in the right places doing the right things. You can read books on strategy and attend courses on corporate vision, but the fact is that without getting the right people on your team, nothing else you do will matter. Your vision is worthless, strategy impotent, and values corrupt without the right people to execute them. And just as important as getting the right people is getting rid of the wrong ones. Keep these losers around and they'll dilute the effectiveness of your great players and pollute your culture. Too many managers are leadership wimps. They won't make the tough calls on poor performers and allow these slugs to continually break momentum, sap morale, and diminish the managers as leaders.

Once you have the right people and get rid of the wrong ones, your job is just beginning, because you must develop the talented people in your charge. If you don't, you'll lose them — and you'll be getting what you deserve.

The good news is that once you have the right people and are continually upgrading their capacities, you can stop thinking incrementally and begin swinging for the fences. The foundation you build gives you the right to be unrealistic and go for more than you would ordinarily think is reasonable.

This book is written from real-world experience in the business trenches and not from the viewpoint of an academic or a researcher. I've had my nose bloodied at the front lines of one of the most competitive businesses in the world — the automotive retail industry — and have made every mistake a leader can commit: hired the wrong people, kept them too long, let the potential of my best people rot on the vine, failed at developing vision, created impotent strategies . . . the list goes on. In my first management jobs I was arrogant, acted more like a cop than coach, and didn't know the first thing about leadership even though I was in a leadership position. In fact, if I could find the first group of people I ever managed, I'd apologize and beg forgiveness. I suspect many of these people were in therapy for years after their stint as my subordinates. The good news is that my mistakes turned out to be great investments because I learned from them and developed strategies that helped me lead some of the most successful businesses in my field and today help clients around the world apply those same ideals. The catalyst for turning around my business career was when I stopped looking out the window for answers and started looking in the mirror. Once I realized that it was my inside decisions and not outside conditions that determined my success, I started focusing ferociously on what I could control. I'm grateful for the opportunity to share these strategies with you in *Up Your Business!* I know how hard you work, the challenges you face, and the decisions you agonize over. I understand what it's like to feel overwhelmed with problems — the challenge of finding and developing great people, and the consternation at having fired the wrong ones, especially if they've been loyal or are your friends.

I'm pulling for you. But I'm not going to let you off the hook with a bunch of Pollyanna happy hot-tub talk. I'll give you effective strategies, presented in simple and direct talk, that you can apply immediately. The only catch is that while they're simple, they're still hard work. But it's even harder work to do things the wrong way, to push the wrong people to do the right things, or to do more of the work yourself because you have the wrong people on board. Don't even think about reading this book without a highlighter, because there is help on every page. Turn *Up Your Business!* into your personal textbook for fixing, building, or stretching your organization. You will find three themes in this book:

1. I focus on the rule, not the exception. Too many leaders exhaust themselves looking for the latter.
2. There are nonnegotiable recurring themes throughout the book: looking in the mirror, leading from the front, dealing quickly with poor performers, pursuing personal growth, and

developing a team. I don't mind saying things twelve different ways if one of them gets through and helps you.

3. I don't expect you to agree with all the strategies presented in
    Up Your Business! However, I do expect you to keep an open
    mind and give them a chance.

Enough talk. Let's get to work.

UP YOUR BUSINESS!

CHAPTER 1

Always Remember, "It's the People, Stupid!"

During the 1992 presidential election campaign, Bill Clinton's inner circle decided that the troubled economy was the theme their candidate would hammer to win the White House. Whenever a Clinton staffer invested time, energy, or resources strategizing or articulating foreign policy, world trade, or environmental issues, a cohort would bluntly chastise him with the words, "It's the economy, stupid." This not-so-gentle reminder became a mantra that created laserlike focus and steered the campaign to victory.

FIRST THINGS FIRST

Leaders wanting to fix, build, or stretch their organizations must employ the same tenacious resolve and embrace the business version of this mantra — "It's the people, stupid" — as the catalyst of measurable and sustainable growth. All organizations have goals,

1

and most have strategies. Both, however, are irrelevant if the right people aren't in place to execute them. In fact, a great dream with the wrong team is a nightmare because bold goals pursued by mediocre people still result in mediocre results. Grand plans designed at off-site meetings and facilitated by costly experts are rendered impotent when employed by the marginal, mediocre, or moronic. Most organizations suffer from a reality gap. The chasm between the leader's forecast and the realities of his people's abilities renders their goals unrealistic from day one.

Up Your Business! Bullet	**If your dream is bigger than your team, you've got to give up the dream or grow up the team.**

Business leaders have no control over weather, the economy, interest rates, or competitors' actions; yet pondering or worrying about these issues often consumes much of their day. What a leader *can* control is who joins or leaves the team and how to develop those on board. Unfortunately, most leaders make poor use of this liberty. To fix, build, or stretch an organization, a leader must exercise one of leadership's greatest privileges proactively and aggressively: deciding whom to keep and whom to lose.

Dave Maxwell, after being hired to turn around Fannie Mae in 1981, related how the mortgage giant was losing $1 million per day and had nearly $60 billion in mortgage loans underwater.[1] Naturally, the board was anxious and, when they met with Maxwell, they asked him about his vision and strategy for the company. Maxwell replied that asking where the company was going and how it would get there was the wrong first question; that before he made the journey his first order of business was to get the wrong people off the bus and the right people on the bus and to make sure the right people were sitting in the right seats. Then, he replied, they could focus all their energy on taking the bus somewhere great.

Soon after the board meeting, Maxwell met with his twenty-six key executives and laid it on the line.[2] He told them the trip ahead was going to be difficult, that there would be major changes and tough decisions to make, and that people would be stretched and held accountable — but that for those who endeavored, the rewards would be great. He also told them that if they didn't think they could stomach the ride nobody would hate them if they left.[3] Confronted with this challenge, fourteen of the twenty-six executives voluntarily exited the bus.[4] The good news was that those who remained were totally committed, and Maxwell filled the vacant slots with some of the brightest minds in the finance business. Now he and his team were ready to take the bus on a ride to unprecedented heights. And what a ride it was. During Maxwell's reign, the same company that had lost $1 million per day was making $4 million per day and beating the general stock market returns 3.8 to 1 between 1984 and 1999.[5] Maxwell retired while still at the top of his game, and the dream team he had attracted and developed drove the bus to equally impressive peaks. With focused discipline, Maxwell corrected the board's errant focus on vision and strategy, fixed his organization, and showed the world, "It's the people, stupid."

GET PROACTIVE: GO FROM HUNTED TO HUNTER

I sometimes wish I could find the man who gave me my first shot at management and apologize. I'd beg forgiveness for all the wrong people I hired who abused our resources, lowered team morale, and consistently broke our momentum. Don't get me wrong; I did have a recruiting, interviewing, and hiring strategy. In fact, I can describe it in one word: reactive. My strategy was to wait until we were shorthanded, run a worthless ad, and hire someone I liked with little regard to whether the person could do the job required.

Fortunately, I've learned a thing or two about building a team since then. In fact, I can sum up my current team-building strategy in four words: hire slow, fire fast. Leaders must be more proactive and deliberate in selecting employees. If you want great people you'd better be prepared to go find them yourself. You must go from waiting to be hunted to being a hunter. At the same time, you must remove poor performers more quickly. Both these concepts will be presented in detail throughout this chapter.

Unfortunately, much as I used to do, most managers don't re-cruit, interview, or hire until they're desperate. Soon, pressured by time and the need for coverage, they begin settling too early, too cheaply. Before long, however, they realize that a bird in the hand is not better than two in the bush if it's the wrong bird. (If you haven't read the book *Hire with Your Head*, by Lou Adler [Wiley, 1998], get it. In addition, go to Lou's web site, www.powerhiring.com, where you'll find one of the most valuable resources available to reinforce and coach you in the strategies for building a team.) Then, when managers realize they do have the wrong person, they cross their fingers, give a half-dozen second chances, and fail while trying to fix the unfixable for far too long.

Up Your Business! Bullet	**As desperation rises, standards fall.**

Personally, I can't think of a better way for a leader to invest his or her time than in finding great people for the team. In fact, you have a choice of either investing time doing this or spending your time pushing the wrong people to do the right thing. Or, even worse, doing more of the work yourself because you have the wrong people. Since it's going to take plenty of work regardless of which path you choose, it's advisable to work in a manner that makes your future less frustrating and more productive. To build a team of eagles, you'll have to get past one of the most pervasive cop-outs in business: "There's a shortage of talented people where I live." I deliver approximately 150 speeches or training presentations annually, and it doesn't matter whether I'm in Manhattan, in Brunswick, Georgia, or in Devils Lake, North Dakota; every time I speak to managers I hear this whimper. Everyone likes to think their situation is unique, that finding good people is an impossible task reserved especially for them. I hate to be the one to kick the crutch out from under you but here is the fact: There is no shortage of talented people in any market area. The Creator didn't suddenly stop churning out talented people. It's just that the most talented people already have jobs! They're not perusing the want ads or knocking on your door with hat in hand. I don't say these next couple of sentences to be condescending or sarcastic, but your best job candidates are not the unemployed. I understand there are exceptions — focus on the rule. Some of these people have waited for their thirty-nine weeks of unemployment benefits to expire and are reentering the marketplace reluctantly and with a chip on their shoulders.

This begs the question: What is your strategy for attracting passive job candidates into your workplace? You know, the happy, productive people getting the job done for someone else? In the following pages, I describe six strategies to up your people and your business.

CREATE AN EAGLE ENVIRONMENT

The best performers expect differentiation. They won't work where they are treated like average or bottom performers. They want to have more input, schedule flexibility, stretch assignments, fewer rules, increased discretion, and pay based on performance (not tenure, experience, or credentials) — and, most important, a great leader to work with.

What is your *Eagle Value Proposition* (EVP) to attract top performers? If a 9 on a scale of 1 to 10 walked in to apply today, what is your compelling EVP that sets you apart from the competition? If you can't be specific or impressive here, you have work to do, because eagles are attracted to mountaintops, not to landfills. Landfill environments are those with marginal expectations, equal rewards and support for top and bottom performers alike, burdensome rules, abusive schedules, and poor leadership. Landfills don't attract eagles. They attract rats, roaches, pigeons, and buzzards. We'll delve deeper into differentiation in Chapter 3. For now, suffice it to say that if you expect to attract more eagles or develop and retain the ones you have, you'll need to build an environment where they can flourish. This also means you'll need to eliminate from your workplace environment demotivators that break the spirit and momentum of your best people. Here's a partial list of the offenders — what we'll call "Landfill Symptoms":

- Too many rules
- Poor training procedures
- Lack of feedback on performance
- Lack of differentiation for rewards between top and bottom performers
- Lack of stretch assignments and meaningful work
- Promotions based on tenure and experience rather than results
- Weak leaders
- Tolerance of poor performers
- Too many or unproductive meetings

- Nepotism
- No room to grow
- Rigid scheduling
- Unclear vision, mission, and core values

You must pay constant attention to this list. Keep weeding out these motivational land mines because just about the time you get things the way you want, one of them resurfaces. Unless and until you make the workplace environment your number one recruiting tool, eagles will keep flying over your landfill. On the other hand, life gets good when eagles come looking for you. It takes a while for word to get around, but if you build it — an eagle environment — they will come.

| Up Your Business! Bullet | **Eagles and turkeys don't eat the same food.** |

MAKE RECRUITING EVERYONE'S RESPONSIBILITY

Think about the last time a great salesperson blew you away with polish and professionalism. Or how about that special occasion when a dynamic waitperson made your night out memorable with personality and service. You can probably still picture these people, and chances are you've told others about the experience. Did you try to recruit these people? If not, why? Normally, the managers who would never think of adding these people to their talent pipelines are the first to lament that there are no talented people where they live. To take this a step further, think of how many people currently working in your company have had similar experiences and missed the opportunity to recruit. The prime reason no one recruits star performers like these is lack of awareness. Recruiting is never talked about,

7

valued, rewarded, or encouraged. And until it is, you'll continue to let golden opportunities slip away. If you're going to up your business, you've got to make recruiting everyone's responsibility. To go from hunted to hunter, give your best people Eagle Calling Cards they can put in the hands of superior performers everywhere they find them. An Eagle Calling Card is the size of a business card. Use the following example as a template to adapt to your own organization.

Front of card:

Congratulations!
I noticed your great service today! We're always looking for eagles to join our team. Call me, Dave Anderson, at 650-867-9000 to discuss the opportunity in total confidence!

Reverse side of card:

Flexible scheduling! Top Gun Club for top performers! Our average employee made $60,000 last year! Full health and life insurance! Generous 401K! Paid vacations! Sign-on bonuses! Great initial and ongoing training! Promotions based on performance, not tenure! You'll be surrounded with winners driven by a vision to be the best!

Another strategy that creates awareness of the importance of building a talent pipeline is to pay recruitment bonuses. Pay a meaningful bonus — at least $500 to any employee who refers an employee you hire. Pay it on the spot. Don't wait six months to make sure the person works out. If you don't think they're going to be there in six months you shouldn't be hiring them in the first place. Besides, the idea is to find reasons to pay the bonus so employees are encouraged to bring in referrals, not to attach strings to make it tougher for them to collect. Even if you pay some bonuses where the people hired don't work out, the long-term benefits of higher morale within the person referring the candidate, increased awareness of recruitment overall, and the occasional breakthrough hire you'll reap are well worth the dollars invested. Anyway, when you calculate how much you waste with conventional hiring methods through want ads or otherwise, the bonus you pay is a bargain.

Up Your Business! Bullet	**The only way you can hire eagles is if you talk to eagles.**

Turn Your Web Site into a Recruitment Post

If your web site isn't already a compelling recruitment post you're blowing it! Every day you have passive job candidates using your site. They're not looking for work; they're looking into your goods and services. Many of these people are successful and productive for another employer. This is your chance to plant a seed, intrigue them, and recruit them — and once the initial web design is complete, it won't cost you a dime! The majority of web sites waste this recruitment occasion with a mundane "Employment Opportunities" icon. Once you click on it you are greeted with a laundry list

9

of job openings and are invited to call or e-mail for more information. To say this approach is weak and uninspiring would be kind.
If you're going to attract eagles in this decade you had better kick
your online hiring campaign into high gear. Here are five strategies
to up your chances of snagging a passive eagle candidate.

1. Use an oversized "Join Our Team of Eagles!" icon and ditch
   the formal and boring "Employment Opportunities."
2. Once candidates enter the "Join Our Team of Eagles" area of
   your site they should be met with employee testimonials from
   your happiest workers:

   > "I've worked at Saga Communications for ten years
   > and absolutely love it! We have ongoing training,
   > special rewards for top performers, great core val-
   > ues, a dynamic leadership team, generous pay and
   > benefits, and I belong to a supercharged team of
   > winners!"
   >
   > — *Dave Anderson*
   > *Sales Manager*
   > *danderson@saga.com*

3. List compelling job descriptions. Try this one on for size:

   > "Sales Opportunity: We're looking for high-octane
   > winners to join our team of sales eagles. You'll get
   > the best training in the business and the support of
   > a super team. The ideal candidate will be able to
   > manage his or her own business-within-a-business,
   > hit our high standards, and grow fast with our com-
   > pany. We understand that a compensation package
   > needs to be very aggressive to continue to build our
   > team of eagles. Apply online on this page and we'll

10

be in touch soon to arrange a meeting of our minds. All replies held in strict confidence."

4. Allow candidates to submit a short (five-line) online application. The shorter it is, the more likely they are to fill it out. Primarily, you want to gather contact information to follow up with and conduct a phone interview. A choice of brackets for desired income is also useful for determining candidates' state of mind. The application should go straight to the general manager or head of Human Resources. Once you receive the application, respond immediately!

5. Use your advertising media to drive candidates to your web site to apply. For instance, your billboards, newspaper ads, radio spots, and other avenues should include the phrase "Join Our Team of Eagles! Apply online at www.saga.com." You should also have signs on your premises encouraging people to inquire about "Eagle Opportunities" or apply online. Giving the online-application option will increase the number of candidates you get to consider because many who are currently employed are uncomfortable with an initial face-to-face conversation.

USE TECHNOLOGY AS YOUR EDGE

Invest an hour of your time surfing the following web sites:

www.careerbuilder.com

www.monstertrak.com

www.monster.com

What you will find on these sites and more like them is precisely where recruiting and hiring are headed. You can post compelling job descriptions, peruse postings by job candidates, and retrieve data based on geographical areas and job classifications in order to customize your hiring and recruiting approach. You can take advantage of services that notify you immediately once a job candidate publishes a resume matching your preset criteria. Monstertrak.com specializes in marketing to more than 600 college campuses, helping you market your offerings to the next generation of the best and brightest. Eagle candidates are using these sites daily as they contemplate industry or career changes or geographic relocations, or once they get the itch to step out and find a greater opportunity than their current circumstances offer. Many local newspapers also offer their own versions of these sites and are worth a look as well. To up your quality of people and your business you must enter this arena. In fact, there's a good chance your competitor is already there.

Raid Talent Pools When and Where Uncertainty Reigns

If you are serious about getting proactive, you'll raid the talent pools of other businesses the moment you hear word of a potential buyout, merger, takeover, or downsizing. You can leverage the uncertainty found in these situations by finding out who their best people are (if the company is a competitor, you may already know), taking them to lunch, and beginning a courtship process with your business. At first, their reaction may be to give the new owners or current arrangement a chance. But once pay plans start getting cut, their friends get the axe, and the new sheriffs in town begin micromanaging, they'll be ready to make the leap. Just make certain they're in your talent pipeline when they do.

As you make contacts and begin building a talent pool, it's important that you stay in touch with those in your pipeline. If you have a company newsletter or e-letter you send out, put them on your list. Make an occasional call or forward press releases about your company's growth or other accolades that let them know you're still interested and they're missing out on where the action is.

DON'T MAKE WANT ADS THE CENTRAL PART OF YOUR HIRING STRATEGY

There's no doubt you've hired good people from classified ads in your local paper from time to time. However, it's estimated that want ads attract the bottom 30 percent of performers. One key reason is that the top people aren't reading them! While you may snag a diamond every once in a while, you'll exhaust yourself sifting through the coal mine to get it. These solicitations normally bring in a combination of the frustrated, the terminated, the curious, and the confused and mystified — people barely doing enough somewhere else not to get fired who want to come test their options at your place. Many of these applicants make the Osbournes look Amish. I know there are exceptions, but as I declared in the opening of this book, I don't believe in looking for the next exception. You can wear yourself out personally and deplete corporate resources sifting through a flock of turkeys to find the eagle. While you should keep some presence in the classifieds for people new to your area and those looking to change careers, these should not be the focal point of your recruiting strategy. Think about it: If they bring in the bottom 30 percent of performers, even if you hire the cream of the crop you're still just getting the best of the worst!

Be Careful What You Ask For
Hiring expert Lou Adler recommends that when you do place an ad in the paper, you make sure to word it so that it attracts people

13

looking for challenges and opportunities, not those just looking for a paycheck. The difference in quality between the two candidates is staggering. Here's an example of each style of ad to help clarify this strategy (material used by permission of John Wiley & Sons, Inc.):[6]

Type I: Typical ad attracting those just looking for a paycheck:

Sales

Thirty-year old jewelry retailer is looking for motivated individuals to join our professional sales team. Prior sales experience helpful but not necessary. You must possess great attitude and desire to succeed. We provide training, health and dental insurance, and 401k retirement plan. We offer a guaranteed monthly draw against commission. Must have high integrity and maintain a strong team concept.

This ad is typical and attracts anyone with a pulse. And you've coached the applicant to talk about what a great team player they are and fake a great attitude during the interview.

Type II: Ad attracting those wanting a challenge and opportunity:

Sales

We're a mover and shaker in the retail jewelry industry and need a self-starter who can build and manage his or her own business and complement our team of sales eagles. If you've got the horsepower to take over this critical position, hit our high standards, and grow fast with our company, send in your resume or apply online at www.eagles.com. Include a separate write-up describing the most significant impact you've had in your current job. We realize that a compensation package needs to be very aggressive to continue to build our team of eagles.

One of the key differences between the two ads is that the second one causes the candidates to sell themselves, whereas the first ad does all the selling. When you sell a job too early you cheapen it. The second ad will also scare off the worthless who want to just get by and pick up a paycheck. On the other hand, it will intrigue top performers and get their juices flowing. An old adage declares, "Be careful what you ask for because you're likely to get it." The same holds true for your recruiting strategies.

What you'll notice when you run the ad attracting people looking for challenges and opportunities is that it will bring in far fewer candidates. This is a blessing. In fact, if you're measuring the effectiveness of your employment ads based on the *number* of people they attract rather than the *quality* of the people they attract, you're using a deficient measurement metric. Would you rather have forty people to sift through looking for a gold nugget, or only four — two of whom you want to hire?

Myles Dolan Jr. is vice president of Millennium Marketing, a New Jersey–based financial services provider to 200 retail automobile dealerships nationwide. Millennium hires finance managers and, in the past, when running a traditional classified ad, would attract twenty to thirty applicants, resulting in fifteen interviews and approximately five placements. According to Myles, when he decided to change his approach and run the sample ad attracting candidates looking for opportunities, only six candidates applied — but four of the six were placed in positions. Dolan explained what happened: "The quality of the candidates was much higher based on the expectation level the ad created. Each of the six candidates actually had resumes, which normally ran below fifty percent when we'd run the old ad. It has always astonished me that these folks think they can interview for a six-figure-income job without a resume. The phone pre-interview was also an excellent tool."[7]

15

People are not your greatest asset; the *right* people are. The wrong people are your greatest catastrophe. Mediocre people are your greatest drain on resources.

UP YOUR BUSINESS! ACTION THOUGHTS

GET PROACTIVE: GO FROM HUNTED TO HUNTER

1. Lose the mentality that your work roster is "all filled up" and start building your pipeline of talent by marketing to passive job candidates.
2. What will you have to stop or start to make your workplace environment your number one recruiting and retention tool for eagles? Be specific and be bold!
3. Design and print Eagle Calling Cards and give them to your management team to begin distributing.
4. Designate significant recruitment bonuses for employees referring workers to your business. Designate a meaningful amount and pay them on the spot.
5. Enhance your web site to create a compelling recruiting presentation to passive job candidates visiting your site. Post employee testimonials and intriguing job descriptions, and provide a short online application.
6. Use all your ad media to drive traffic to your web site to apply online.
7. Review and incorporate local and national recruitment web sites into your strategy.
8. With your key managers, designate a "raiding party" that descends on vulnerable businesses being acquired, merged, or downsized and recruits their talent pool. Stay in touch with those in your talent pipeline.
9. When you do use newspaper want ads, design them to attract people looking for challenges and opportunities, not just those looking for a paycheck.

EMPLOY GUERILLA INTERVIEW TACTICS

Once you find high-potential candidates your job isn't finished. In fact, it's just beginning. You must have an effective interview strategy in place that accurately assesses the people wanting to join your team. In fact, when you take time to contemplate the cost of hiring the wrong person, often because there's no real interview or hiring strategy in place, it is staggering! Get some Maalox ready before going over the following four penalties for hiring recklessly:

1. Calculate the *cost of lost production* between the poor candidate and your top-echelon performers. In many job functions this is the easiest cost to figure. And while it may be substantial, it pales when compared to the next three.

2. Try to put a price on the *cost of broken momentum* poor performers create. While this figure is not possible to quantify, let your imagination go to work here.

3. Attempt to determine the *cost of having lower morale* throughout your workplace as a result of having the wrong people on board, people who are not carrying their weight or contributing to organizational goals. While you're at it, factor in what it costs for your good players to have their personal performance compromised because they're carrying the weakling's load.

4. Now for the real killer: What is the *cost of running your personal credibility as a leader into the ground* because you can't choose capable people — and everyone knows it? To compound this cost, add in the extended penalty to your stature when you don't remove these people as quickly as you should and your

17

solid players secretly call your standards, leadership, and judgment into question.

| Up Your Business! Bullet | **The best time to fire people is before you hire them.** |

Why are so many of the wrong people hired by otherwise intelligent and effective managers? Too many interviews wing the hiring process or have faulty systems in place. Use the following nine interview strategies or adapt them to what you currently do so you can up the quality of candidate you bring on board.

CREATE AND STICK TO PREDETERMINED INTERVIEW QUESTIONS

The time you invest in preparing for an interview will be far less than the time required to rehabilitate the wrong candidate if you make a bad decision. Creating and sticking to predetermined interview questions will help you avoid a fatal flaw of interviewing: talking too much and letting the interview turn into a sales pitch. Your questions should revolve around past behaviors and performance. The key here is to determine what the candidate has actually done to get results in past jobs. Until you determine competence, factors like appearance, personality, education, and experience are mostly irrelevant. Keep in mind that the interview itself should be a fact-finding mission, not a casual conversation. You're better off asking fewer questions and then going deeper with follow-up questions than you are in presenting a wide array of queries covering general topics. The deeper you dig to follow up on the answers the candidate gives, the more exaggeration you'll weed out.

DISCIPLINE YOURSELF NOT TO MAKE AN EMOTIONAL HIRING DECISION

Hiring experts point out that making emotional decisions is the number one cause of hiring errors, and I couldn't agree more because I used to fall into the same trap. I'd get so blown away by how sharp someone looked or how articulate certain candidates were that I wouldn't assess them too toughly because I wanted them to make the cut. I see this same error repeated continually and ubiquitously. Managers make remarks like "Did you see the suit he was wearing? Were those Gucci shoes?" or "She was the most well-spoken candidate I've ever interviewed" or "He's got two degrees and fifteen years of experience." What's missing in these assessments is any meaningful discussion about what the candidate has ever done. Shortly after hiring one of these "apples of their eye" many a manager finds that the gap between interview performance and job performance is a gulf. In fact, I've seen more sales managers surrounded by gregarious, preppy failures than I care to remember. You have to focus on hiring people good at *doing* the job, not just those good at getting it. Some of them have had plenty of practice at the latter. Think about it: What difference does it make if someone went to school at Princeton or Podunk, or whether they went at all, if they've never accomplished anything significant on the job? All a degree that someone earned one, five, or ten years ago means is that at one time they knew a lot. It doesn't mean they can get the job done in your workplace.

During the interview process, when your emotions get too involved you stop assessing the candidates. You will maximize their strengths, minimize their weaknesses, and start selling the job too soon. When this happens you lose leverage. On the other hand, if you are turned off by appearance or personality in those first few minutes you'll get bored and start to exaggerate the candidate's weaknesses while playing down his or her strengths. This is unfortunate because some applicants are rendered temporarily incompetent by the glare of an interview spotlight. Stick with the candidate by asking predetermined questions, keeping your emotions in check, and dialing in on job competence.

A technique that minimizes the impact of the first visual impression is a short phone interview. Thus, when the candidate shows up you are less likely to be swayed by appearances since you have already tested substance during the phone questions. I can recall interviewing a finance candidate on the phone and being favorably impressed and thus anxious to meet him in person. However, once the applicant showed up he sported the worst hairpiece I had ever seen in my life, and it horribly distracted me. (It's tough to take someone seriously when you keep waiting for the thing on top of his head to sit up and beg for a peanut.) Fortunately, because of the phone interview, I was interested enough in this person to get past the distraction and he made an exceptional hire. (His signing bonus was converted to a hair allowance.)

DIG DEEP INTO THE APPLICANT'S TRACK RECORD

You won't become as overwhelmed by experience, education, personality, and appearance if you dig deep into the track record of the applicant with precise, behaviorally based questioning and diligent follow-up questions. Remember, until you determine job competence none of those other factors mean much anyway. Why put so much emphasis on track record? You do so because the greatest predictor of future performance is past performance. It's not the only predictor and it's not a sure thing, but it is the greatest predictor. Not to oversimplify, but winners tend to stay winners unless the job or workplace environment changes drastically. The opposite of this reasoning means that losers tend to stay losers unless the job or workplace changes drastically. In fact, if someone was an average performer at Place A, average at Place B, and average at Place C, he's probably not going to change in the moving van on the way to your place. Again, this isn't always the case, but stop looking for the exception and focus on what happens most often. While you look for the next exception, you'll lower hiring standards, give too much benefit of the doubt, and settle for less than your organization deserves. Playing Russian roulette with your hiring standards is a death wish for your culture and credibility.

Another reason you should focus more on past accomplishments than past experience is that when you don't, the best candidates get turned off. On the other hand, weaker applicants are relieved when you accept what looks good on paper rather than delving into what they've managed to accomplish. They can hide behind tenure and credentials without ever having impacted anyone or anything.

Here are two typically weak interview questions used all too commonly by misguided managers:

- *"Tell me about your strengths."* While this is an oft-accepted and legitimate-sounding interview question, it doesn't do an effective job of determining competencies. Think about it: How do you really expect someone to answer this question? If they're applying for a sales position, they're likely to say, "Well, I'm a people person. I've always gotten along well with people." Well, that's real nice, but the world is filled with likable failures. In

21

fact, Hannibal Lecter was a people person, but I wouldn't want him waiting on my customers. What the question fails to determine is what the person has ever done.

- *"Tell me about your weaknesses."* This one is really a joke. Do you really think people are going to 'fess up for you? Can you imagine an applicant saying, "Well, I'm going to level with you: My biggest weakness is that I'm a procrastinator. Sometimes I can't even manage to get up in the morning. The alarm goes off and I dream I get up but I don't. In fact, I'm amazed I'm even here today."

  Or how about this one: "The biggest weakness I have — and I've been working on it quite some time now — is that I'm a thief. I steal money, food, and pens. And I have this cocaine habit. But that's really a strength because I'm motivated to make a lot of money." Absurd scenarios, aren't they? Yet managers keep asking these questions and reaping a banquet of useless answers.

Following are four interview questions that dig into track record, give you a better measure of competencies, and help you find the people you need to up your business. Customize the words to fit your needs:

- "Describe for me the most significant impact you've had in your current job and explain the keys to pulling it off." I know of no better question to determine what an applicant has actually done. You will uncover volumes about someone when they explain what they think their most impressive accomplishment has been in their current job. After they answer, dig deep with follow-up questions to weed out exaggeration. For instance, in automotive retail sales, the national average for a salesperson is ten vehicle sales per month. Thus, when the applicant relates how selling eight cars one month during the zero-percent-financing special was the most significant thing he's ever done, you can look at your watch, gasp that you're out of time, point to the door, and keep looking for real help.

- "One of our objectives is to increase sales by twenty percent next year. Can you name for me the most relevant experience you've had doing something similar in a past job?" With this question, you determine whether the applicant has ever done anything close to what you need him or her to do. Oftentimes, there may be too large a reality gap between what you need accomplished and what the candidate has ever done. This might be acceptable if you have ample time to develop someone, but if you need him or her to have an instant impact and hit the ground running, he or she is probably the wrong candidate.

- "One of our goals is to get each of our salespeople up to an average monthly sales count of sixteen units. If you got the job, how would you go about accomplishing this?" A strong candidate will not rattle off quick-fix answers here. Instead, he or she will ask you questions: "How do you currently train your salespeople?" "Where is their greatest room for improvement?" "What current and clear performance expectations are set for them and are they held accountable for reaching them?" Only after a good candidate makes a diagnosis will he or she begin to prescribe solutions.

- "We expect anyone working for us to make some mistakes and cost us some money. What is the most significant mistake you've made in any job and what did you learn from it?" This question helps you determine whether you're interviewing a risk taker or a pretender. Good people take shots and they make mistakes, but they also have their share of breakthroughs. If someone answers that they can't recall any major mistakes you have either a liar or a play-it-safe maintainer. Either way, keep looking.

Up Your Business! Bullet	**The most successful people aren't those who fail the least. The most successful people are the least afraid to fail. When they hit a wall they bounce, they don't splatter.**

Wayne, a client who attended my workshop on interviewing and hiring, told me how immediately after the class he interviewed a sales candidate and asked what his most significant impact was at his current job. The young man replied that he had increased his capacity from being able to wait on three tables at once to five tables at once. His biggest mistake at any job was forgetting about a party of four for twenty minutes. My friend told me that the applicant was attractive, well groomed, and had a great personality, and that if he had interviewed him a day before the class he'd have assessed him as a high-energy kid who only needed a shot to prove himself and hired him. Instead, the application went into the discard box and Wayne kept looking for a stronger hire.

CLEARLY DEFINE AND EXPLAIN JOB PERFORMANCE EXPECTATIONS DURING THE INTERVIEW

During the interview you should explain performance expectations for the job at hand. You're going to be discussing these with the person after hiring, so you may as well lay the groundwork in the interview. If your company has minimum acceptable performance standards, this is the time to discuss them. Minimum performance expectations should always relate a negative guarantee, not a positive guarantee. In other words, if the standards are met, it doesn't mean the person automatically keeps his or her job. Criteria like attitude, integrity, and customer care must also be factored in. What a negative guarantee means is that if employees don't maintain those standards they will be written up, be put on probation, or lose their job. We'll talk more about clear performance expectations in the next chapter. For now, remember that if you want superior performance you must first define it. By establishing what is expected in no uncertain terms during the interview you will charge up the winners because the best people will try hard to hit a standard if they know what it is. On the other hand, you'll scare off the mediocre looking for a place to park and pick up a paycheck.

KEEP HIGHLY DEVELOPED LEADERS INVOLVED IN INTERVIEWING, RECRUITING, AND HIRING

The Law of Attraction states that you attract into your business what you are, not what you want. I wish I'd known this law when I was building my first team. I didn't like interviewing or recruiting so I delegated it to junior managers. Let's call them 4s on a scale of 1 to 10. Here's the problem with my former strategy: If you have 4s conducting interviews, they will attract 2s and 3s because lower-level managers won't bring anyone on board they see as a threat. They are looking for the easy-to-control, the compliant candidate. Netscape cofounder Marc Andreessen's "Rule of Crappy People" says that bad managers tend to hire very bad employees because people anywhere close to their own abilities intimidate them. Weak managers look for people who won't make waves, who will be easy to control and will do as they're told. To compound the problem, think about what is going through an eagle candidate's mind when a 4 is grilling him during an interview. I bet it's something like this: "Life is too short to work for an idiot. I've got to find someone serious about hiring great people." Top leaders take recruiting and interviewing personally. They also have a better eye for talent: They can see what's there and — equally important — what's not.

The best candidates are often independent, aggressive, and a bit quirky. They'll intimidate weak managers. It's up to a highly developed leader to bring this eagle on board and draw out his or her best while helping the candidate find a team fit.

BUILD YOUR TEAM AROUND INDIVIDUAL EXCELLENCE, NOT HARMONY

When you keep highly developed leaders involved with interviewing, recruiting, and hiring, this strategy evolves naturally. While harmony and camaraderie are important to every team, they should not be the first things you look for in a candidate. Instead, great teams are built around individual excellence. You must have the talented people in place first. With a good coach at the helm and the right people on board you'll start winning. Harmony and camaraderie will be an extension of that success. After all, what good does it do you to have a bunch of harmonious 3s and 4s on your team who can't get the job done? While the ship is sinking, they can hug and sing campfire songs, but they won't have what it takes to save it.

I spent many childhood years growing up in a Texas neighborhood where I was a perennial team captain and my rival was a kid named Randy. For six years, Randy and I chose sides for football, baseball, and basketball. For those same six years my teams always lost and Randy's always won. As a manager in the making, I naturally blamed my team. However, as I grew older and wiser and began to reflect, the truth hit me: We'd lost for six straight years because I'd picked my friends while Randy had picked the best players. I'd chosen my brother, my neighbor, my best friend: all

26

kids I knew I could get along with — and control. Randy, however, picked the biggest, the fastest, and the meanest. I wanted harmony and he wanted to win. The truth was, though, that as we continually lost we had very little harmony on the team. On the other hand, Randy's victory streak caused his team to bond like brothers. Winning has a way of doing that when a good coach is at the helm.

HIRE PEOPLE WIRED FOR THE WORK

Excellence is impossible without talent, but you can't teach talent. You can teach skills and knowledge, but you have to hire talent in. If you could teach talent there would be hundreds of Michael Jordans, Eric Claptons, and Robert De Niros. Teaching a job skill to someone who is void of talent for the work at hand is simply a form of damage control. You'll get the person to the point where they won't hurt you too badly, but they'll never be excellent because excellence is only realized when working in an area of strength. People get by when they work in areas of weakness, but they get great when they work in areas of strength. Use predictive testing that gauges competencies — not preferences — to determine if someone has a talent for the job. I suggest you focus on competencies because preferences are mostly irrelevant. In reality, I would prefer to sing for a living, but should anyone ever have to hear me sing? Absolutely not! I can assure you that my joyful noise would not be yours. Competency tests are no guarantee of great performance, but extensive research (conducted by Caliper Corporation of Princeton, New Jersey) shows that they are three times more likely to identify a talented candidate than when you hire without using them.[8] While talent is a great head start, keep in mind it is only potential. There are plenty of talented people who never use their gifts. This is why you must dig into their track record to determine what they've ever done with their talent.

In fact, some of what Caliper reports should simultaneously give you hope and pause. What should give you hope is that one of every four people from nonsales jobs who were randomly tested scored higher for sales aptitude than those currently making a living selling. This opens many possibilities for recruiting passive job candidates into a workplace. What should give you pause is that their testing also showed that 55 percent of people currently in sales shouldn't be selling. They don't have the attitude, drive, or empathy. Another 25 percent should be selling something other than what they are; perhaps they sell a tangible like cars or homes when they are better suited to selling intangibles. This leaves just 20 percent who have a chance of being excellent in their current sales arena.[9] Here's the catch: The eagles and turkeys often look alike, dress alike, and sound alike. But there's something inside the eagle the turkey will never have: talent. These candidates are analogous to a diamond and a piece of coal. They both are primarily made of carbon. The diamond, however, has something in its makeup the coal never will. Bearing this in mind, can you imagine how futile it would be to take a piece of coal to a jeweler and ask him to polish it up and turn it into a diamond? Yet that's what managers try every day as they train, motivate, and coach people who have no talent for the work at hand.

| Up Your Business! Bullet | **Taking a stronger whip to a dead horse won't move the sucker.** |

MAKE IT TOUGH TO GET ON BOARD

The easier you make it for someone to join your organization, the easier it is for them to leave it when they decide the grass is greener elsewhere. What people gain too easily they esteem too lightly. On the other hand, when you conduct a rigorous and serious interview the candidate appreciates the job more and is likely to work harder to validate your confidence once hired. The Marines are the only branch of the military that exceeds recruitment quotas every year, and they do so with a fraction of the budget other service branches use. The money is not any better and the work isn't easier, so how do they do it? They sell *exclusivity.* Not everyone can be one of them. You don't join them strictly for what you get; you enlist because of what you have an opportunity to become. Find ways to sell exclusivity in your organization. Creating an EVP (Eagle Value Proposition), as discussed earlier, is a great place to begin.

Southwest Airlines does an exemplary job of selling exclusivity and recruiting proactively. Southwest is unique in that they are the only airline to be profitable for three consecutive decades. If you've ever flown them you know their people are different. They are free spirits, energetic, and a touch unpredictable. Southwest recruits, interviews, and hires year-round. In fact, for every 105,000 applicants they hire just 3,000.[10] It is statistically tougher to get on at Southwest Airlines than it is to get into Harvard. Their results speak for themselves, and no one has ever had to remind Southwest that "it's the people, stupid." What is your ratio of applicants to those you hire? Though they would never admit it, in many organizations it's about two out of three. (And the only reason it's not three for three is that one couldn't pass the drug test or background check.)

WHEN IN DOUBT, KEEP LOOKING

As mentioned previously, the cost inflicted on your organization when you bring the wrong person on board is nearly incalculable. Not only the cost in missed productivity, but the cost of broken momentum, lower morale, misuse of resources, and your own diminished credibility. If you were sick and couldn't find a good doctor, you wouldn't let a bad one start hacking away on you; you'd keep looking for a good one. Bad doctors make life worse and so do bad employees. When in doubt, keep looking. When you panic-hire and bring in the wrong person just to fill a hole you will pay for that mistake over and over again — and so will everyone forced to work with the nonperformer.

DILIGENTLY CHECK REFERENCES

You can't afford to take shortcuts verifying references and past income. Reviewing W-2's for the past several years will help determine whether someone is on the way up or down. While law prohibits the person with whom you're checking a reference from divulging personal information, he or she is not prohibited from talking about performance issues. Thus, make it easier for the person to talk openly by using a script similar to this:

> "Since law prohibits us from discussing personal issues about John Doe, let's focus on performance issues. . . ."

At the end of your questioning, make one last stab at insight with this question:

> "If you could whisper one piece of advice in John's ear that would help him succeed in a new job, what would it be?"

Once when I asked this question, the person on the other end of the phone paused, sighed, and then remarked to me, "I'd tell him to be less abusive of his people and to work more as a team player." This one sentence told me more about the candidate than everything else I had gleaned from the reference check. Needless to say, I passed and kept looking.

Another tactic to use when checking references is to speak with the applicant's subordinates. Often, these people are less schooled in what they can and cannot say and will enlighten you with insights not revealed when checking with a superior or with Human Resources.

SET THE CANDIDATE UP FOR COUNTEROFFERS

Whenever a great candidate tells his current boss he's leaving, the games begin. Knowing in advance that an astute employer will pull out all the stops to keep an eagle, you can gain the upper hand by planting a seed that sets the candidate up for the counteroffer. Use a variation of this script to render impotent your opponent's retention efforts:

> "Jane, keep in mind that when you give your notice ABC Company is probably going to make you a counteroffer. In fact, I'd be shocked if they didn't. One thing we've seen over time is that when an employee accepts a counteroffer and stays, her relationship with the company is weakened and they become a bit suspect. Future upward mobility is diminished and things can become very frustrating for you. Besides, it hardly seems right that it would take your leaving for ABC to wake up and show their appreciation. In fact, the thought is a bit offensive, isn't it?"

DEBRIEF NEW EMPLOYEES

Great people you hire from other companies normally know other great people within that organization. Debrief the new employee for referrals of coworkers who may want to join them in their new adventure. Find out who was a great performer, what they liked and didn't like, who just had a pay-plan adjustment, which departments may be downsizing, who is suffering under an abusive boss, and who might be a diamond in the rough whose potential the current employer has failed to notice, recognize, or reward.

UP YOUR BUSINESS! ACTION THOUGHTS

EMPLOY GUERILLA INTERVIEW TACTICS

1. Create and develop the discipline to stick to predetermined interview questions.
2. Talk to yourself before the interview to create the self-awareness not to make emotional hiring decisions. Stay focused on substance.
3. Dig deep into the applicant's track record. Focus more on past accomplishments than past experience.
4. Clearly define and explain job performance expectations.
5. Keep highly developed leaders involved in recruiting, interviewing, and hiring.
6. Build your team around individual excellence, not harmony.
7. Since you can't teach talent, test for it. Hire people wired for the work.
8. Do you make it tough enough to get on board? What can you do to sell exclusivity?
9. When in doubt, keep looking. Don't settle.
10. Diligently check references. Ask performance questions.
11. Head off trouble. Set the candidate up for a counteroffer.
12. Debrief those you hire and get referrals.

DECLARE WAR ON POOR PERFORMANCE

Thus far we've focused on the human capital aspect of your business and have incorporated the mantra "It's the people, stupid" into your philosophy. You now have tools to build an exceptional pipeline of talent by becoming a proactive recruiter. You are also equipped to evaluate the candidates you find with high-impact interview techniques. However, you will defeat your purpose of bringing great people on your team if you deal ineffectively with the poor performers currently on board or fail to deal with them appropriately if they develop over time. It's like taking your favorite drink and gradually watering it down. Even though the drink was vital on its own, by diluting it you weaken its effect and render it undesirable. The same happens when you let the wrong people water down your roster of great players. Taking action on poor performers requires an iron hand in a velvet glove. Without the iron hand you are reluctant to confront poor performance and hold others accountable, and without the velvet glove the process can be demeaning and insensitive. To fix, build, or stretch your organization you must develop a greater sense of urgency in dealing with the poor performers on your team. My "Weak Link Manifesto" helps explain this detrimental impact: The weak links on your team determine the pace and overall success of the team. Just like a weak link in a chain determines what the chain can pull, regardless of the strength of the other links, the weak links on your team will determine how far you go and how fast you get there.

When you put the impact of poor performers in this light, you begin to grasp the devastation of their deficient performance. Whenever and wherever it exists, life cannot continue with a business-as-usual approach. While it's often considered politically incorrect to discuss poor performers and their lackluster results frankly, it's essential we do so. Poor performance is a debilitating disease. If you had a debilitating disease in your body you wouldn't ignore it. You'd be alarmed and would take swift, appropriate action. But when poor performance takes root in a business, we often act like it's not happening, like it will fix itself — or worse, like we can live with it as long as it doesn't get much worse. But it doesn't take six poor performers to wreak havoc on your bottom line; it only takes one!

| Up Your Business! Bullet | **You can't afford to take a casual approach to mediocrity. You don't handle mediocrity — you devastate it.** |

Granted that we all have equal value as human beings, the truth is that people do not create equal value in the workplace. Some people build the team and others drain it. Thus, leaders must take swifter, firmer action to turn around poor performance or root out poor performers. Most business owners I consult with agree that failing to deal swiftly and appropriately with poor performers is the number one reason managers fail. It boils down to a lack of emotional strength. A question I'm often asked in my workshops is how you define poor performance and how long you let someone stay at a deficient production level before taking action. My definition of poor performance is any performance that hovers at or below average with no upward trend. As for how long you let someone remain at this level before taking action, all I can say is *not very long*. An excuse commonly used by management cowards to justify keeping the wrong people is that dismissing them would leave the company shorthanded and overwork the good workers remaining. The fact is, if your good people are being forced to work with weak links, they're already overworked! They'd much rather be overworked carrying their own load than carrying someone else's. Carrying their own load gives them a cause, whereas covering for incompetents is a curse.

Along this same line of thought, you must realize that if you have the wrong people working for you, you are already shorthanded. The only difference between being shorthanded by keeping them or firing them is the paycheck you sign for them twice a month. On the following pages are nine points concerning poor performance that should prompt you to take a second look at how you deal with it in your organization.

1. *Would you rehire the person if given the chance?* If there are people working for you that you wouldn't rehire if given the opportunity, you have an unacceptable situation. Ask yourself this question about every person on your team: "Knowing what I now know about Bill, if he applied for the job today, would I hire him?" In other words, knowing what you now know about Bill's character, attitude, work ethic, and production, would you hire him if he came in looking for work today? This is an important and eye-opening question. You might also ask yourself whether, if this person came and told you he was leaving the organization, you would be terribly disappointed or secretly relieved. If you have someone working for you whom you wouldn't rehire you have an unacceptable situation and must execute one of these three options (the *Three Ts*):

- *Train.* If an employee isn't working out you must look in the mirror first and determine if you have equipped him or her to succeed. If not, do your job and train the person. Training is the most positive of the Three Ts because it invests in the employee and it's more economical to improve a current employee than to start a new one from scratch. However, there

35

are two reasons people don't perform: *can't-do's* and *won't-do's*. A can't-do is a skill issue, and training can make a positive difference in fixing it. A won't-do is a motivational issue. Training won't fix a won't-do. Here's a clue to determine whether you are facing a can't-do or a won't-do: If the person used to do the job well but no longer is, it's not a can't-do, it's a won't-do — and should be dealt with differently.

- *Transfer.* We've all seen people who are cast in the wrong role. Many have a good attitude, a strong work ethic, and high energy levels and would be valuable in another capacity. Stop trying to fix the person and fix the casting error. If you believe there is a legitimate skill match in another position, transfer the person. People aren't disposable, and you can't afford to throw good people away because you don't have the discernment to line their talents up with the jobs that require them. In fact, part of a leader's job is to get people doing what they're wired to do. However, transfers are not an excuse to move people around endlessly trying to find their niche in life. Some managers transfer people so they don't have to fire them. This is dangerous and allows nonperformers to inflict themselves on multiple people and departments over extended periods of time.

- *Terminate.* Think about where you're at: You have someone you wouldn't rehire if given the chance. Training won't make a difference and there are no feasible transfers. What option is left? Terminating, and it's a lousy job. In fact, some leaders lose sleep and get physically sick when faced with terminating an employee. In hundreds of workshops, I've had only one person tell me he enjoyed firing people. (I suggested therapy.) But removing a poor performer from the team is every bit as important as finding and keeping a good one.

One reason termination is so difficult is that oftentimes people don't see it coming. And if they don't, it's an indication you're failing as a leader. If you're blindsiding people when you fire them, you've failed to set clear expectations, failed to hold them accountable throughout the process, failed to impose consequences for continued poor performance, and failed to let them know exactly where they stood along the way. Otherwise, they would have seen it coming. While it's never easy to fire people, it's easier if you're not catching them by total surprise. In fact, in today's litigious society you're asking for legal trouble if you don't have a paper trail documenting poor performance. Regardless of the situation surrounding a termination, tie severance pay to an agreement not to sue whenever possible.

The problem is, most leaders tend to keep the wrong people far too long. Think about yourself for a moment: When have you ever fired someone and then said later, "Gee, I wish I'd kept them another sixty days." Never! Rather, you probably wondered why you hadn't done it sixty days ago, six months ago, or perhaps even six years ago.

Up Your Business! Bullet	**It's not the people you fire who make you miserable. It's the ones you keep that make you miserable.**

I've seen many leaders hide behind compassion as a reason for keeping the wrong person too long. They talk about how "good old Bill" has been with the company for ten years, has a family, and will have trouble finding work in the current business climate. What a crock! If managers are honest, they will admit that the real reason they keep the wrong people has less to do with compassion and much more to do with personal convenience. It's just a lot more inconvenient to go out and find someone else, interview them, and train them with the chance they'll work out no better than the terminated employee. (Better the devil you know than the devil you don't.) In addition, a manager knows deep down that when he fires someone, he failed first and must bear a great part of the blame. When you fire someone, you not only give up on the person, you also give up on yourself — since you couldn't do anything productive with them — and we don't like to give up on ourselves . . . so by giving the person another chance, we're also giving ourselves one. Managers sometimes pontificate that it is harsh or disrespectful to fire someone and that they should keep working with them. Quite frankly, I can think of no greater disrespect you can show than to keep a person in a position where he or she is not considered successful by others, is losing self-esteem, and hasn't a prayer of ever reaching his or her potential as a human being. In fact, doing so is brutal.

Up Your Business! Bullet	**Removing poor performers should be done quickly, professionally, and humanely.**

2. *Keeping the wrong person lowers the collective self-esteem of the entire team.* Everyone, especially top performers, feels cheapened when they have to share work space with people who aren't cutting it, who don't do their share and don't contribute to team goals. In addition, chances are that one of your strong players will have to carry his or her own load plus the weak link's load, and this will ultimately compromise his or her personal performance.

3. *Keeping the wrong person diminishes your credibility as a leader.* This one's a killer. So often a leader talks about high standards, how their workplace is number one, and how it's a special place to work. The problem is, your good performers are listening to what you say at the same time they're observing whom you're allowing to stay in the workplace, and quite frankly, they're confused. "High stan-

dards? We're number one? Special place to work? But Fred, Bob, and Sue are still working here! The boss is talking right and walking left!" When you fail to confront and remove poor performers, people perceive the company as being poorly managed and see you as a chief collaborator.

| Up Your Business! Bullet | **You will lose the respect of the best when you don't deal effectively with the worst.** |

---

4. *Care enough to confront.* Most leaders would rather be well liked and popular than confront poor performance. But how well liked and popular will you be when you have to fire a person who never saw it coming? Great leaders don't let their people live in a gray area. If they're great, they tell them they're great. And when they're failing, they tell them that too and help them turn things around. Confronting a poor performer is a form of tough love. It means you care enough about your employees to help them correct their course and turn around their failings.

5. *Use negative reinforcement as a last resort before termination.* Negative reinforcement is a coaching technique that you use as a last resort to turn around a poor performer before firing him or her. Negative reinforcement attaches a consequence for continued deficient performance. This is key to improving results, because if you want to change the behavior of a poor performer you must first change the consequences for that behavior. In fact, one reason many people keep underperforming is that there has never been a meaningful consequence for doing so. If you don't confront poor performance and present a consequence for it, you unwittingly reinforce it. The bad news is that, as psychology teaches us, behaviors that get reinforced get repeated. Thus, by failing to address it you sanction and endorse more of it. Negative reinforcement says, "Do it or else." It

sounds like a harsh way to manage, but it's harsher to let someone stay in a gray area and surprise him or her with a pink slip because you never had the guts to draw the line and say, "Do it or else." Besides, there comes a time when enough is enough and you have to stop hugging and burping people, pull their head out, and get them going. You're running a business, not the Good Ship Lollipop! The key to negative reinforcement is that you use it only to turn around a poor performer; once he or she turns around, you switch back to positive reinforcement.

6. *Redefine expectations and attach deadlines for attainment.* If someone on your team is not cutting it, the first thing you should do is sit down with that person and redefine what is expected and by when. Then help that person figure out how to get there. When you do this, you take the person out of a gray area, establish a benchmark for accountability, and create greater focus and urgency. Accountability is impossible without expectations. Think about it: How can you sit down with me and say, "Anderson, you're not cutting it," if you've never defined what cutting it is? You can't. So you won't. And so poor performance continues its vicious cycle of destruction in your organization. Good people will try hard to hit a standard if they know what it is. But it's difficult for people to work with focus and resolve if their goal is shrouded in fog. When you redefine expectations you kick the crutch of convenient ignorance out from under the person and shine the light of accountability on his or her performance.

7. *Remove poor performers when you're on a roll—don't wait until the bottom falls out.* Many managers don't deal with poor performance quickly or appropriately because they don't face reality about their people. As a leader, you've got to force realism into every level of your organization, compelling everyone to evaluate their people, their plan, and their results and pulling the trigger by making tough

decisions when any of these falls short. Even more important, you can't let the overall success of your enterprise seduce or delude you into believing that dealing with poor performers is made less imminent by virtue of current results. This allows the invisible creep of mediocrity and entitlement to grip your culture. Too often, leaders don't feel the urgency to deal with the mediocre when things are rolling along. But what's the alternative—waiting until they've broken the momentum and you're in a rut? It's a bit late then, isn't it? You have much more at stake when you're on a roll than when you're in a rut because you have precious and priceless momentum at your back pushing you to higher levels. And if your momentum is broken while you're going 100 miles per hour it hurts much more than if it breaks when you're limping along at 15 miles per hour. When you give poor performers a stay of execution because results are rosy, you let them linger long enough to disrupt your roll and plant the seeds for a rut. You also miss a prime opportunity to send the team a clear message about performance standards, fail to preserve the culture, and miss the chance to enhance your personal credibility and resolve.

Don't misinterpret this point as saying you shouldn't deal with poor performers when the bottom falls out. Of course, you must. The point is that if you continue to wait until you reach that point, you're being too reactive and will never effectively sustain momentum or protect your culture as you should.

Up Your Business! Bullet	**The best time to fix the roof is when the sun is shining.**

8. *Overcome the loyalty dilemma.* One of the toughest things a manager must do is confront a loyal and tenured employee who is no longer cutting it. These are the decisions that make your gut ache

41

and it's made more difficult if you promoted this person initially and must now deal with your own failure in judgment. Keep the following thoughts in perspective as you face your own loyalty dilemmas.

- *Continue to stretch and develop your loyal, tenured people.* Oftentimes, bosses let up on the loyal and let them do their own thing because they've been around so long and seem to need less attention. This is a common and severe error. Human nature is to let up, not to continue going the second mile. Thus, your loyal, tenured people need to have their bar raised, their skills developed, and some expectations and accountability established and employed over time, just as the others in your organization do. Give them stretch assignments, and if they are burned out in a current area of responsibility try to find a good fit for them within the organization that challenges them while it uses their strengths. If you take your seasoned people for granted, you will pay a hefty price in productivity, morale, and weakened culture.
- *Realize that when employees stop performing, their lack of results is the ultimate disloyalty to an organization.* I love yesterday's heroes as long as they're still delivering. But it's crazy to listen to managers make excuses for keeping good old loyal John when John's lack of productivity evinces the ultimate disloyalty and his lack of results can jeopardize the entire team. Loyalty is more than just showing up every day on time. It's more than the hours, days, or years someone puts in. It's what they put into those hours, days, and years that counts. Experience, tenure, and credentials don't substitute for results. A chief concern of every manager should be the high number of unemployed people they have on their payrolls. Many have re-

42

tired on the job. They borrow credibility from who they were and what they did long ago. When their output is down they try to cash royalty checks from yesteryear. There comes a time when your loyal, seasoned people have got to stop belching out the baloney and bring home the bacon. When they chose to stop producing, they chose the ultimate disloyalty.

- *The good of the team must come before the good of any one individual.* The interests of one individual can never come before the good of the overall organization, because if the organization suffers everyone is at risk. If you start making exceptions to excuse nonperformers because they are loyal and tenured, you begin an endless cycle of rationalization. Everyone has personal problems, challenges, and slumps from time to time. But these are not excuses to take a prolonged production holiday. Good leaders subordinate tradition and sentimentalism to the good of the team.

- *You owe more loyalty to the fifteen people suffering under or around the loyal nonperformer than you do to the culprit who has stopped producing.* Often you hear a boss say, "But good old John's been with us fifteen years. What kind of loyalty would we be showing by getting rid of him now?" What this manager should be more concerned with is the people suffering under or around John, coworkers and customers alike. And don't hide behind the fear of the negative message you'd send to others in your organization by discarding a loyal but nonperforming employee. Instead, be much more concerned about the message you'll send about your standards, expectations, and personal credibility when you fail to remove him.

A manager in one of my seminars remarked that he personally liked a loyal nonperformer and felt conflicted when confronted with the necessity of firing him. He mentioned how fun this person was to be around and that he was willing to work any shift without complaint. I told him that if he liked him that well he should remove him from the company payroll and pay his salary out of his own pocket. I then asked, "Now how well do you like him?" He got the point.

Up Your Business! Bullet	**Leaders create an environment where people come to work to prove themselves over again every day. No one gets paid to budget their efforts or pace themselves.**

---

9. *Confront and turn around or remove good performers who violate core values.* What do you do with the hammer, the guy who hits the numbers every month but violates your core values in the process? You confront his performance and attempt to turn him around, but if you can't, you fire him. If you blink on this issue you reduce yourself to a leadership sellout, akin to a harlot who does business with anyone as long as they put cash in the till. I heard Jack Welch discuss this topic very effectively at a Fortune 500 Leadership Conference:[11]

> One of the toughest calls a leader makes is to remove the employee who doesn't share the values but delivers the numbers; the "go to" manager, the hammer, who delivers but does it on the backs of people, often "kissing up and kicking down" during the process. This type is the toughest to part with because organizations always want to deliver — it's in the blood — and to let someone go who gets the job done is unnatural. But we have to remove these people because they have the power, by themselves, to de-

44

stroy the open, informal, trust-based culture we need
to win today and tomorrow.

We made our leap forward when we began removing the people who hit the numbers but violated
our values and making it clear to the entire company
why they were asked to leave — not for the usual
"personal reasons" or to "pursue other opportunities," but for not sharing our values. Until an organization develops the courage to do this, people will
never have full confidence that these values are real.

I have never seen or heard of an instance where a manager removed a negative top performer and overall production and sales
didn't increase almost immediately. I was speaking on this topic at
a convention in Florida when a car dealer approached me after the
speech to relate how her top technician had been a cancer: always
negative, stirring up other workers, playing politics, and doing so
on a regular basis. After she mustered the courage to fire him, sales
increased 30 percent overnight.

A large number of your poor performers must be asked to leave
your organization each year, and you must develop an urgency to
remove them more quickly. It's nothing personal, strictly business.
It doesn't mean they are bad people; it just means they can't work
in your business any longer. Pruning your organization of poor
performers is a lot like trimming trees. If you don't cut off the dead-
wood, eventually the whole tree falls. But if you remove it, the tree
becomes healthier and more productive and you make room for
new productive branches on the tree. Think about the positive impact on your enterprise if you begin stretching your top 20 percent
with more of your time, attention, resources, and support while at
the same time you're moving on the bottom 20 percent more quickly.

When you do this, guess what happens to the middle? It moves up — and moves up quickly. One of your goals as a leader should be to gradually narrow the gap between top and bottom performers, because the wider the gap, the more your culture weakens. And while you'll always have a bottom 20 percent, by implementing many of the strategies in this book you'll find that the day will come when your bottom 20 percent is better than your competitor's top 20 percent. At this point, life gets good!

Up Your Business! Action Thoughts

Declare War on Poor Performance

1. Evaluate your roster and determine whether you would rehire your people. If not, exercise one of the Three Ts to turn things around: train, transfer, or terminate.
2. Be aware that keeping the wrong people lowers the collective self-esteem of the entire team.
3. Which poor performers are diminishing your standards and personal credibility?
4. Care enough to confront poor performers when they are off track and keep them out of a gray area.
5. Use negative reinforcement as a last resort to turn performance around before termination.
6. For whom must you redefine expectations and attach deadlines for attainment?
7. Remove poor performers when you are on a roll—not after the bottom falls out.
8. Which loyal nonperformer must you confront and attempt to turn around before dismissal?
9. Which people are violating core values and must be confronted—regardless of how good their performance numbers are?

Don't Screw Up a Good Thing

Once you've gone through the hard work of recruiting, evaluating, and hiring the right people and made the tough but necessary decisions involving poor performers, your work is not finished; it's just beginning. Now you must retain the winners on your team. You will also need to provide the opportunities and differentiation that help them develop to their fullest potential. This topic will be covered extensively in Chapter 3. For now, let's discuss three strategies you can use to get employees off to a great start and retain them over time.

1. *Intensify the on-boarding regimen.* A new hire's first few weeks on the job are critical. In fact, I believe you can attribute a significant percentage of voluntary departures from an organization to improperly assimilating the person into the culture. The key question a new employee asks him- or herself after the courtship process is whether the new job will live up to expectations. What is your organization's on-boarding regimen? Do you have one? Is it effective? Too often, a person's first few days on the job are spent filling out forms, being overloaded with data, being hurriedly introduced to countless people they'll never remember — all right before they get tossed into the arena to sink or swim. To on-board effectively:

   a. *Formally share and review vision, values, company policies, and performance expectations.* Ideally, you discussed these issues during the interview, and now you will review them. This clarity helps new employees internalize and understand the DNA of the organization, which makes it easier for them to make decisions and interact with others in the future. It also connects them to the business's purpose and plants the seeds of ownership and meaningful work.

b. *Position the person for early victories.* When spelling out performance expectations, set up some short-term-win mile markers that will point to progress and build self-esteem and confidence. These short-term objectives should be reinforced once realized and the subsequent momentum used to move on to bigger objectives.

c. *Make certain the person's strengths are being leveraged.* There is nothing more frustrating than doing work for which you're not wired. Make certain the person is starting off in your organization in an area of personal strength. You can move him or her on to stretch assignments in more diverse areas later.

d. *Appoint a mentor.* Assign a peer to show the person the ropes, answer questions, make sure he or she meets the right people, and remove initial roadblocks. Choose this person carefully. The last thing you want is to assign Charlie with the chip on his shoulder, who will give dissertations on "how things really are around here." Pay the mentor extra for time spent with the new person. If you run a sales organization you may also want to financially vest the mentor in the new hire's production. Then you'll have people who are really pulling for the new employee rather than starting a pool to see how long he or she lasts.

e. *Provide ongoing feedback and support.* Meet with the new person often to give feedback, offer support, and make yourself available for questions. Communication at this stage is vital. Good things the person does must be reinforced quickly;

when the person goes off track his or her course should be corrected just as quickly so the deficient behaviors don't become habit.

f. *Conduct a "fresh eyes" meeting with the new employee.* Do this within thirty days of the start of employment. Before the new employee's vision has been dimmed by your own orthodoxies, ask questions like: "What do we do here that's dumb?" "What has or hasn't lived up to your expectations?" "What could we do to be easier to deal with from a customer's point of view?" "What should we begin doing to make it easier for other new employees to get off to a fast and productive start with our organization?" In addition to providing you with invaluable insights, these questions will send a strong message to the employee that you are open to change and that his or her opinions are important in the future.

2. *Motivate the person as a unique individual, not like another head in a herd of cattle.* Take the time to discover what motivates the new employee, and then make certain you pull the right trigger to bring the best out in that person. Weak managers use the same canned, planned, generic approach to motivate people, but the best leaders know that motivation is the people's choice, not the leader's choice.

Up Your Business! Bullet	**Positive reinforcement and motivation are in the eyes of the receiver, not the giver. You've got to know them to move them.**

Some people are turned on by public recognition; others prefer to be recognized in private. Many are moved first and foremost by tangible rewards and others by increased latitude and discretion. Find out what makes each of your people tick. It's much more efficient to motivate everyone the same way, but it's not effective. Keep in mind that people's motivations change over time and that it's your job to stay attuned to what moves your people; it's not their responsibility to let you know.

3. *Don't micromanage.* Micromanagement works in the short term, but it means that your people won't grow. If you feel you need to make every decision, have every idea, and do all the talking, let me break some news to you: Relax, you're not that good. Micromanagers rarely know as much about what needs to be done as the people they're harassing to do it. When you have the right people on your team you don't need to micromanage them. In fact, if you do, you'll lose them. Your people deserve a certain level of trust and discretion the moment they join your team. They should not have to earn it. They should be given the benefit of the doubt or you shouldn't have hired them in the first place. How they respond to the trust and discretion you give them will determine the increased or decreased levels you grant them in the future, but *you* must trust first. Great managers don't become overinvolved. They don't create complexity where it doesn't belong. They don't break their best people's momentum or sap their morale. If you can't trust or delegate to the people around you it's your fault, not theirs.

4. *Clean up the joint.* Review the Landfill Symptoms listed earlier in this chapter and know that if you allow these demotivators to take root in your workplace environment you'll never retain eagles. These land mines will slow down, devastate, and debilitate your best people. It's your job to remove them.

Up Your Business! Action Thoughts

Don't Screw Up a Good Thing

1. What will you do to intensify on-boarding efforts? Make it meaningful, not merely a formality.
2. Do you know how to motivate each person on your team as a unique individual? Care enough to discover what makes each one tick and pull the right trigger. Keep in touch with individuals' motivations as they change over time.
3. Don't micromanage. If you have to tightly manage your people you've made a hiring error. Whose way do you need to get out of?
4. Clean up the joint. Ridding your workplace of demotivators is endless work. You can't afford to give any of the demotivators listed earlier safe quarter in your business. Which must you take action on immediately?

ACCEPT YOUR RESPONSIBILITY

Let's stop looking out the window for a while and look in the mirror. One of the chief mistakes a manager makes is to underestimate his or her impact on organizational results while overestimating the impact of subordinates. Quite frankly, nothing gets better in a business until the leaders do. And when you have problems or fall short of your potential in a business unit you don't fix it at the bottom or in the middle of the organization. You fix it at the top. As we conclude our chapter on why "It's the people, stupid!" we need to discuss the biggest make-or-break factor in any enterprise: the leaders. Many times during the year our company is approached to train an organization's sales department, and we unapologetically turn the business down if we have not trained the leaders first. Why? If we can get the leaders good they'll get their people good, but if the leaders don't improve, no success a client manages to wring out is measurable or sustainable. Quite frankly, it's easier for most managers to look out the window for answers to their organization's ills than to glance in the mirror. And because they do, they often come up with the wrong cure. What you misdiagnose you will mistreat. Your business is no exception.

In fact, I'm often sadly amused when I hear managers run their people down, because as they do they confess their own leadership sins. If none of your followers are any good, what do all those "losers" have in common? You! In my two-day leadership workshops I spend half of the class teaching the leaders how to develop themselves before we move on to developing others or the organization. The reason for this is very simple. It's the *Law of Attraction*. What this law states is that leaders don't attract into their business what they want; they attract what they are. In other words, on a scale of 1 to 10, if someone is a 6 as a leader, there's some bad news: A 6 doesn't attract 8s, 9s, or 10s. Here's some more bad news: A 6 cannot develop someone into an 8, 9, or 10 because you can't take someone on a leadership journey you've never been on yourself. In one class (before I had a chance to explain this law), I had a manager tell me, "Dave, where I work, I'm surrounded by losers! My people have a weak work ethic, marginal character, and do just enough to get by." I had to tell this manager to stop before he dug a deeper hole for himself and asked him, if none of his people were any good, to name for me the one thing they all had in common. I could tell by his flushed cheeks he got the point.

Listed next are four strategies that will help put the importance of getting the right managers in its proper perspective.

1. *Institute ongoing leadership training within your organization.* We'll cover this in depth in Chapter 3, but for now suffice it to say that one of senior management's biggest mistakes is to overestimate the leadership ability of their managers. Many of these managers have strong technical ability but don't know how to lead. They can budget, forecast, organize, and solve problems but they're weak at casting vision, creating the right culture, evaluating talent during an interview, making the tough decisions quickly, knowing how to treat and motivate people as unique individuals, turning around a poor performer, instilling accountability, and developing bench strength throughout their organization. They excel at tactics but don't think strategically. They maintain but they don't stretch. They chart results but they don't chart the course. They problem solve but don't problem predict. They defend the status quo but fail to challenge the process. They work hard on their jobs but don't work hard on themselves. They focus on the bottom line but never look at the horizon. They focus their time on what it costs to do something but ignore the cost of neglecting it. They command but don't communicate. They hoard decision making and power, and thus they never develop a team. Please don't misunderstand; management and leadership are equally important. Management without leadership means you can't grow what you keep, while leadership without management means you can't keep what you grow. Unfortunately, most people in management positions today have been trained more exhaustively in management and lack a balance of leadership skills. This is precisely why so many organizations today are grossly overmanaged and severely underled.

The good news is that leadership is developed, not discovered. It can be learned if an organization provides the training and creates the conditions for one to use what they learn. This goes beyond sending your managers to semiannual retreats where they whitewater raft or rappel down a cliff to learn teamwork. It also goes further than sending them to a guru's seminar at the local hotel where they're led around blindfolded through the lobby with grapes atop their heads to learn trust. It's not that these occasions aren't helpful for leadership development. The point is that what you do to train your leaders in between these meetings is more relevant. Leadership training must be process oriented to be effective. You provide knowledge and let the trainees quickly apply what they learn in real-life situations within your business, then offer feedback on their efforts. This training will include putting them into stretch jobs, increasing latitude and discretion, and pushing more and more power and decision making down to lower levels.

Up Your Business! Bullet	**Life will not just come along and improve your people. In fact, time and experience can make them worse if it's the wrong experience. You must deliberately pour yourself into your team in order to grow it.**

It's vital to remember that having a leadership title does not make you a leader. All a title does is buy you time: to earn influence or to lose it, to get the job done or to blow it. It's also worth pointing out that leaders don't automatically have followers; they have subordinates. How you act as a leader determines whether the subordinate ever turns into a follower. In fact, some leaders don't even have subordinates. They have subjects and have a longer road to earn followership. And for those leaders who are members of the lucky sperm bank and have attained their positions through blood or marital ties, please get real: Leadership is not genetic. In fact, there have been enough heirs who lost family fortunes and enough deposed monarchs throughout history to make this evident. Lead-

54

ership is earned. It is not assumed. In fact, if you are in a blood-tie position, you must work doubly hard to develop your leadership skills, connect with your people, and earn results since others are likely to harbor resentment and strong doubts about your abilities, sincerity, and legitimacy as a leader. Their attitude is "Let's see what you can do with what you've been given." Ultimately, it is the followers who decide if the person they report to is a leader.

2. *Measure managers by whether they improve their people.* I can think of no better way to measure managers than by whether the people they lead improve. Many managers increase sales and production within their businesses by adding bodies rather than by making the people already there better. The measurement metric you use depends on the job function and is up to you to determine. I have found no better way to focus managers on developing their teams than to tie a substantial portion of their compensation to the improvement of their people rather than to the department overall. Think about it. If people are improving on a person-by-person basis, the department will grow exponentially. This is a more valid measurement than looking strictly at overall results within the enterprise, since factors like cost cutting can boost a bottom line with no regard to whether people got better, and adding extra people can augment the top line with no regard as to whether those on the team improved.

3. *The good people you're looking for could be right under your nose.* Many times at a seminar a manager will ask me where he can find good employees. I always give the same answer: Start with what you've got. The good people you're looking for might be right under your nose. Have you set clear expectations, trained them with the skills necessary to succeed, given fast and frequent feedback on their performance, learned how to motivate them as unique individuals, and provided a culture that encourages success rather than

inhibiting it? If not, there's no sense in bringing in new people and subjecting them to the same abuse! When a business owner asks me where she can find good managers, I give her the same answer I do for finding good subordinates: Start with what you've got. If you have a manager who isn't cutting it, look in the mirror before you look out the window and determine if you've created the conditions necessary for him or her to succeed.

4. *Bad managers should be given less rope.* When all is said and done, if you have a manager who isn't getting the job done and you've done all in your power to ensure his or her success, you must make a decision about this person quickly. Before you do, exercise your responsibility to any manager not performing well: Redefine what is expected and by when, and help the person determine a plan to get there. Please make a note that earlier, when we discussed the "train, transfer, or terminate" option for someone you wouldn't re-hire, it goes double for managers. Bad managers should be given less rope and less time to get the job done than an underperforming subordinate because bad managers make life worse more severely and more quickly than any other position in an organization. In fact, when a bad manager hangs himself he tends to snag a lot of other people with him. If you bond with bad managers for old times' sake or because it seems more convenient to put up with the devil you know than to go find one you don't, you're putting that manager's department and people on the endangered species list.

To fix, build, or stretch your organization to where you want it to be, you must become less tolerant of bad managers. This is why clear expectations must be set forth up front, fast and frequent feedback offered on their performance, and ongoing training supplied to make them more competent. You should also perform due diligence to guarantee they are uninhibited by unnecessary rules, red tape, and lack of discretion.

<table>
<tr><td>Up Your
Business! Bullet</td><td>**If you think you must make every decision, have every idea, and do all the talking, relax! You're not that good. The surest way to lose good people is to abuse them with micromanagement.**</td></tr>
</table>

UP YOUR BUSINESS! ACTION THOUGHTS

ACCEPT YOUR RESPONSIBILITY

1. Realize that nothing gets measurably or sustainably better in an organization until the leaders do. If you misdiagnose your organization's ills, you'll mistreat them.
2. Since most organizations are overmanaged and underled, install ongoing and effective leadership training in your business. Describe your current ongoing management training program. If you have good people, you have an obligation to develop them.
3. Measure your managers by whether their people are improving. Tie a meaningful portion of their compensation to this metric. Who in your organization is growing people? Who is simply maintaining them?
4. Before looking outside for different or better people, start with the ones you already have.
5. Become less tolerant of bad managers. Move more quickly to redefine expectations and to turn them around or remove them.

Further Up Your Business

The Importance of Creating Stressful Interviews

Of all the strategies presented in this chapter to up your business, the most common area I continue to find managers struggling in is conducting high-impact interviews. An interview is one of the most important tasks a leader undertakes as he or she evaluates who will join the team. This is serious business! It's time to put your game face on and discipline yourself to hire slower. To that end, and as counterintuitive as this may appear, I recommend that you find ways to make interviews more structured and tougher on the job candidate.

For some reason, many managers have gotten the idea over the years that an interview is supposed to be some kind of warm and fuzzy "get to know each other" session, a casual conversation, or, worse, a sales pitch. Think for a moment about all that is at stake during an interview: This is your best opportunity to evaluate someone you are considering bringing on board who will affect your customers, your other employees, and your results. Misjudging the candidate can literally cost you a fortune. This is why I have said for years that hiring should be an elimination process and that the best time to fire is before you hire.

While there are many traits you're looking for in an interview, one of the most important is this: Can the potential employee handle stress? I cannot think of a position in practically any business where this ability is not essential. Yet we often find out the hard way that the employee has little or no tolerance for stressful situations and reacts poorly when caught in difficult circumstances. The best way to find out if employees can handle stress is to make your interviews more stressful and not to wait until you've hired them to make this discovery! Here are three tips to toughen up your interview process:

1. Don't worry so much about putting the person at ease during the interview. Limit small talk. Don't be unfriendly, but do be professional and serious. You'll have a chance to become friends if you hire the candidate, but for now you need to have your game face on and dispense with too much casual conversation. Serious candidates expect a serious interview. Remember, they've got to sell you. You're not supposed to worry about selling them . . . until you're sure you want them.

2. Stay on track. Have prestructured questions and stick to them. When the applicant gives you a general answer, dig deep for specifics. This helps weed out exaggeration and shows that you are not some gullible boob who is going to accept everything he or she says at face value.

3. Ask some stressful questions — provocative and unexpected are the most effective. Again, you're better off finding out how candidates handle stress before they're on your payroll. Halfway through the interview, look the applicant in the eye and ask, "How would you feel if I told you the interview wasn't going very well at this point?" See how the applicant responds. Some of them will blame you and say you haven't given them a chance or that you asked the wrong questions, and so on. This tells you a lot about them, and it's better to uncover this victim mentality before they're cashing your paychecks.

C. S. Lewis wrote that if you have rats in the cellar, you're more likely to see them if you go downstairs suddenly, before they have a chance to hide. The suddenness of your approach doesn't create the rats. It merely reveals those already there. The same holds true when you ask a sudden, provocative question during an interview: It doesn't create an ill-tempered, sarcastic, or defensive person. It merely reveals the ill-tempered, sarcastic, or defensive person seated before you.

CHAPTER 2

Abolish Corporate Welfare

Create a Culture of Merit

DEFINING A CULTURE OF ENTITLEMENT AND A CULTURE OF MERIT

One of the most overlooked organizational aspects that must be addressed to fix, build, or stretch an organization is the workplace environment. Managers work within this environment all day but do little to work *on* it. And that's a travesty because environment dictates behavior and behavior dictates results. Thus, if a leader wants better outcomes from the employees, he or she must first focus on enhancing the environment in which that behavior is found. To fully appreciate the relationship between environment and behavior, you only need to look around to see it in action. Think about it: When you go to church, you find people behaving a certain way. Why? It's a result of the environment they're in. When you go to a

61

ABOLISH CORPORATE WELFARE

library, a nightclub, or a ball game you witness the same relational principle at work. The identical cause-and-effect connection is evinced by your workplace environment. How your people behave on a day-to-day basis is a direct result of the culture you have created. If people are motivated, energized, and passionate about what they do, the environment gets much of the credit — as do the leaders who created it. On the other hand, if people drag their feet, go through the motions, and produce the bare minimum possible, the environment shares much of the blame — as do the leaders who are presiding over it.

Many leaders are uncomfortable talking about corporate environment or corporate culture because they think it sounds too warm, soft, and fuzzy. They'd rather talk about hard numbers. But the fact is that you won't get the hard stuff — numbers — until you pay attention to the soft stuff — culture. The numbers are simply the end result of what is taking place within the context of the environment.

Up Your Business! Bullet	**Culture determines what your people feel and how they behave. This, in turn, determines their results.**

One of the most debilitating workplace environments is a culture of *entitlement*. Many businesses today find themselves entrenched in this mire and don't know how it happened or how to get out. In this chapter, I'm going to offer a brief history of how entitlement reared its ugly head in society and business, outline symptoms of this culture, define the opposite culture — a culture of *merit* — and coach you on how to move your environment from entitlement to merit so you can abolish all forms of corporate welfare in your organization.

THE ROOTS OF ENTITLEMENT IN THE WORKPLACE

In her book *Danger in the Comfort Zone* (AMACOM, 1995), Judith Bardwick explains how entitlement spread throughout America in the years after World War II, when there were too few employees to fill jobs in a booming economy and it became virtually impossible to get fired.[12] Because of this shortage, countless people doing marginal work were rewarded with promises of lifetime job security and began reaping regular raises without regard to whether they earned them based on performance. However, you can actually trace entitlement's roots in our country's culture and psyche to the earlier period of FDR's New Deal, which established numerous social programs and subsidies to help stabilize the economy. Although World War II rudely and temporarily rooted out entitlement, it found a more welcome and willing host in the postwar years because the seeds had already been planted.

ENTITLEMENT INFECTS BUSINESS

In fact, since the New Deal, entitlement has spread like a plague through society as well as business. It is in evidence everywhere from public schools where teachers are admonished to work with the weaker kids; to inner cities where consecutive generations of American families are supported by government welfare; to Indian reservations where entitlement has created an expectancy of handouts for over a century, resulting in a diminished self-esteem and work ethic that has spawned widespread poverty, illiteracy, and alcoholism. It wasn't always this way in our nation. As our country was getting started the proposition was very simple: If you didn't work, plant, or hunt, you didn't eat. As we were growing and be-

63

coming an industrial power the proposition was equally clear: If you wanted to cash in on the American Dream you could; the only catch was that you'd have to work for it. If you didn't want to work, there were no food stamps, welfare checks, or telethons to see you through the tough times.

As you look around today, you find that society has become filled with spoiled brats. In our instant-gratification age, everyone wants to cash in and claim their prize now with little regard for paying the price. Instant breakfast, blink-of-an-eye access to information over the Internet, instantaneous access to communication via cell phones and Palm Pilots, promises of quick weight loss or hair gain, fast marriages, faster divorces, shortcuts to college degrees, six-day courses to learn Chinese, four-hour flights to Paris, on-the-spot credit decisions on car purchases, and ten-minute answers on million-dollar mortgages. We see the unemployed win a hundred million dollars in the lottery and former strippers and White House interns gain fame, fortune, and television shows without virtue of accomplishment.

We're also living in an era of victimhood. In fact, our new national mantra, "It's not my fault," has turned therapy, psychology, and psychiatry into booming growth industries. This flame of wretchedness has been fanned out of control by lawyer-leeches who coddle and encourage their derelict clients, signing on for no money down and a cut of the action. Our jaws drop as we hear of smokers being awarded billions because the tar that, for decades, they knowingly and deliberately coated their lungs with made them sick; we watch in disbelief as klutzes who spill hot coffee in their lap are made rich by our courts; and we can only marvel as we witness the Jerry Springers of daytime television parade a conga line of losers and misfits in front of millions of viewers five days each week.

So, what does this have to do with fixing, building, or stretching your business? Everything! Because you and the people working for you and with you are all subject to the influence these corrupt and perverted mind-sets create in your workplace environment, which in turn influences people's behavior and, of course, their subsequent results.

Up Your Business! Bullet	**Where you are in your life is a result of the decisions you've made in the past. It is your inside decisions, not outside conditions, that determine your success or lack of it.**

Following is a baker's dozen of symptoms of an entitlement culture. Evaluate your business as you read through this list, and realize that most organizations have multiple cultures. Under the same roof you may have one sector thriving within a culture of merit while another lies in the stench of entitlement.

Thirteen Symptoms of a Culture of Entitlement

1. People gain promotions and remain in jobs because of tenure, not because they are the best individuals for the job. In fact, when one is considering candidates for promotion, longevity, credentials, and experience often substitute for results.
2. Christmas bonuses are given out because it's Christmas time, not because people earned them.
3. End-of-year raises are doled out because it's the end of the year, not because people went the second mile.
4. Dollars are dumped into black holes to fund monthly incentive programs and contests that enrich everyone without regard to whether they deserve to participate based on past performance.

65

5. Managers hold sugarcoated, politically correct employee reviews and evaluations rather than telling people they're not cutting it.

6. Managers set no-brainer performance standards designed to make people feel safe and comfortable rather than stretch them with a higher bar.

7. Managers spend equal amounts of time, energy, and resources on employees evenly across the board rather than pouring resources into the top performers who have earned it based on past results.

8. Managers would rather be well liked and popular than confront poor performers and hold others accountable for results.

9. Overall, employees focus more on what they are owed than on what they owe the company or their coworkers. Many have retired on the job.

10. People have an expectancy that more and more should be done for them and whatever is done is never enough.

11. Yesterday's heroes — who have stopped performing — continually borrow credibility from past accomplishments and try to cash royalty checks from who they were and what they did long ago.

12. Employees have a "quota" mentality, believing someone should or shouldn't get a job or opportunity because of race or gender rather than results.

13. Pressure to perform has been supplanted by pressure to conform.

Do any of these symptoms sound familiar? If they do, you're not alone. In fact, they are pervasive throughout our country. If they don't sound familiar, congratulations, and rest assured you will find principles throughout this book to help you preserve and build on your culture of merit. Now examine nine traits of a merit culture.

Nine Traits of a Culture of Merit

1. A merit culture mandates that the strongest people in your workplace must be fully supported and leveraged and the weak links weeded out.
2. A culture of merit distributes recognition, rewards, and opportunities based on what people earn and deserve, not equally across the board.
3. A culture of merit holds people accountable and shows that if you can't meet minimum performance standards you lose your job, because leaders are not afraid to fire those who can't cut it.
4. A culture of merit does not allow tenure, experience, or credentials to substitute for getting the job done.
5. A culture of merit doesn't blindly accept or tolerate an employee for what he or she is, but creates an environment hostile to mediocrity and presents a positive peer pressure to perform. People worry more about letting their teammates down than letting the boss down.
6. In a merit culture people want to be held accountable, to be told how they're doing. Living in a gray area demotivates them.
7. A merit culture welcomes the championing of heroes and the punishment of slackers.
8. In a culture of merit, *termination* is not a bad word. Everyone understands that when an employee is forced to leave the company it is not for personal reasons or to explore other options; it's because he or she flat out didn't get the job done.
9. In a merit culture everyone comes to work to prove them-

selves over again every day. No one merely goes through paces or budgets their efforts.

KEEP SOCIETY AND BUSINESS MIND-SETS IN THEIR PROPER PLACES

To create a culture of merit in your workplace it's imperative that society's politically correct tendencies not be allowed to seep into your business psyche. For example, society's entitlement model says: "Weaken the strong to strengthen the weak." This is evinced in tax rates that increase as you make more money and in organized sports that give kids equal playing time rather than allocating opportunities in proportion to their performance. It is amplified when affirmative action gives preferences based on ethnicity or gender rather than accomplishment. A merit culture espouses the opposite of this philosophy. It dictates that your strongest people should be supported, rewarded, and leveraged while you either turn the weak ones around or weed them out. Society's mind-set says that everyone should have equal access to opportunities and resources, whereas a merit model dictates that treating people fairly doesn't mean you treat them all alike. It means they are treated in a manner they earn and deserve, and that they haven't all earned — nor do they deserve — equal amounts of your time, resources, or opportunities.

Think about it for a moment. Is there any fairer way to treat someone than in accordance with what they have earned and deserve? In fact, who are the only people in your organization who would have a problem getting only what they earned and deserved? Obviously, those who haven't earned much and don't deserve much! Society's entitlement model says that if you can't make it on your own, government programs will subsidize the tough times and that if you can't afford a lawyer, one will be given to you.

Please note: I'm not judging the value of these models, but simply pointing out how society's mind-set and agenda conditions and can influence your business thinking. What you see and hear in politics, on the news, and on television takes root in your business psyche, diluting and perverting the performance-based philosophy required to create a culture of merit in a business. As a leader, you must keep society's mind-set, which is rooted in entitlement, separate from your business mind-set, which must be rooted in performance. If you confuse the two your business descends from a meritocracy into a welfare state, from leader to laggard.

Up Your Business! Bullet	**Seek improvement over being approved. Your job is not to make people happy; your job is to get them better. Get them better and they start to get happy.**

FAMILY VERSUS TEAM MODEL

Let me put the difference in mind-sets in yet another perspective. To build a merit culture and weed out entitlement you must run your business more like a team than like a family. While having "one big happy family" sounds ideal, as with society's entitlement model, there are serious flaws with a family mind-set when put in the perspective of the performance-based culture needed in business.

For instance, family models are too forgiving and accepting to work well in business. In a family, no one is judged; everyone is accepted and benefits strictly because they belong — not because they perform. Family models are too generous and too tolerant to serve well in a culture of merit. No one can be fired from a family. Membership in a family is the epitome of entitlement; it is assumed and not earned.

On the other hand, people on a team must prove themselves and earn their way, and they are judged and rewarded based on their contribution. There is pressure to perform. Team members are held accountable for results, not best efforts, and nonperformers find themselves off the team.

A CULTURE OF MERIT BRINGS FORTH DISCRETIONARY EFFORT

A healthy, productive merit culture will create the conditions where employees put forth discretionary effort. *Discretionary effort* is the extra level of performance people give when they want to do something as opposed to when they feel they must do something. Discretionary effort is like loose change in an employee's pocket: It's up to the leader to get the person to spend it. It's the difference-maker between employee compliance and commitment.

Behaviorally speaking, discretionary effort will occur only when expectations are high, employees are motivated, and productive behaviors are positively reinforced. Positive reinforcement is a key element in building a culture of merit where results are consistently spectacular because employees have become "and-then-some" people: They do what is required and then some. They hit their forecast and then some. They deliver to a customer what they promise and then some. In fact, a merit culture presents a positive peer pressure to do so.

ENVIRONMENT DICTATES BEHAVIOR

Since environment dictates behavior, it is the key to effective execution and lasting results. Thus, organizations with erratic or unspectacular outcomes can find their problems rooted in poor or defective environment. It's important to note that as you move from entitlement to merit, your culture will not change significantly until you actually get results — and get them quickly. Your change must develop roots to sustain the new culture. And lest we forget, the culture is ultimately the responsibility of the leader.

Up Your Business! Bullet	**Building, protecting, and reinforcing a merit culture takes endless attention and work. A leader in that organization must be less of a show horse and more of a plow horse. He or she must perform cultural due diligence day in and day out.**

UP YOUR BUSINESS! ACTION THOUGHTS

DEFINING A CULTURE OF ENTITLEMENT AND A CULTURE OF MERIT

1. Survey your business environment and employee attitudes to determine whether entitlement is gripping your culture. Which departments need the most immediate attention?
2. Assess the leader of each individual department and determine the leader's effectiveness at creating the department's culture.
3. Evaluate the amount of consistent discretionary effort you are getting from employees. If they are just going through the motions or doing the bare minimum possible, what does this tell you about your environment and your leadership? How will you turn it around?
4. What will you do to redefine and enhance your workplace culture?

Five Steps to Move from Entitlement to Merit

1. *Decide where the new bar of expectations should be set.* Remember that when a goal is too high or too low, people don't get involved. Thus, your challenge is to find that optimal point that keeps people stretching and at the same time believing they can reach it. This is art and not science. Psychologists estimate that motivation is the highest when there's about a fifty-fifty chance of reaching an objective.

2. *Clearly redefine the performance expectations and deadlines.* This creates a benchmark for future accountability. In fact, without defining expectations, holding people accountable is impossible. When you redefine these expectations, it's an ideal time to raise the bar. In many organizations the bar is so low people keep tripping over it. They have expected so little for so long, many have retired on the job. Some ruts are so powerful you don't even know you're in them. To get out of a rut you must disturb the equilibrium by clearly redefining higher standards.

3. *Meet with your employees one on one to discuss the new expectations.* Explain why they are important and what's in it for them once they meet expectations as well as the potential consequences of failing. You should also discuss strategies for reaching the objectives and offer your help to get the person there. Involve the employee in the plan to reach the new targets, because people will buy into and support what they help create.

4. *Maintain pressure to perform.* Every business needs pressure to perform in order to build and sustain a merit culture. I define *pressure to perform* as clear and high performance expectations, fast feedback on performance, and accountability for results.

Quickly reward progress toward the expectations and just as quickly confront shortfalls. Delayed consequences lose their punch and are rendered ineffective, so hurry to get toe to toe with your employees either way. Maintaining pressure to perform also means establishing positive consequences for reaching an objective and punishing consequences for failing to do so. Consequences are either carrots or sticks, and it's up to you to leverage them effectively and appropriately. Behavioral science teaches that if you want to change a behavior you must change the consequences for that behavior. Thus, to fix, build, or stretch your organization you must learn to coach with consequences.

5. *Stick to your guns.* Understand up front that entitled people go into denial when suddenly there is pressure to perform. In fact, many will wear brave smiles while they conceal a barely controlled state of panic at the thought of having to actually get back to work and produce again. Thus, they secretly hope that if they keep their heads down and give your new demands the "kiss of yes," those demands will eventually fade away as so many other flavors of the month have over the years. This is why you must maintain pressure to perform long enough to let people know the good old days are over and what you are doing is not an experiment. It's natural for people to resist change and pressure to perform, so you're safe in expecting it. They may not come right out and whine, because resistance often comes in code. In other words, people will start doing and saying subtle things in an attempt to subvert your efforts. When this happens, call them on it quickly. If you don't confront this behavior you are, in effect, reinforcing it and will see more of it. Here's the danger: If you don't stick with your new standards of performance expecta-

tions and accountability, and fail to maintain a consistent pressure to perform long enough to change your environment, entitlement will reestablish itself in your culture stronger than ever before and make it much more difficult to weed out in the future.

While I don't believe in or advocate shortcuts in general, there is a significant shortcut to changing a culture: Change the leaders. Try to change their attitudes and behaviors first. If that doesn't work, you have the option of physically changing them. Either way, nothing changes a culture like changing the person responsible for it.

UP YOUR BUSINESS! ACTION THOUGHTS

FIVE STEPS TO MOVE FROM ENTITLEMENT TO MERIT

1. Follow the prescribed steps for moving from entitlement to merit. Spend enough time clearly determining the message you want to send and the direction you wish to head in before embarking on the journey.
2. Commit to sticking with your new performance expectations long enough to anchor them in your culture.
3. If a drastic and/or immediate culture change is needed, consider changing key personnel.

THE MANDATE OF PRESSURE TO PERFORM

If you listen to the feel-good Pollyanna pundits, you will follow their karmic advice and work hard to create a stress-free workplace. Do so at your own peril, because this philosophy is insane! Chant or burn incense if you like, but be warned that in a stress-free workplace nothing gets done. You'll have to go in every day and ring a bell to wake people up! While too much pressure to perform is detrimental to performance, so is too little. As discussed previously, a leader must work to create that optimal amount of pressure, because as negative as this sounds, there is something we must acknowledge about human nature: It's inclined to slide backward, not forward. In fact, going the second mile is an unnatural act. Anyone going the second mile does so very deliberately. Granted, it is possible to discipline oneself to go the second mile so often that it has become second nature, but for most people in the workforce it sounds a bit troublesome. Understanding this about human nature, leaders are remiss if they don't establish expectations and impose accountability to pull people through the natural tendency to let up. Face it: We aren't at our best when life is too safe. We get fat, lazy, rusty, and complacent and lose our edge. This is why effective leaders don't apologize for stretching their people. Instead, weak leaders should apologize for the unforgivable act of allowing people to calcify in a mold and rot in a comfort zone. Your best people will respond positively to a continuing pressure to perform that keeps them sharp and brings out their best. Your weak people will find it stressful, will become disabled, and may leave your organization. Alleluia! Because either way, you win.

Up Your Business! Bullet	**We are not at our best when life is too safe. In fact, too much certainty is cause for depression. Uncertainty keeps you alert, interested, and engaged.**

UP YOUR BUSINESS! ACTION THOUGHTS

THE MANDATE OF PRESSURE TO PERFORM

1. Embrace and act upon the idea that without consistently communicated high expectations, accountability, and a positive pressure to perform, your people will let up, and this let-up can turn into a stall. Who has let up and must be quickly addressed?
2. Don't apologize for expecting and drawing the best out of your people. Top performers expect it and respond to it.

ENTITLEMENT AND THE QUESTION OF SUCCESSION

In a culture of entitlement, conventional wisdom will tell you to promote the person with the most tenure and experience. After all, the logic goes, we owe it to them to repay their loyalty. This philosophy can be found infecting government jobs, unions, and universities and is absolutely debilitating when trying to build a performance-based merit culture. Henry Ford put it well: "Asking 'who should be the leader?' is like asking who should be the tenor in the quartet. Of course, it's the person who can sing tenor."

Let me suggest who is next in line for a promotion in your organization: It's the person who can best get the job done. After all, you're running a business, not the royal family. Leaders express concern that they'll send the wrong message about the importance of loyalty and paying your dues if they don't promote the tenured, loyal person. The truth is that you send a much stronger detrimental message by not rewarding results and failing to promote the best person for the job.

76

UP YOUR BUSINESS! ACTION THOUGHTS

ENTITLEMENT AND THE QUESTION OF SUCCESSION

1. Get past sentimentalism and tradition and realize the next person in line for a promotion is the one who has earned it based on past performance, not on tenure, credentials, or years of experience.
2. Which slots are currently opening up or are already open that will require filling? Based on results and performance, who are the best people for those jobs?

FURTHER UP YOUR BUSINESS

TO BUILD A CULTURE OF MERIT, YOUR ORGANIZATION MUST DWELL ABOVE THE NECK!

More and more, people simply amaze me today. They've become experts at concocting explanations and victim stories to explain away their lack of success. And I'm not talking about the people dwelling at the bottom rungs of the corporate ladder but the leaders — or should I say, people in positions of authority that have leadership titles.

As a result of meeting, listening to, and observing thousands of managers and business owners over the years during my 150 annual speaking dates I've found I can divide the thinking and actions of people into two groups: those who live "above the neck" and those who dwell "below the neck." As you read over the differences between the two, evaluate where you and your team spend your time thinking and working.

77

Below-the-Neck Traits
Think about what you find below people's necks:

1. Pointing fingers. "Below-the-neck leaders" embrace the time-honored tradition of professional victims to blame other people for their lack of results — the lousy team, the stupid boss, the incompetents they are forced to work with — but the blame game doesn't stop there. The list includes parents, teachers, coaches, and old girlfriends. One thing is for certain: When you blame someone else you temporarily take the spotlight off yourself. But since you can't change what you don't acknowledge, blaming only perpetuates the misery you seek to resolve.

2. Twiddling thumbs. Since taking action involves risk, below-the-neck leaders have embraced the mantra that "this indecision is final." They discuss but never decide; study the race but never join it; stick their toes in but never take the plunge. As they sit still and conditions around them worsen they claim to be a victim of circumstances even while they author their own demise.

3. Covering behinds. When things turn south the strategy of choice for a society of below-the-neck leaders has been to blame outside conditions rather than inside decisions. Let's blame the weather, the economy, the war, the time of year, the inventory, the crazy competitor, the rise in interest rates, and how about the full moon while we're at it? By blaming outside conditions weak leaders cover their own behinds and make sure there is a stable of scapegoats to take the spotlight off their own inadequate and failed leadership.

4. Sitting on behinds. In this ultimate bond with denial, below-the-neck leaders pretend not to see problems and thus absolve themselves from having to do anything about them. They are addicted to a "wait and see" strategy that turns into a sinkhole

when possible solutions get stalled behind a dam of inaction. By taking no action, these people think they're being optimistic when they're simply engaging in wishful thinking. When things collapse they look and act confused and frantically react to the crises triggered by their own immobility.

5. Kicking the cat. In this phase of victimhood below-the-neck leaders are so deluded by their own incompetence they not only blame others, they fire them. They subscribe to the mistaken notion that by putting a fresh rider on a dead horse they will be able to move it — an outrageous fantasy as long as the poor leader who created the crisis continues to infect it with his or her failure to step up and take responsibility for its lack of success.

6. Constipation. Corporate constipation takes place when the below-the-neck leaders indulge in a diet of the five points above. Over time, the whole system gets stopped up. People stop growing, results plateau, and morale comes to a standstill. What these organizations need is an enema of urgency brought on by an injection of pressure to perform, accountability, and leaders who will look the hideous reality that has created their problems in the eye and take massive action to remedy it.

Above-the-Neck Traits
Now think about what you find above the neck:

1. Eyes that focus on reality. "Above-the-neck" leaders look reality in the eye and make the right and hard decisions to bring vitality to their organization.

2. Ears that listen. Above-the-neck leaders lead with questions. They don't just tolerate feedback or dissenting opinions, they insist on it. They know that only as they create an organization where the truth is spoken and heard can they make

sound decisions and avoid developing blind spots brought about by yes men and too much reliance on oneself.

3. A face that looks in the mirror. Above-the-neck leaders work as hard on themselves as they do on their jobs. They focus on self-improvement, developing self-discipline, and holding themselves accountable. They accept that nothing gets better in their business until they do.

4. A mouth that accepts responsibility. Above-the-neck leaders accept responsibility. They're not afraid to say "It's my fault" or "I screwed up." But they know that accepting responsibility is more than making confessions. It is taking corrective action boldly and quickly.

5. A brain that thinks of solutions. Above-the-neck leaders focus on solutions. They focus on facts more than feelings and devote their resources and energies to those things they can control rather than whining about conditions they cannot.

6. A nose that sniffs out opportunity. Above-the-neck leaders have a nose for opportunity. Since they accept responsibility and don't waste time blaming or looking for scapegoats, their time and energy are freed up to think in terms of playing to win rather than playing not to lose. Below-the-neck leaders exhaust themselves defending their actions and trying to maintain the status quo; above-the-neck leaders grab the prize while the whiners rub their eyes.

It's time for leaders living below the neck to step up and stamp out the age of victimhood in their business, and they can start by holding themselves to the high standards found in a culture of merit. Otherwise, their own deficient actions, attitudes, and abilities aid and abet a culture of entitlement in their business. After all, nothing creates more corporate complacency than a whiny, entitled leader.

CHAPTER 3

Develop Your Human Capital

How to Train, Coach, Mentor, and Retain Eagles

Thus far, you've journeyed through two key steps for fixing, building, or stretching your organization: You've taken a fresh look at the significance of finding and keeping the right people, and you have become more aware of the importance of the environment in which they work. Now it's time to roll up your sleeves and develop the human capital in your charge. Talent rarely arrives fully developed, and one of a leader's greatest responsibilities is to take the human capital he or she is entrusted with and make it more valuable tomorrow than it is today. Thus, creating and committing to a process of training, coaching, mentoring, and differentiating your people is the next discipline you must incorporate into your leadership repertoire. In this chapter I'll present strategies for accomplishing these ends as well as outlining how to accelerate the growth of your best people with effective delegation and how to deliver the fast, brutally honest feedback they need to grow.

Developing people starts with the right mind-set from the leadership in an organization. To judge from the number of companies who poorly or inconsistently develop their people, this mind-set needs urgent attention. Many managers don't invest the time or money necessary to develop their teams because they see training as an expense rather than an investment. Instead, they act as though time and experience alone will improve their people. On the contrary, the wrong experiences can make people worse, not better. Experience can be helpful when optimizing but not when innovating, because it's difficult for people to discover new lands using the same old map. Managers use excuses that training is difficult to quantify and that people serious about their careers should be willing to invest in themselves. These are cop-outs. Often, managers with this dinosaur mind-set were never trained, coached, or mentored themselves so they don't appreciate or value the developmental process.

Up Your Business! Bullet	**If you don't invest time and money in good people, you don't deserve them. In fact, you deserve to lose them, and probably will. It's just a matter of time.**

To develop human capital you must focus less on the cost of training your people and more on what it costs to neglect it. Yes, training is expensive. It takes plenty of time and money. But if you ever get hung up on the cost of training your people, consider the cost of their ignorance. Think about it: What does it cost to have a receptionist who can't handle calls with courtesy and efficiency? What's it cost to have a salesperson who can't greet a customer without offending him or her, who can't close a deal, overcome an objection, set an appointment, or ask for a referral? Here's one that will keep you up at night: What's the financial penalty when you have a manager who is ignorant of how to motivate or interview, who cannot create and cast a compelling vision or turn around a poor performer?

When managers do train their people, it's often ineffective. There's a substantial gap between training people and training them effectively. To grasp the difference, imagine a group of shopping-mall security guards battling a group of Navy Seals, or Barney Fife fighting Rambo, and you'll understand the difference between someone who is trained and one who is trained effectively.

Up Your Business! Bullet	**There is one thing worse than training people and having them leave your organization: It's not training them and having them stay!**

As you examine your strategy to train and develop your people, consider incorporating the factors discussed in the next section into your regimen.

How to Train Effectively

Train, Don't Just Educate

In my travels I get the opportunity to attend numerous training meetings, and one thing many have in common is that they are not real training meetings — they are educating meetings. Training meetings get people involved. Attendees are writing information down, practicing presentations or other job functions; salespeople are role-playing scripts. Educating meetings, on the other hand, are styled such that an instructor is presenting information — usually too much and with a boring delivery — and those in attendance are merely spectators, staring back, eyes glazed over, mentally disengaged from what is going on. If the attendees aren't doing most of the work in your training meetings, they aren't nearly as effective as they should be. To fully appreciate the difference between training and educating, consider the following. If your kids came home from school and told you they were taking sex education classes, you'd probably be okay with that. But if they walked in one day and mentioned they were going through sexual training, you'd have a totally different reaction! Think about your training meetings: Are people involved, and are their senses engaged in what's going on? People learn and retain better when they are involved, hands-on, and taking action. As Mark Twain declared, "Anyone who carries a cat home by the tail will learn a lot more about cats than someone who merely watches a cat."

CONSCIOUSLY HONE YOUR PRESENTATION SKILLS

Training and managing are two different skill sets. As important as training is, few companies train their trainers to train. Chances are, you are involved with some type of training in your current job. It may encompass one-on-one instruction or classroom-style presenting.

To improve your own speaking skills read David People's book *Presentations Plus* (John Wiley & Sons, 1992). This book is a must-read for everyone holding any sort of presentation or training meeting. If you want to improve your presentations, buy this book. It's a fun, fast read that will build your confidence.

Keep in mind that your purpose in conducting a training session or meeting of any genre is to relate and not to proclaim. Don't become so enamored with the sound of your own voice that you pontificate when you should be connecting, influencing, and teaching.

STRIKE AT THE ROOT: MANAGEMENT TRAINING MEETINGS

One of the most neglected aspects of any training program is a focus on consistently training the managers. There are training meetings for new hires and sales training meetings, but rarely do top leadership teams get together to learn together. On the other hand, management meetings are common, often too common. These are gatherings at which leaders discuss budgets, ad strategies, and forecasts. Management meetings are important to control the technical aspects of an organization, but only management *training* meetings deliberately develop the leadership capacities of your managers. Management training meetings can center on discussing strategies for motivating employees or turning around poor performers. They cover interview and recruiting techniques, effective leadership styles, strategic thinking exercises, and more. Books, videos, and audio resources on pertinent topics are helpful to guide and facilitate these meetings. When you think about it, what could be a better use of your time than getting together to grow the people charged with growing your business?

UP YOUR BUSINESS! ACTION THOUGHTS

HOW TO TRAIN EFFECTIVELY

1. Make certain your training meetings are getting people involved—that the attendees are players, not spectators.
2. Develop your training skills and delivery style so your meetings are interesting, engaging, value-adding, and entertaining.
3. Make training your managers a priority. Sending them off to an annual seminar doesn't cut it. Initiate internal, ongoing management training meetings.

Up Your Business! Bullet	**Get your managers good and they'll get their people good.**

THE GOOD, THE BAD, AND THE UGLY: COACHING YOUR PEOPLE WITH FAST, FREQUENT, BRUTALLY HONEST FEEDBACK

If you're serious about getting better performances from your people and developing them to their fullest potential, you must deliver feedback on their performance quickly, honestly, and consistently. People can't grow when they live in a gray area. Good coaches understand the importance of feedback. In fact, perhaps the best definition of *coaching* is the combined acts of observing, analyzing performance, and delivering fast feedback. The best coaches are leaders who lead from the front. They spend enough time in the trenches to discern what is really going on and offer meaningful feedback on performance. The alternative is to be locked in your office atop the ivory tower and rely on intuition or secondhand information to make judgments and espouse advice. Remote-control leaders who spend more time with things than with people are the least effective managers. They haven't the credibility or the insight to help others grow. Thus, if you are going to develop people, you're going to have to actually spend time with them. I've seen leaders who can impress others at a distance, but only those who get up close can affect people.

THE GOOD: POSITIVE REINFORCEMENT

Positive feedback is a form of positive reinforcement. Positive reinforcement is like oxygen. It's the tool of choice for leaders wanting to improve the behaviors that will improve results. Psychologists tell us that behaviors that get reinforced get repeated. Thus, if someone is doing the right thing, makes a good decision, or engages in useful action, the leader had better reinforce it if he or she wants to see more of it. I've heard my share of old-school managers asking why they should reinforce or compliment someone for doing something they're getting paid to do in the first place. This Neanderthal attitude displays a glaring ignorance of how human nature works. In fact, by failing to reinforce worthy performances you can extinguish them.

The key to positive reinforcement is to deliver it quickly, because delayed consequences lose their punch. Again, this is why leaders who stay engaged at the front lines of their business are better coaches, since you must be proximate to reinforce — and especially to reinforce quickly. Think about the trainer who gives the porpoise a fish for completing a jump through the flaming hoop: When does he give the reward? Immediately! He doesn't wait a week, a day, or an hour. Such delayed approaches would be impotent in trying to develop the habit of jumping through the hoop on command. The problem is that most managers seem to know more about training mammals than about getting better behavior out of their people. Think about how quickly you and your organization give positive reinforcement. For instance, getting a paycheck or bonus is a form of positive reinforcement. It brings closure to work well done and allows the employee to focus on the next matter at hand. Bearing this in mind, how timely is your delivery of this type of positive reinforcement? The same goes for acknowledgment of having a great day, week, or month. If you take these accomplishments for granted you're sending the wrong message to your workforce and will eliminate the productive behaviors you want. People's performance will be uninspired and results will be inconsistent. Don't worry about overdoing positive reinforcement. I've never heard anyone tell a manager, "You know, boss, the problem with you is that you reinforce me too much." The key is to reinforce the right behaviors. People must deserve it; otherwise it won't mean anything when they get it.

Another key aspect of positive reinforcement is that it is always in the eyes of the receiver, not the giver. In other words, it must mean something to the person getting it or it's ineffective. If the porpoise jumps through the hoop and its trainer offers it a carrot, it probably won't be as inclined to jump through again. If what you are using as positive reinforcement doesn't cause a behavior to be repeated, it is not effective. Change your approach. Don't wait for the performer to adapt to your efforts.

Another benefit of positive reinforcement is that it's contagious. When a leader creates a culture where people are publicly and quickly championed for good performance, he or she starts a chain reaction and establishes a value that followers will emulate. Reinforced people reinforce other people.

The Other Side of the Coin

If behaviors that are reinforced and rewarded are repeated, consider this: If someone is doing a poor job and you don't confront it, aren't you in effect reinforcing it? You bet you are. This is how managers unwittingly encourage and breed poor performances. Since they never address them, they in effect endorse them and can expect to see more of them. And you really can't fault the poor performer, who is only behaving in a way that's been reinforced in the past. Thus, when coaching people for better behaviors and results it is just as important to confront poor performances quickly as it is to reinforce good ones quickly. This takes constant attention but is an essential part of a leader's job. Personally, I'm not going to let someone have eight bad days in a row before we sit down and talk about it. Eight bad hours is stretching it. On the other hand, I can't afford to let my best players have victory after victory without getting in there and letting them hear about how well they're doing. This affirmation brings a sense of closure for past good works and provides the incentive they need to work hard and earn acclamations in the future.

| Up Your Business! Bullet | **What gets reinforced gets repeated. What gets punished doesn't. It's that simple.** |

THE BAD: EMPTY FEEDBACK

Empty feedback is the result of poor and inattentive leadership. It occurs when managers give no feedback, good or bad. When employees are doing well they don't hear about it, and when they do poorly they are not confronted. In simplest terms, this means that people performing productively are less likely to continue to do so since their behaviors aren't being reinforced; at the same time, those slouching or underperforming continue their derelict duty since it is not addressed. By virtue of their neglect managers guilty of empty feedback extinguish productive behavior at the same time they unwittingly encourage slack efforts. Managers that won't come down off their hierarchy horse, who stay locked in their offices — presiding rather than leading — and who otherwise fall out of touch with their people are the biggest perpetrators of empty feedback. Their aloofness creates performance casualties at all levels. These weak leaders are often the most likely to look out the window and curse their people's performance when the real problem is staring back at them in the mirror.

89

| Up Your Business! Bullet | **No news is not good news when coming from the leader.** |

The Ugly: Negative Reinforcement

As bad as the term *negative reinforcement* sounds, it is a legitimate aspect of coaching. There comes a time when enough is enough. You've dangled carrot after carrot, given endless pep talks, and begged and pleaded for performance until you're worn out. You don't want to fire the person yet, but you desperately need to turn them around. Enter negative reinforcement. Negative reinforcement attaches a consequence for continued poor performance. In essence, it says, "Do it or else." Behavioral science teaches that if you want to change someone's behavior, you've got to change the consequence for that behavior. Consequences can be either carrots or sticks. In the case of negative reinforcement, it's the stick. The fact is, you've used negative reinforcement instinctively throughout your whole life. It's what you did to stop your kids from beating up their little brother and coloring the walls with crayons. It's how you teach your pet not to unleash its facilities on your carpet or chew the sofa. It's a key reason that, after you suffer the consequence of a speeding ticket, you become more aware of your speed and change your driving habits to abide by the limit — at least for a while.

The key to negative reinforcement is to use it strictly to turn around poor performance. Once the performance improves, you switch back to positively reinforcing the person. Continuing to negatively reinforce people to improve their performance is exhausting for you and the person. In fact, if you have an employee who responds only to negative reinforcement — who does the job only when threatened with a consequence — it's a sure sign you have the wrong person. When you sit down with an employee and give negative reinforcement, it's important you document your conversation and both the expected target and the consequence in writing and put these in the employee's file. This creates a vital paper trail you'll need later if you must follow through and terminate that employee. You should also help the person map out what he or she must do to turn this performance around, and offer support and encouragement. As important as it is to let people know where they stand, you can't just let them know and then leave them there.

It's also important that even after you negatively reinforce someone you begin to positively reinforce their new behaviors once the person displays the actions you're looking for. Also, it's important to keep in mind that trying to help someone form a new habit will take four to five times the reinforcement you think it should — so stay after it.

Negative reinforcement is a form of tough love. It means you care enough to confront people and get them out of a gray area as you show them the route to better performance. Effective leaders leverage both positive and negative reinforcement appropriately. You can't just walk around dangling carrots or spend all your time wielding sticks and expect to coach people to higher levels of performance. You must employ a combination of both, swiftly and consistently. It takes constant attention and commitment but, when all is said and done, it's well worth the payoff you get when people improve their performance.

Constructive Feedback
Constructive feedback is designed to improve the behavior of an employee by coaching and showing him or her how to improve performance. Constructive feedback is not saying, "You really screwed

that up!" In fact, that type of feedback is debilitating. *Constructive feedback* is given when you point out a deficiency in a behavior but offer help on how to make it better next time. As leaders, we need to receive constructive feedback so we can keep growing, and your people need to hear it from you so they continue to grow as well.

A chapter on feedback wouldn't be complete without a statement of how important it is that you continue to get it for your own performance. While you can help others grow by giving it, you grow by getting it. The problem is that most leaders don't ask for it and still more aren't interested in hearing it. Some managers declare that they have an open-door policy and that people can come in and give them feedback any time they like. The sad fact is that most people won't, and those who do are always the same people. A real open-door policy allows the leader to go through the open door and ask the tough questions to subordinates and superiors alike: "What can I do better? How can I help you better do your job? What do I do around here that destroys momentum and attitudes and that I should stop doing?" It takes courage to ask these questions, and honest answers often hurt. But I know of no better way to build trust and openness and to grow your own leadership skills.

A business owner who attended my leadership seminar told me that he had devised a survey he passed out to employees that allowed them to rate him from 1 to 10 in several areas and turn the surveys in anonymously. One of the categories he asked to be rated in concerned his effectiveness as a motivator. He then told me he had only scored a 2 in this category. He told me, "Dave, in order for me to score two, there were a lot of ones that showed up on the surveys to bring my average down. I had to take a hard look in the mirror. I thought that overall I was a productive force in the workplace, but I discovered I was actually destructive and acted on the feedback to change my approach."

UP YOUR BUSINESS! ACTION THOUGHTS

THE GOOD, THE BAD, AND THE UGLY: COACHING YOUR PEOPLE WITH FAST, FREQUENT, BRUTALLY HONEST FEEDBACK

1. Feedback is necessary for people to grow. It must be fast, consistent, and brutally honest.
2. Behaviors that get reinforced get repeated. You can't take them for granted.
3. When you don't confront poor behavior, in effect, you reinforce it and can expect more of it.
4. Empty feedback is the result of poor and inattentive leadership. It snuffs out good performance and encourages subpar performance.
5. Negative reinforcement is a tool to turn around poor performance because it attaches a consequence for continuing to perform poorly.
6. If you want to change someone's behavior you must change the consequences for that behavior.
7. Constructive feedback lets people know what you think of their performance but doesn't leave them there. It shows them how to improve it.
8. Actively and earnestly seek out feedback for yourself that will help you grow and improve as a leader and as a person.

I can recall when I was director of training for a large automotive training company and I was being trained to conduct a three-day sales workshop. The company broke me in to holding their classes by letting me have my first shot in a small town, so if I botched it I wouldn't offend too many people. They also sent a small panel of judges — solemn-looking women who sat in the back of the room with frowns on their faces, making notes of my successes and victories while I conducted class. After the first day of my first class, I sat down with my judges to receive their feedback on my performance. I felt pretty good about the class and was looking forward to being acclaimed during this review. I was in for an eye-opener. They started the feedback session by covering the things I had done well. There were three things on that list. (Keep in mind this was an eight-hour class!) Then we discussed the areas where I needed to improve. I can still remember to this day that there were sixty-seven things on that list. It took three and one-half hours to cover it. This feedback session was one of the toughest things I had ever been through. I felt like I had been stomped on and run into the wall. I wasn't excited about hearing what they had to say. In many instances, I didn't think I needed to hear what they had to say. But the fact was that I did need to hear it, and it helped me tremendously. The next day there were only twenty-two items on the list, and the third day there were only six. Pretty soon, those sour, dour judges stopped following me around as I earned their confidence to hold the classes without supervision.

Be aware that you're getting feedback every day if you're paying attention. For instance, if you have an open-door policy and no one's coming through it, that's a form of feedback on how you're perceived as a listener and as being open to change. If you have good people who continually leave your organization, that's also a form of feedback on your role as a leader and motivator. If you are in charge of people who aren't getting much better, this is a serious indication of your hiring, training, and coaching skills. Suffice it to say that feedback is all around you. You just need to care enough to open your eyes and ears and realize it's the key to growing yourself.

THE KEY TO ONE-ON-ONE COACHING AND TRAINING

An important part of effective feedback is one-on-one coaching sessions you have with your employees. One-on-ones are much less rigid than formal performance evaluations and give you a greater opportunity to connect with and build relationships with team members.

Early in my management career I attended a seminar that advised me to hold one-on-ones with my salespeople. This sounded like a great idea. The problem was that they never told me *how* to conduct them. Thus, my one-on-ones weren't very effective. In fact, they were similar to indictments. I'd bring each employee into my office, effectively swear them in, and read a list of ten charges against them. Soon, no one wanted to have a one-on-one with me.

Fortunately, I discovered an effective five-step method for holding high-impact one-on-one coaching sessions. Follow this process the next time you go behind closed doors with an employee and your impact will increase exponentially.

STEP 1: ASK

Start the one-on-one by asking the person questions. This opens people up and gives them air. Ask about their goals, their strategies, their progress or frustrations, how they think team morale and output could be improved, and how you can help them better do their jobs.

The "ask" step is counterintuitive to most managers because the natural tendency is to start a one-on-one by telling. However, effective leaders always diagnose before they prescribe. Think about how a doctor treats you. Before writing out a prescription or rattling off a snappy answer, the doctor is careful to find out what ails you. Just as you'd have little confidence in a doctor who prescribes a solution before diagnosing your ailment, your "prescriptions" won't be well received until your people feel you're tuned in to what's really going on with them and their careers.

Up Your Business! Bullet	**People don't understand until they feel understood.**

STEP 2: LISTEN

After you ask questions, have the good sense to zip it and listen without interrupting. Don't judge or jump down the employee's throat or you'll sabotage the one-on-one and wind up presiding over its disintegration. While listening, don't shift from being a coach to becoming a know-it-all problem solver. Teach your people to discover their own answers by asking them what they think their options are and what they think will or won't work. Many leaders have a hard time listening because they're used to doing all the talking. But it's important to remember that leadership is a dialogue, not a monologue, and you can never learn a thing while talking. After all, no good idea ever entered the head through an open mouth.

Up Your Business! Bullet	**Big leaders monopolize the listening. Small leaders monopolize the conversation.**

STEP 3: COACH

Only after going through steps 1 and 2 are you ready to credibly coach your employee. At this stage you should make suggestions and offer solutions that haven't been discovered yet. You should also focus people on what they can control and not let them assume the posture of victim. Otherwise, one-on-ones tend to turn into therapy sessions. You'll also find that if you diligently work through steps 1 and 2, the person will be more open to what you have to stay at this point since he or she feels understood and believes you have a better grasp of the situation.

STEP 4: REINFORCE

This is your opportunity to praise and reinforce the behaviors and results the employee has displayed. Ideally, you will have done this earlier, closer to the actual time of the action, but this gives you a chance to reaffirm those behaviors or mention them for the first time if you've missed prior opportunities to reinforce. When it comes to reinforcement, err on the side of giving too much of it rather than thinking you're overdoing it. I've never had anyone say, "You know, boss, the problem with you is that you reinforce me too darned much."

STEP 5: STRETCH

Challenging the person and establishing accountability for future action and results is an effective way to end a one-on-one. This step gives you a chance to redefine what is expected, encourage stretching and growth toward the objective, and set a benchmark for future accountability.

I recommend you start a one-on-one binder with dividers for each of the people you hold these coaching sessions with. The binder can contain notes from prior meetings, the employee's current results, charts, graphs, and so on. How often you hold these meetings is up to you, but keep in mind that the more often you conduct them the less time they'll require. Personally, I wouldn't want more than a week to pass without having a one-on-one with my top people. (I'll discuss the importance of paying attention to your top people as a priority later in this chapter.) You may also find it helpful to schedule one-on-ones instead of waiting until you have everything else done before trying to hold one, or you'll find they'll never get done. These coaching sessions should be a priority. They offer an unmatched opportunity to connect, build relationships with, listen to, learn from, teach, coach, guide, and hold accountable the valuable human capital you have the privilege of leading.

UP YOUR BUSINESS! ACTION THOUGHTS

THE KEY TO ONE-ON-ONE COACHING AND TRAINING

1. One-on-one coaching sessions should be a top priority to develop your people. Schedule them as a priority.
2. Follow the five-step process and avoid the fatal flaw of talking too much or turning one-on-ones into dress-down sessions. They should be developmental, not punitive.
3. Focus people on what they can control, and organize your one-on-ones with a binder.
4. Spend more time with how-to's than should-be's. People learn faster and retain more when multiple senses are involved in the learning process. Keep people engaged in the process by making sure they are doing, not just listening or watching.

ONE-ON-ONE TRAINING

One-on-one *training* differs from one-on-one *coaching* in that you're performing a task with the employee, hands-on. When training someone to do a task, the best method is to first perform the task and have the employee watch you do it. Then, do it with the employee. Finally, he or she does it while you watch, after which you offer reinforcement and feedback on his or her performance. Too many managers would rather sit in their office chairs and talk about what good performance looks like than climb into the trenches and show people what it looks like. If you've been spending more time saying should-be than showing how-to, it's time to climb down off the hierarchy horse and lead by personal example rather than by personal convenience.

| Up Your Business! Bullet | **Your people would rather see a sermon than hear one.** |

THE MAGIC OF MENTORING

Mentoring is not for everyone whom you are directly responsible for leading. It is reserved for those with the most upward mobility: the ready, willing, and able. After all, your job as a leader is not to smack someone in the head with a bat and drag them around the bases. Every leader needs an inner circle of leaders in whom he or she invests more time, energy, and resources. John Maxwell, in *The 21 Irrefutable Laws of Leadership* (Thomas Nelson, 1998), describes the Law of the Inner Circle:[13] "Those closest to the leader determine the leader's success." Bearing this in mind, it is obvious how your inner circle is going to make or break your long-term leadership success. After all, you can't do it alone. Who makes up your inner circle? What are you doing to pour yourself into these people? These are the team members you know will produce the greatest return on investment in production and results. Mentoring gives you the opportunity to build depth and multiply yourself through these key people in your organization. Here are three steps to effective mentoring.

99

STEP 1: LAY THE RIGHT FOUNDATION

This starts with sitting down individually with each of your mentees and letting them know you've identified them as people with high potential and that you want to help them map out a growth path. Go over each person's strengths and discuss what you see as the next level of performance or job competency they should reach on their career paths. Discuss skill gaps they have that must be closed to reach these new levels, and together devise a plan to close those gaps. An important part of closing skill gaps is *delegation.* This word makes most leaders cringe because they've been burned by past efforts to delegate and have martyred themselves into doing the job themselves if they want it done right. Thus, overburdened by the menial and mundane, they plateau and fail to grow those around them. Here are ten keys that will help you delegate to accelerate the growth of your best people.

a. Delegate, don't dump. Dumping is when you toss a file of forms on someone's desk Friday at 4:00 P.M. and say you need them done by Monday at 9:00 A.M. This is abusive and creates delegation resistance. People feel like their reward for doing good work is having more work tossed at them by an ungrateful louse mandating an unreasonable deadline. Instead, explain why the task is important and that it is part of their development process.

b. Do the task with them. By performing the task with them a time or two before letting them run with it, you'll have a chance to show how it should be done, gauge their aptitude for the task, and build their confidence.

c. Delegate to people's strengths. Know your people well enough to hand off jobs they are wired to do. The whole idea is for

100

them to gain a victory, build confidence, increase their competence, and be ready for the even bigger assignments. You can't attain this if you're throwing them into arenas where they have little background or aptitude.

d. Clearly communicate what you want done and by when. Clarity is power, so be specific. Have them paraphrase back to you what you want done to determine their level of understanding.

e. Don't micromanage. Don't give them a ten-step plan to attain the outcome. If you do, they'll never take ownership. The task will still belong to you, and if it doesn't work out they won't accept responsibility since they were just executing the plan you administered. Instead, delegate outcomes without providing step-by-step methods. Advise people of minefields to avoid, but let them use their own ingenuity and energy to attain the outcome. Micromanagement is always easier in the short term, but your people won't grow.

f. Give the tools they need to get the job done. You have every right to ask that something be done but no right to expect it to get done if you don't provide the authority and resources necessary to pull it off. Clear away obstacles for your employees and make sure they have the discretion they need to make it happen. Set up directed autonomy. This is where the person can go to a certain point on his or her own without having to check with you.

g. Communicate throughout the process. Delegation is not an excuse to take a totally hands-off posture toward the task at hand, since you still own the ultimate responsibility for accomplishing it. Depending on the duration of the task, meet with the person periodically — not to micromanage but to offer support, answer questions, get updates, and keep your finger on the pulse of what's going on. This also presents positive accountability to keep the employee focused on getting the job done on time.

h. Expect and accept a certain number of mistakes. You can't grow people in a sterile and antiseptic manner. Sometimes it gets messy. People will make mistakes. In fact, mistakes are part of the growth process. The key is to use the error as a teaching opportunity and not as a battering ram. It's also important that you let the person know up front that you expect people who try new things to make mistakes, but that you don't expect them either to get defensive about them or to repeat them.

i. Avoid delegating to people who don't share your vision. You don't need to fight these battles just to prove a point. The fact is, when you delegate to people who aren't on the same page as you, they have a chance to sabotage the process — whether consciously or unconsciously — to prove they were right and you were wrong.

j. Lose your insecurity. Many leaders don't delegate because they are insecure. They fear giving power away and don't want to take the chance that anyone else might be as good as they are at a task. Other times, some managers won't hand off tasks because they get a high personal return from executing the task and don't want to let it go. And occasionally you find managers who won't hand tasks off because they think they're indispensable and are convinced no one else can do anything as well as they can. If you have any of these mind-sets, you will never grow a team. Your selfishness will curse you by immersing you in work you shouldn't have to do and will curse your team by stunting their growth. In addition to frustrating good people while they are in your employ, you can also count on running a good number of them off.

The number one reason good people leave an organization is to pursue personal growth opportunities elsewhere.

If you are a pompous leader and believe yourself to be indispensable, let me take the pressure off you: You're not that good! No one is. As Charles de Gaulle said, "The graveyard is filled with indispensable men." Let's face it: The day will come when you leave this earth and those you leave behind will put you in a box, lower you into the ground, shovel dirt on your face, and go back to the church to eat fried chicken and potato salad while they discuss the upcoming ball game that weekend. In other words, life goes on with or without you, so, if you'll forgive my bluntness, get over yourself — everyone else has!

Delegating doesn't diminish your importance. In fact, delegating multiplies your importance. Just as one candle's lighting another doesn't diminish its own light but multiplies it, so it is when you grow others. Delegation also offers you the exciting opportunity to hand off your weaknesses to others who are stronger than you in a given area. This frees you up to spend more time working in your areas of strength, which is the only way you can attain excellence. Part of growing up as a leader is looking in the mirror and knowing what you're wired to do and what you're not, and having the good sense to supplement your weaknesses with a strong team. In four decades, I'm somewhat embarrassed to say I've only found two personal talents: writing and speaking. I can't sing, dance, draw, paint, sculpt, fix, or build anything; I'm not good at any sport and can't play musical instruments. And I'm okay with this because I've finally realized that the mantra of "jack-of-all-trades and master of none" was a recipe for obscurity in business and in life. Life is simpler when you have only two strengths. It's easy to decide what to do and what to hand off to your team. I'm more effective and much happier than I was when I thought I had to do it myself if I wanted it done right. My people are happier as well, as they get chances to grow and contribute at higher levels of responsibility.

Giving your people stretch assignments is your opportunity to accelerate the growth of your best people. It's a win/win/win situation. You win because you're freed up to do more of what you're effective at. Others win because they become more competent, grow personally, gain confidence, and become more valuable to the organization. The organization wins by allowing people at all levels to be more productive and effective and by ensuring its long-term vitality through building a bench of more effective people at all levels. As a final note on delegation, consider it an opportunity to get rid of your weaknesses. Working in areas where you're no good drains you, and part of the joy of building a great team is surrounding yourself with others who complement your strengths and neutralize your weaknesses.

Up Your Business! Bullet	**Weak managers want to be needed. Real leaders want to be succeeded.**

STEP 2: HELP THEM DEVELOP A PLAN FOR PERSONAL GROWTH

The second step to mentor your high potentials is to help each develop a plan for personal growth. The best way to teach this is when you model your own personal growth program. A *personal growth program* is a discipline you develop to deliberately upgrade your own competencies. It may be something as simple as reading one book or listening to one compact disc per month on a topic in your field. If necessary, buy the first book or tape and put it in their hands. Tell them you'll get together in a month and cover the key points they gleaned from the work. Start a library at your business. This will put a visible priority on personal growth. The key to a personal growth plan is that it must be deliberate and measurable. If you read every once in a while, when you find the time, you don't have an effective personal growth program. There is nothing to hold you accountable or to measure your progress. Just like an exercise program, a personal growth program takes discipline and commitment. I'll discuss in Chapters 5 and 6 the importance of your developing this discipline and modeling personal growth before you can credibly expect others to adopt their own plan.

Up Your Business! Bullet	**As you add value to others it comes back to you multiplied. But you must add value first. That's why you're called the leader: Leaders go first.**

STEP 3: DELIBERATELY MAKE YOUR PEOPLE LESS DEPENDENT ON YOU

As you build a team you should do so with the goal of continually making them less dependent on you. In fact, the only way you can create this condition is to make your people more competent. In my first sales management job, I had this concept backward. I thought that the more my people relied upon me, the better a leader I was. I'd take the day off and my home phone would ring twelve times with my minions asking advice and permission on a number of trivial matters. I'd hang up the phone at the end of the day, sit back in my overstuffed chair, and proudly tell my wife about the job security I had at work. After all, what would these people do without me? I was the shepherd and they were my sheep. When it came time to take a vacation, it never failed: My team's sales would tank.

With my corrupt understanding of effective leadership, I'd point out to my spouse that every time I took a few days off my boss must gain a whole new appreciation for my value since nothing got done in my absence. Wrong! Wrong! Wrong! If I'd had a clue about being an effective leader I'd have realized that my people's failure in my absence was an indictment of my leadership, not an endorsement of it. I'd have known that the fact that I made all the decisions and had to sign off on all ideas that weren't my own was a reflection of leadership weakness, not strength.

I had created a state in my people known as *learned powerlessness*. When people are in this state they have become too dependent on the leader and they stop taking initiative. They won't make a decision, seize an opportunity, or make a change on their own. If you instill this state in your team you'll lose good people and plateau whatever and whomever you lead. Your ego may be fattened by people's reliance on you, but the esteem of your followers is diminished.

Up Your Business! Bullet	**The truest measure of your leadership is how well your people perform in your absence, not how they perform while you breathe down their necks.**

What are you doing to make your people less dependent on you? The following are two places to start.

Exhibit More Trust in Those You Lead
Trust is reciprocal. So is distrust. Whichever you exhibit to followers comes back to you multiplied. This may sound like a basic question, but I'll ask it anyway: Do you trust your people? If you answered in the affirmative, here's another question: How much money can they spend, on the spot, to solve a customer problem without any management sign-off? If your answer is that they

can't, because you want them to run each situation by you, you are communicating distrust. You don't trust either their character or their competence, or you'd give them discretion in this area. And if your response is that if I knew your people I'd understand why you can't trust them, you should look in the mirror — because the fact that you have people around you incapable of making a five-dollar decision is not a reflection of them as followers. It's a reflection of you as their leader.

Oftentimes, leaders declare that after their people earn trust and prove themselves they'll push power and increased discretion down to lower levels. Unfortunately, it doesn't work this way. People should be given a prescribed benefit of the doubt or you shouldn't have hired them in the first place. How they live up to this trust will determine whether their boundaries are broadened or withdrawn in the future, but you must trust them first. And don't fool yourself into thinking that increasing trust and broadening the discretion that goes with it will spur your people to turn the inch you're giving them into a mile. Quite the opposite — you'll find that people who have been given trust have a powerful incentive not to screw up.

Up Your Business! Bullet	**It is impossible to develop people you don't trust. If you don't trust them, you shouldn't have hired them — and shouldn't be keeping them — in the first place.**

When you do empower people with trust, you have an obligation to train them to use their power wisely, because choice without competence is dangerous. Give them directed autonomy. This is where you set limits bordered with boundaries. People are allowed to make decisions within these parameters before having to check with you. As they make good decisions you should increase their autonomy in proportion to their success. If they abuse their power you must deal with them accordingly. This may include counseling, retraining, reprimanding for repeat offenses, or removing discretion.

Push Decision Making Down the Hierarchy
Find ways to make fewer of the decisions yourself. When people bring you problems, rather than rattling off a quick-fix response, ask what they think should be done. If what they suggest makes sense, let them run with it. If your people have become conditioned to relying on you for the trivial, it may take some time to wean them off you, but by getting them in the habit of discovering their own answers you'll build the competence and confidence within them they need to grow.

| Up Your Business! Bullet | **Treat your people like partners, not peons.** |

It's vital that you empower intelligently. *Empowerment* is probably one of the most overused words and most abused concepts of the past decade. In fact, when I hear a manager talking about empowerment, my first impulse is to reach for the Maalox. Clearly, not everyone in an organization deserves the same level of empowerment. The key is to establish prescribed powers everyone shares in and then to elevate or diminish those limits based on proven performance. Empowering recklessly is dangerous. In fact, I've been inside many organizations where micromanagement would have been a more appropriate style of running the business than empowerment. Incidentally, if you are going to hire the wrong people, I highly suggest you micromanage them! It's a pitiful strategy for growing a business, but if you're going to bring morons on board, empowering them will only exacerbate the misery.

Studying history is my hobby. I find you can learn volumes about leadership when you do: people who did it well and people who screwed it up. We can learn from both. When you study the Civil War, you find a classic example of an empowering leader versus a micromanager. President Lincoln was a great empowerer. He'd take a general, tell him what he wanted done, provide unwavering support, and get out of the way. However, Lincoln's mistake was empowering the wrong generals. For the first couple years of the war, Lincoln empowered incompetents, and the North failed to win a major battle. However, to his credit, the president didn't stay with the wrong general too long. He'd normally give them a matter of months and if they didn't get the job done, he'd replace them. After six attempts at finding the right general-in-chief, he appointed Ulysses Grant.[14] Grant, while unorthodox, was a winner. His victories turned the momentum on the western front of the war.[15] As often happens with sudden popularity, though, criticism came with the territory: Some congressmen started taking shots at Grant. In fact, a delegation approached Lincoln at the White House and complained that Grant was a drunk and shouldn't be leading the army.[16] President Lincoln reportedly instructed his aides to find out what brand Grant drank so he could distribute it to the rest of his generals and win the war!

Leading the Confederacy was Jefferson Davis, and he was blessed with the most talented generals in the divided country. When the Civil War began, the best and brightest generals in the United States joined the Confederacy. There was one big problem: Davis was a micromanager. He meddled in everything, became involved in many areas, and created complexity where it didn't belong. He was more interested in being right than in what worked; and when he should have been thinking like a revolutionary, he thought like a bureaucrat. Managers today can learn a poignant

---

UP YOUR BUSINESS! ACTION THOUGHTS

THE MAGIC OF MENTORING

1. Lay the foundation for effective delegation. Don't delegate recklessly!
2. Help your key people develop a plan for personal growth. Modeling personal growth yourself will accomplish more than a hundred speeches on the topic.
3. Make your people less dependent on you by trusting them and pushing decision-making power down the hierarchy. The more you exhibit trust, the more trust comes back to you from your employees.
4. Empower intelligently. Empower the right people. Micromanage the wrong ones until you can turn them around or force them out.

---

lesson from Jefferson Davis about the penalties of micromanaging good people, slowing them down, breaking their momentum, and lowering their morale. A more recent example would be the devastating impact Jacques Nasser's micromanagement style had on Ford Motor Company. No one could question Nasser's work ethic. Unfortunately, it was directed toward doing things personally that he should have built a team to do. You must know when to micromanage and when to empower. Lean very heavily toward empowerment, but empower the right people.

As a leader, you can err on the side of micromanagement or you can err on the side of letting people try things. I suggest you err on the side of letting people try things. The benefits of higher morale, more capable people, and potential for breakthrough will more than offset the cost of an occasional mistake.

Up Your Business! Bullet	**There is no greater waste of time than doing something well that needn't be done in the first place.**

DON'T TREAT UNEQUALS EQUALLY

One of the most common management mistakes is to treat everyone on the team the same. Managers motivate, reward, and allocate time, resources, and opportunities equally across the board. In fact, when they do distribute these things unequally, it's normally in favor of the bottom-rung performers, with the result that top people — the strengths of the organization — are ignored. But the only way you can fix, build, or stretch your organization to new levels is by leveraging its strongest people, not trying to repair the weakest ones — many of whom shouldn't be on the team in the first place.

The *Pareto Principle,* also known as the *80–20* rule, stipulates that 20 percent of the people do 80 percent of the work. In other words, there are people in every workplace who are substantially more valuable to the organization than the others are. This brings up an important question: What are you doing to reward, equip, empower, and motivate your top 20 percent? Do you treat your top 20 percent the same as your bottom 20 percent? If so, what message does that send about your appreciation and support of excellence in your business? And what's it costing you to let your strengths atrophy as you misuse rewards, time, energy, and resources?

When conducting workshops, I often hear two objections to "giving your best to your best." People ask about all the high-potential people in the middle and at the bottom of the organization — how will you ever develop them if you're spending all your time with top people? Another complaint is that it's just not fair to spend more time, money, energy, and resources on those already doing well. These are legitimate concerns. First, I don't believe your highest-potential people are in the middle or at the bottom of the ladder in most organizations. Over time, you may find a few there, but to a large extent your highest-potential people are those already excelling. These people have clearly demonstrated that they have the skills, habits, attitudes, and talents to be better than average. And for the most part, many got to that point without much time or attention from you.

REDEFINING FAIRNESS

As for the fact that it doesn't seem fair to more fully support your top 20 percent, let's redefine fairness: Treating people fairly in business doesn't mean you treat them all alike. Treating people fairly means you treat them in a manner they've earned and deserve, and they haven't all earned — nor do they deserve — the same amount of your time and attention, or the same pay plan, schedules, or opportunities. Fairness doesn't mean sameness. Fairness means justice, and justice means you get what you deserve. Think about it for a moment: What could be fairer than treating people in accordance with what they have earned and deserve? In fact, who are the only people in your organization who would have an objection to getting strictly what they earned and deserved? The laggards, of course: those who don't earn or deserve much — the people who want the maximum return possible for the least effort and results. In addition, I'm not advocating that you ignore anyone. What I am suggesting is that you reallocate adequate time, energy, resources, and rewards to support and stretch your top people. As a matter of fact, if anyone is ignored in most organizations it's the top people. Obviously, everyone in an organization must be held to the same high standard of character, customer care, and work ethic. But beyond that, rewards and resources should be distributed according to what people have earned and deserve based on performance.

| Up Your Business! Bullet | **Give your best to the best and less to the rest.** |

A manager who worked for me struggled to grasp the "give your best to the best" strategy. Charles was honest, fair, and good-hearted. He told me he had always prided himself on trying to be everything to everyone. I told him that while I could appreciate his intentions, no effective leader had ever endeavored to be everything to everyone. All great leaders identify with and pour more into their high potentials, their inner circle from whom they know they'll gain a greater return. Charles, still skeptical, asked for an example. I asked him if he thought Jesus was an effective leader, and he vigorously nodded. I then asked if He had spent equal time with everyone. Charles replied that Jesus spent most of his time with the twelve disciples. I agreed and then asked the key question: Did He spend equal time with each of the twelve? The answer is no. There were three — John, James, and Peter — who sojourned on special field trips, were exposed to different experiences, and received extra attention. After all, Jesus had three years to get the job done and twelve uneducated men to equip. He knew they weren't all going to get it like He'd want them to get it, so He invested in those who would bring the greatest return after his departure. I told Charles the good news: You don't have to invent great new leadership principles. Success leaves clues, and you can emulate what other great leaders have done. Giving your best to your best is nothing to apologize for. Ignoring them and failing to develop their full potential is worthy of apology.

Up Your Business! Bullet	**When you go to a horse race you don't put your money on a nag just to improve its self-image.**

THE TOP 20 PERCENT CLUB

While running the sales operations for a $300 million dealer group, the leadership team and I decided to put greater emphasis on encouraging and rewarding excellence. We had bold goals and knew we couldn't reach them without leveraging our strengths, so we started what we called a "Top 20 Percent Club." For instance, in a dealership with twenty salespeople, more focus and attention would go toward fully developing our top four. Since we were a volume-oriented organization, we decided that top unit sales would be the qualifier. We ran the contest quarterly. Salespersons who made it into the top 20 percent club earned a cash bonus. Since top performers are recognition oriented, the dealer would take them out to lunch as a group each month, anywhere they wanted to go, and let them order anything they wanted to eat. In addition, each top 20 percent club member would receive the help of a temp (temporary employee) four hours each week to unburden them from the curse of all top salespeople: paperwork. The temp would make follow-up calls and handle mailers, cards, and other administrative tasks, freeing our top people up to do more of what they did best: sell!

We also trained our managers to hold one-on-one coaching sessions with their top people first. We wanted to make certain our stars were listened to, challenged, and motivated as a priority. Psychology teaches that humans love attention and that from the day we are born we're wired for it. Some people like more attention than others, but no one likes to be ignored. Another lesson of human nature is that when someone feels like they're not getting enough attention they'll change their behavior until they do. Just as a baby cries when ignored, adults will do something, consciously or unconsciously, to get someone else's attention. This is evinced in relationships, at the workplace, and on sports teams. Bearing this knowledge of human nature in mind, think about this: Who are the last people in your organization you want changing their behavior just to get your attention? The top people, of course! But that's exactly what happens. Oftentimes a manager will tell me that the top person is negative, comes in late, or does something that creates distractions. If they don't feel special, appreciated, significant, and supported, you can't blame them! In fact, it's only human nature for them to do something to wake you up.

When the management team and I discussed the top 20 percent club concept, there was a fear the top people would become arrogant and selfish if a special club were designated for them. We overcame this possibility by clearly establishing ground rules up front and at the outset. We told our top performers that with additional privilege came responsibility and that we would hold them to a higher standard and expect them to act more like leaders. When we began treating them in accordance with these higher expectations they responded well. Our top performers saw themselves differently because we treated them differently, and their improved self-image was reflected in their performance. We found them spending more time assuming a mentor's role and endeavoring to get the strugglers up to speed.

Predictably, one group of employees who were alarmed at the prospect of a club to stretch and reward our top people were our marginal performers. In fact, it made them squirm. After our new standards had been defined and more focus put on creating excellence, the bottom 20 percent of the team began filtering out of our organization and moving to employers where their mediocrity was accepted.

Up Your Business! Bullet	**When you set the bar high the winners will love it and the losers will leave it. Either way, you win.**

A client attending one of my presentations returned to his dealership to stretch his top performer. He told me that Harvey had averaged forty-three car sales per month. When you bear in mind that the average sales for the industry is ten, you can grasp Harvey's value to their business. Unfortunately, management had ignored him for years, letting Harvey fend for himself while they wasted time pumping up and propping up the bottom dwellers. When the managers approached Harvey they told him they didn't feel he had maximized his potential yet, but they knew he'd need help from them to reach a higher level and offered assistance. Harvey replied that if he weren't buried in sheaves of paperwork and administration he could sell more cars. The managers assigned an assistant to help Harvey and free him up to do what he did best: sell cars. In sixty days, Harvey raised his sales from forty-three to sixty-four cars per month, totally destroying the conventional wisdom that mandates you wear yourself out repairing the weakest team members.

Up Your Business! Bullet	**If you spend all your time trying to turn strugglers into survivors you'll have little time left for the rewarding work of helping your good people become great.**

If you run a small organization, a top 20 percent club may not seem feasible. But if you stay flexible you can send the same message about your standards and stretch your best people with a "president's club" or "top gun club" that rewards all performers attaining prescribed performance targets. You may also change your benefits and criteria from time to time, but the simpler you keep it, the better. Too many qualifiers or regulations confuse matters and cause people to lose interest.

UP YOUR BUSINESS! ACTION THOUGHTS

DON'T TREAT UNEQUALS EQUALLY

1. Identify your top 20 percent and commit to investing disproportionate time, energy, resources, and rewards into these strengths.
2. Remember that fairness doesn't mean sameness, it means justice. And justice means giving people what they earn and deserve.
3. Find ways to use your treatment and support of top people as a recruitment tool.
4. Stay flexible and design a top-performer club that best suits your organizational needs. The simpler you keep qualifying criteria and the clearer you make the reward structure, the more motivating it is.
5. Reward your best people proactively, fairly, and intelligently.

THE FINANCIAL FACTOR

Occasionally a top performer will threaten to leave — or actually will leave — for a bigger paycheck elsewhere. While you can't prevent this from happening, you can limit the frequency by doing the following:

1. *Compete on dollars and win on culture.* I've never seen a top performer who was offended by money. However, it takes more than money to attract and retain eagles. The cultural aspects

that make up your environment (as discussed in Chapter 1) are key factors. Be fair with financial remuneration or you will lose more stars than you should, but build an environment that addresses such intrinsic human desires as trust, room to grow, association with a great team, meaningful work, and recognition — benefits that are difficult to quantify financially.

2. *Be proactive with raises.* One of the most senseless decisions a manager can make is to allow eagles to leave over financial differences, only to offer them more money to return at a later date. If you'd pay more to get a solid performer back, pay them now so they don't leave and create distractions, take other key players with them, lower morale, and break your momentum. In fact, if you proactively approach an employee with a raise before he or she has to go through the agony of soliciting one from you, you'll get away with paying less money. Your making the move first builds greater inner satisfaction and self-esteem within the employees, making them less focused on what they were going to ask you for — an amount that is normally more than the preemptive raise you gave them.

3. *Get a trade-off.* When you are approached for and decide to give a raise, get something in return. Ask the person which new responsibilities the person would be interested in assuming to justify the increased pay, or what the person would be willing to learn to augment his or her value to the organization. What you'll bargain for depends, of course, on the person and situation.

4. *Keep your ego in check.* Don't let personal pride interfere with making the right compensation decisions for your best people. It helps to remember that the most expensive people on your payroll aren't the highest-paid people: The most expensive

people on your payroll are the unproductive people. I recall an entrepreneur who should have known better boasting to me about how cheaply he was able to hire his new general manager. I told him that before long, he'd know precisely why he exacted such a bargain, because it would show up in his lack of results.

5. *Differentiate according to results more than tenure and credentials.* Weight compensation packages more heavily toward performance, not tenure, credentials, or experience. Otherwise, the dreaded entitlement discussed in Chapter 2 will sink its roots into your organization and debilitate your culture.

If you don't give extra support, recognition, rewards, and opportunities to your top 20 percent, what have you given your middle 60 percent to emulate? Nothing! And the problem is that if your middle 60 percent isn't trying to become like the top 20 percent they tend to become more like the bottom 20 percent by default. Use the power of your top 20 percent to neutralize the negative influence of your bottom 20 percent.

Up Your Business! Bullet	**You must pay eagles more. If you pay peanuts, expect to get monkeys.**

ENCOURAGE CONFLICT AND DISSENT

You cannot grow a high-performance team until your leadership style dictates that truth trumps harmony. An old cliché declares that great teams are composed of members who all love one another and bask in perpetual harmony. Wrong! The best teams I know fight. But they fight about issues, not personalities. And just

119

as important, they have the ability to have a brutally honest discussion, anchored in conflict, make a decision, and then put their differences behind them and emerge as a team once again.

| Up Your Business! Bullet | **A real team concept is not one in which everyone gets along. It's one in which everyone puts the team first, regardless of personal differences.** |

A culture that embraces — insists on — dissent and conflict must start with the leader. With this in mind, ask yourself: Can your people challenge you without fear of negative consequences? Can they tell you, with all due respect, in the proper tone and place, that they think you're wrong and that they have a better way? If they can, you'll get the best they have because they'll bring their all to you. But if they can't, you'll develop blind spots because people will become accustomed to telling you what you want to hear instead of what you need to hear.

As a rule, leaders talk too much at their staff meetings and are too domineering. Unfortunately, this "let the boss do all the talking and all the thinking" mind-set carries on after the meeting as people go about their jobs. As an observer, I've sat in disgust in meetings where heads bounce up and down like a bunch of bobble-heads while the boss gives a soliloquy. Everyone is all smiles and gives the "kiss of yes" to what is being ordained right before joining hands, singing Kumbaya, and leaving to play golf. If something like this happens at your workplace you can rest assured of one thing: As your team skips cheerily down the yellow-brick road, the tough issues aren't being looked at and the path you're on will take you smack into a wall of irrelevance.

At staff meetings an astute leader is a questioning machine, not an answering machine. He or she states the issue at hand without giving a personal opinion on resolution, insists on input from the meeting participants, and ensures that ideas are not fire-hosed and everyone is heard. The leader then processes what has been discussed and presents his or her view, while encouraging the team to shoot some holes in it, until resolution is achieved. This doesn't mean the leader runs things as a democracy: While everyone has an equal voice, they don't all have an equal vote. However, since conflict brings about clarity, you're less likely to make poor decisions and walk onto a minefield.

Up Your Business! Bullet	**Too much harmony is cancerous to decision making. Conflict brings clarity. It ensures that every side of an issue is examined. The bigger the decision or risk, the more conflict you need.**

UP YOUR BUSINESS! ACTION THOUGHTS

ENCOURAGE CONFLICT AND DISSENT

1. Teach others to think for themselves and express their views honestly and openly by encouraging productive conflict and dissent from your team, especially at your staff meetings.
2. Hire and promote people with a team concept: Even though they may differ, each member sets his or her own agenda aside and puts the team first.
3. If you really want truth over harmony, you'll have to earn credibility from your team, especially if you haven't welcomed it in the past.

Great teams challenge the leader and one another without its becoming personal, and once the decision is made they unite behind it. They don't hold grudges. Some managers don't seem to get this last point. They have their say at a meeting, but when things don't go their way, they leave the meeting to pout, whine, complain to somebody, or call somebody to vent. The best advice you can offer these malcontents is that if things don't go their way and they want to call someone after a meeting, they should call U-Haul to come and get them. Otherwise, their cancer will pervade your culture and future meetings. Colin Powell put this principle very well:

> When we're debating an issue, being loyal to me means giving me your opinion whether you think I'll like it or not. At this point, disagreement stimulates me. But after the decision has been made, the debate ends. From this point on, being loyal to me means getting behind the decision and executing it as if it were your own.[17]

Up Your Business! Bullet	**To grow your team, you must assume the role of facilitator at your meetings rather than dictator.**

As your people become accustomed to challenging one another and meeting tough issues head on, you can expect to see conflict. In fact, conflicts always arise when you have people who care about what they're doing, think for themselves, and aren't afraid to speak out. Resist the temptation to jump in and referee these disagreements. Encourage your people to work things out among themselves whenever possible. If your team becomes dependent upon your jumping in and solving their problems, they'll never develop into a highly functional unit.

FURTHER UP YOUR BUSINESS

GET NEW HIRES OFF TO A GREAT START!

Throwing new hires into the fray of their job without proper orientation and culture inculcation is a leadership failure. After hiring the wrong person at the outset or having an ineffective manager under which an employee suffers, sloppy on-boarding processes are the primary culprit for poor employee retention.

While it often takes ninety days to gain a clear picture of how someone will do in their position, the first thirty days are the most essential to setting the stage for productive employment. To create even more urgency to get new hires off to a good start, realize that human resources studies show that within the first two weeks new employees have already either made up their minds that the workplace is what they expected or decided to continue with their job search — while continuing to collect your paychecks. Very early on new employees begin to sense that their basic needs for survival either will or will not be met at a particular job, and they will then react accordingly. I once conducted a forty-five-minute tele-seminar for clients on the topic of getting new hires off to a great start, and the feedback was such that I felt I should share the information on a broader basis. As a result, I decided to include it in the revised version of this book.

Following are five steps to incorporate into your current on-boarding process to get employees off to a fast and productive start and improve your retention of them for the long haul.

1. Highly structure their first day. During the first day of employment new employees are both excited and nervous. Without

structure, their excitement will wane and their nervousness may turn to negativity. To pull this off, the following should take place:

a. The direct supervisor should take a primary role in assuring that the new hire's first day is busy, focused, and productive. Don't hand off new hires to a subordinate on the first day. As their boss, you should take an active leadership role in guiding them through their first day on the job.

b. Use a checklist with the most vital tasks to be accomplished that day. Your checklist should contain things like a tour of the business, a review of performance and behavioral expectations, a detailed explanation of the pay plan, and the like. Each point on the checklist should be signed off on by the employee and supervisor and given to Human Resources for placement in the employee's file.

If you structure the first day right, there will be no real time for training. There will be plenty of time for training in upcoming days. The first day should be primarily focused on getting the employee acquainted with others, comfortable with the surroundings, and familiar with procedures and policies. Once these basic needs of security and safety are met, the employee is ready to move on to developing competencies and contributing to the team.

2. Set forth training objectives for the next thirty days so the employee knows up front what he or she is expected to learn. You may also assign a mentor to help with the designated areas. For instance, in sales, this may mean that in thirty days you will teach and expect the salesperson to learn a meet and greet, an appointment phone script, key investigative questions, a referral script, and the like. Even if the employee has experience in your industry it is important that you teach him or her to do things your way. At the end of

thirty days test the person on the assigned training tasks. Put these expectations in writing and have the employee sign off on them.

3. Establish product knowledge goals for the first thirty days. You should focus your energies on your best-selling products first. You may wish to assign the salesperson one or two "products of the week" to learn about in depth. Assign a mentor to do presentations on these products with the new employee, and let the new hire know you will test him or her on these products at the end of a prescribed period of time. If the new employee is not in sales, customize this point so he or she learns the most vital aspects of his or her job: mastering certain reports, computer functions, and so forth.

4. Assign and pay a mentor to help the new employee master the tasks you've given. This person should be someone with a positive attitude who shares the company values. Depending on your pay scale, $250 per month or so is a good place to start when paying a mentor.

5. Personally meet with the new employee at least once weekly during the first month to formally gauge progress, make yourself available for questions, and reinforce his or her sense of belonging to the organization. You cannot just meet with a person once the first day without fast formal follow-up and expect to build a strong relationship with the person.

By following the prescribed activities and others like them, you will accomplish the following:

a. Make a much better impression on the new employee as a professional organization.
b. Give the direct supervisor the opportunity to establish a strong relationship with the new hire.
c. More quickly calm a new hire's apprehensions and anxiety,

which will help him or her reach higher levels of productivity faster.

d. Improve your chances of retaining the employee for the long term.

e. Create greater clarity of what you expect and by when, which eliminates confusion and excuses for nonperformance.

If you've ever studied Maslow's motivational hierarchy of needs then you know that until a person is satisfied that he or she can survive and will be able to meet basic life needs, no speeches about being part of a great team or having the potential to make unlimited income will stir an employee for very long. New employees begin to make decisions about whether or not this basic survival need is being met very early on the job. If they are tossed to the wolves with no guidance or training; if they suspect that management doesn't really care about them but only about what they produce; if they draw the conclusion that they're working in an unprofessional workplace that burdens them with poverty wages while promising a sky-is-the-limit income — their basic instinct to survive will lead them first to mentally check out of the workplace and soon thereafter to leave it physically.

CHAPTER 4

It's All Right to Aim High if You Have Plenty of Ammo

Most managers set goals for themselves that are outrageously safe and keep themselves within limits that are embarrassingly small. If you build the foundation in your business as set out in Chapters 1 through 3 you have created the necessary platform and earned the right to shoot for big, bold goals. In fact, if you set a goal and can clearly see every step necessary to achieve it and have no doubt that you will, your goal is too small. Goals aren't supposed to be no-brainers or slam dunks. You shouldn't be able to sleepwalk there. You must believe in your heart you can reach it but it should cause you to scratch your head a bit, consult with others, think outside the box, and even become a bit uncomfortable. Within the context of that tension and uncertainty you'll come up with breakthrough ideas you'd never have dreamt of if you were plodding along with steady-as-she-goes, incremental thinking. Michelangelo was right

127

when he said, "The greatest danger for most of us is not that our aim is too high and we miss it but that it's too low and we hit it."

| | If you can reach your goals with a business-as-usual approach, your goals are too small. Effective goals force change, risk, and out-of-the-box thinking. |
| Up Your Business! Bullet | |

The "Bunt": The DNA of Leadership Wimps

There is scarcely a bigger betrayal of a leadership position than to have built a strong foundation of the right people in the right places doing the right things and then to deliberately underestimate a forecast. Managers do this with conscious intent and sometimes unconsciously as well, because they've been conditioned to set numbers they know for sure they can hit, which makes them look good. Most do so without any regard for or understanding of how it diminishes their team. When you deliberately underestimate a forecast you project that underestimation out on your people and devalue their potential. In effect, when you lay down a bunt at forecast time, you're saying to your team, "This is all you're capable of doing." Managers with the right foundation should be swinging for the fences, not bunting their way through a career. Incredibly, though, some don't even bunt. They, in essence, stand there and hope for a walk — a free pass — to get by without having to lay it on the line. Some would be content to be hit with a pitch if it would get them around the bases without their having to commit to swinging hard for bold results.

Sometimes managers use the excuse that it's demotivating to set a goal high and miss it. But is it any better to set a goal that is safe and small and hit it? Think about it: If you set a goal that requires

128

no stretching, no change, and no risk and you are assured of hitting it via the "let's not rock the boat" approach, and then you reach the goal, can you really feel any significant sense of accomplishment? If you set a sure-thing goal that doesn't cause you to stretch, learn, or risk and hit it, is this really your definition of success? It wouldn't be mine. On the other hand, if you set a goal that's quite a reach and fall short of it but by stretching for it you wind up doing better than you would have done had you played it safe, would you define this as failure? I can't imagine you would. When it comes right down to it, whether you're hitting or missing your goals is irrelevant. The question is, should your goals even be your goals in the first place? People who brag about hitting their targets don't tell the whole story. If the targets were low and easy, the fact that they hit them doesn't reveal much about them or their organizations. On the other hand, if your goals are a stretch and you miss them, but in try-ing to hit them you finish stronger than you would have had you played it safe, the fact that you fell short of your target doesn't tell the entire story. Quite frankly, the managerial whine that setting goals too high and missing them is demotivating is nothing more than a cop-out espoused by cowardly, wimpy, sissified managers who don't have the guts to lay it on the line.

If you have built a foundation of the right people in the right places doing the right things and you still undersell your team with lame, tame goals, you have all the makings of a leadership wimp. Stop treating your tenure as a leader like a dress rehearsal, and go for it! You have one shot to get this thing right, and you'll never im-pact your people or organization or reach your own potential by playing not to lose instead of playing to win. Sometimes you're ready to reach but the people around you try to use their experi-ence to douse your dreams. Instead of stoking your flames they soak them. These people can often leave you discouraged, disappointed, disgruntled, defeated, and depressed. If you've built a foundation of the right people in the right places doing the right things, don't ever allow anyone to project their definition of reality on your team, your dreams, or your life. I don't care who they are. They've got no business shrinking your thinking. The best revenge is getting the job done and making them choke on their words, because there is nothing more embarrassing than watching someone do something you said couldn't be done.

Granted, there are times when you must play it safer, build your foundation, and settle for more conservative estimates of what you can accomplish. I'll cover these scenarios in Chapter 6.

Up Your Business! Bullet	There are two ways you can fail when you forecast: failing to go far enough and failing by trying to go too far. The most successful organizations fail via the latter route because they know that only by trying to go too far do you find out how far you can go.

In today's marketplace, shooting for safe, steady growth is not enough. One sudden setback can derail your momentum and consume whatever marginal gains you racked up. You must unlock the play-to-win mind-set in your team, and to do so you'll have to remove the fear of thinking big. At one time, many managers did shoot high. They motivated their teams to think big and new, but after the leader established the bold goal and missed it there was such a penalty for failure that one thing was assured: No one else ever dared to dream big again. One thing is for certain, you don't do big until you think big. After all, no one ever went out for a stroll, happened to get lucky, and wound up at the top of Mount Everest.

SETTING STRETCH GOALS

While he was chairman of General Electric, Jack Welch made stretch goals famous and turned them into an institution.[18] Welch understood a manager's tendency to play it safe in order to look good and wanted to take the fear out of swinging for the fences. He would have each division manager set a normal departmental forecast that was realistic and achievable and then set one higher — much higher — to the point of almost seeming unrealistic. Then the team would focus on what they'd have to do differently and uniquely to move from attaining the normal forecast to reaching the stretch. It was this higher level of thinking that brought forth breakthrough strategies that the team wouldn't have generated by thinking incrementally. To take the sting out of failing to reach a stretch target, Welch set up mile-marker bonuses that rewarded progress past the normal goal even if the efforts fell short of the stretch target. He didn't want people with a normal forecast of 10

131

and a stretch target of 14 who wound up at 12 to feel like losers because they fell short of the stretch goal. Welch found that by reaching for what appeared to be impossible his teams often did the impossible, and even when they fell short they ended up doing much better than they would have done had they played it safe. The stretch atmosphere replaced the grim, heads-down determination to be as good as one had to be and shifted the focus instead to how good they could become.

| Up Your Business! Bullet | **When little is at stake little often happens. Breakthroughs don't take place in safe environments.** |

My management team and I took over the management of a dealership that had lost $60,000 the month prior to our arrival. Our instructions from the top were to stop the red ink by breaking even the next month and then to stay in the black from there on out. Somehow, breaking even didn't sound inspiring, so our team got together to discuss what our real forecast should be. We determined that based on the gross sales of the store the monthly net profit should be $200,000, and we made that number our goal. I can honestly say that when we set the goal we weren't sure how we'd get there. But this was a sign the goal was big enough, and within the context of uncertainty and the positive pressure we put on ourselves we got busy devising the steps it would take to pull it off. I cannot tell you with honesty that we hit the $200,000 mark that month, because we fell short. But we didn't miss by much. We netted $193,000 that July and learned a valuable lesson: We'd never have hit that number had we been focused on breaking even, because we'd have been at a totally different level of thinking. If I had asked my team what we'd need to do to break even, they'd have come up with one set of answers. But by asking instead what we'd have to do to reach $200,000, we came up with an entirely different set of answers. The lesson is that if you want bigger and better answers, ask bigger and better questions. Here are four other keys that helped us have a breakthrough month:

1. *We cleaned house.* "Always remember, it's the people, stupid" was a guiding premise as we removed the deadweight employees who had rested on their laurels and failed to perform. We never even replaced many of these people, because the mediocre results they were producing were easily made up for by promoting and bringing in the right people.

2. *We moved quickly.* We didn't tamper, tinker, and tweak. The business was in desperate straits that required massive action. We erred on the side of moving too quickly.

3. *We believed in our hearts we could hit the goal.* We didn't set some pie-in-the-sky number that we had no confidence we'd hit. We felt it was attainable but knew it couldn't be reached with a business-as-usual approach.

4. *We built a foundation for future success.* We didn't simply put the business on growth steroids while slashing expenses just to give us a short-term boost and look like heroes for a month or two. By putting the right people in place first, then having them devise the most effective processes and strategies, we built a sustainable foundation that went on to make more money in the next six months than the dealership had made in the past five years combined.

| Up Your Business! Bullet | **When the goal is too high or too low people won't get involved. Psychologists say motivation to hit a goal is highest when there's about a fifty-fifty chance of pulling it off.** |

Up Your Business! Action Thoughts

Setting Stretch Goals

1. Stretch goals should be set from a position of strength: having the right people in the right places doing the right things.
2. Reward progress over and above a normal forecast even if the effort falls short of the stretch goal itself. This takes the failure out of thinking big.
3. You must believe you can hit the stretch goal, or it will have no integrity and you won't be credible as you communicate it.
4. Stretch thinking and forecasting will change the culture of your business. Decide how you can work them into your business.

The Role of Strategy and Tactics

As important as bold goals are, they are impotent without strategy. In fact, you can hold a series of meetings and brainstorm goals all day, but the plan to reach them is where the money's at.

| Up Your Business! Bullet | **Vision without strategy is hallucination.** |

One of leadership's greatest privileges is to determine the direction for your organization. In fact, effective leaders are expected to see more, see farther, and see sooner than their people on a day-to-day basis. But you'll never earn the buy-in for your forecast unless you include others in the strategy.

| Up Your Business! Bullet | **People support what they help create.** |

One of the most effective meetings you'll ever have is when you bring your team together and tell them: "Here's where we are. Here's where we need to go. This is why it's important, and here's what's in it for you when we pull it off. Now, what do we have to do to get there?" This starts the process moving forward, generates buy-in, and evokes ideas you'd never have come up with on your own. Contrary to what the old command-and-control management manuals would have you believe, it is not top management's job to create the organization's grand strategy. Its function is to create the context for the strategies to be developed rather than all the content.

Now that the pressure for mapping out each step of the strategy and inventing 100 percent of its content is off your shoulders, let's cover one of the biggest mistakes managers make when helping to devise and facilitate their organization's strategy: They confuse strategic thinking with tactical thinking. To help clarify your thinking on the role of vision, strategy, and tactics, consider the following.

VISION IS THE "WHERE"

This is the most important element of the grand strategy because all subsequent strategies and tactics are based on it. I believe that in most businesses a yearly vision is most effective, since it gives people a greater sense of purpose for the year at hand. Vision gives meaning to the workplace, offers purpose, and enrolls people in more of a campaign or cause than a mere job does. People will quit a job; they'll die for a cause. While the vision is normally the leader's or leadership team's prerogative, it should take into account the dreams and aspirations of the people throughout the organization. Effective yearly visions are measurable, bold, and clear.

Up Your Business! Bullet

Without vision, you can't credibly devise a strategy. After all, what are you preparing for? Without a vision, your people become victims of big-picture blur.

Strategy Is the "What" and Tactics Are the "How"

Don't confuse strategy with tactics. *Tactics* are blocking and tackling: the number of phone calls salespeople make, earning more gross profit per unit, tweaking the steps to your selling process, and the like. On the other hand, effective *strategies* change the rules of the game in your marketplace. They alter customer expectations and have the power to change industry economics. Organizations with the best strategies dominate over tactically obsessed companies because it's easier to win the game when you make the rules. It takes hard work to create breakthrough strategies and even more to implement them. In fact, the only time strategy is easy is if you're content to be an imitator.

Up Your Business! Bullet

Until you move from tactical to strategic thinking you will work longer and harder, often at the wrong things.

Effective Strategies Attack Centers of Gravity (COGs)
Center of gravity is a military term for a high-leverage target that, upon being hit, brings forth a substantial return. Situation dictates strategy; thus, the centers of gravity in your business may include key personnel, target customer groups, competitors' weaknesses, and flaws in your current systems and procedures. Choosing the right strategic pinpoints is paramount because the most extraordi-

nary effort you can produce is pointless if it is not focused on the right target.

A strategy to determine the most precise pinpoint possible is to question down with the *Five Why's*. For example, the manager running a sales department that is having trouble closing enough deals might be tempted to target-train salespeople on more proficient closing techniques or scripted closing verbiage. But when the manager questions down with the Five Why's, the pinpoint changes and becomes much more precise:

1. Why aren't we closing more deals?
   Answer: The customers aren't excited about the product.
2. Why aren't customers excited about the product?
   Answer: The salespeople's product demonstrations seem to be missing the mark. They don't create excitement.
3. Why don't the sales team's product presentations create excitement for the customer?
   Answer: The salespeople are talking too much and giving too much information. The customer looks overwhelmed and confused.
4. Why are the salespeople overloading the customer with too much product information?
   Answer: They're not finding the customer's "hot buttons" and thus aren't sure what to focus their presentation on. Thus, they talk about everything.
5. Why aren't the salespeople finding the customer's hot buttons?
   Answer: The questions they are using to qualify the wants and needs of the client are shoddy; sometimes they don't ask them at all and jump right into the presentation.

After questioning down with the Five Why's the sales manager's pinpoint is much clearer. Rather than teach the salespeople thirty new closing techniques — in an attempt to sell prospects a product they're not excited about — the training will focus on how to better investigate for wants and needs with a proper line of questioning and then focus the presentation primarily on those buying motives. Use the Five Why's to make sure you're investing your time and resources in pinpoint targets that will bring the return you're looking for, or else you'll squander time, money, and morale mistreating a problem you misdiagnosed.

Up Your Business! Bullet	**Identify and hit the 20 percent of targets that will produce 80 percent of the impact.**

Effective Strategies Attack Multiple COGs Simultaneously

To borrow again from military terms, this simultaneous approach to hitting COGs is known as *attacking in parallel*. Whenever you implement a strategy you are working against a current system and the defenders of the status quo. The natural tendency is for systems to bounce back to their former state and repel new efforts. They unconsciously conspire to resist change and preserve the status quo. A parallel approach provides more opportunities for creating momentum and overwhelming current systems resistant to change before they have a chance to repair themselves. In fact, the greater number of COGs you hit in the least amount of time, the higher your probability of creating lasting change. The alternative to implementing strategies in parallel is to use a *serial approach*. With a serial philosophy, you put all your focus on one target before moving on to another. This option is mostly chosen by the managers who play not to lose rather than play to win. They tweak, tinker, and nudge rather than offering up a full court press. The problem with throwing all the weight of your efforts against one front is that one setback or delay can derail the entire process and stop

138

your efforts in their tracks. Your progress, energy, and enthusiasm stall while you regroup and determine your next move. In short, you move too slowly to unfreeze the status quo and change your current systems.

| Up Your Business! Bullet | **Multiple actions, leveraged against the right targets, reduce the duration of effort and thus conserve resources.**[19] |

With this in perspective, you should be able to avoid the common management pitfall of confusing strategy with tactics. One method for keeping this in perspective is that strategies innovate while tactics optimize. For example, while at a meeting recently, a business owner proclaimed to the group that his key strategy for the coming year was to do a better job of cutting costs. This sounds great, and cost control is certainly important, but it's not a strategy — it's a tactic. In fact, cost cutting is the tool of choice for managers seeking instant gratification, the low-hanging fruit that temporarily puts profitability on steroids and makes a leader look good fast. It's like taking a hit of morphine: The pain is deadened temporarily, but without surgery you become addicted to the quick fix. Since cost cutting is a tactic, it is easily imitated and offers you no competitive advantage. In addition, cost cutting eventually brings a diminishing return. And while you're wringing out the last 5 percent of efficiency on the cul-de-sac of counting beans, a competitor with a breakthrough strategy will leapfrog right over you.

Let's face it: You can cut all you like, but you can't shrink your way to greatness. You have to perform your way to greatness. It takes a lot more work to build top-line growth and gain market share by out-strategizing, out-hustling, and developing better talent than your competitors. Ultimately, that's the test of leadership,

139

not how efficiently you wield a knife. At the end of the day, leaders grow things — they don't make them smaller.

YOU CAN'T SHRINK YOUR WAY TO GREATNESS

As you consider your own strategies and tactics, here are three warnings on the dangers of trying to shrink your way to greatness. I include them because these tendencies are as pervasive as they are flawed.

Cost Cutting Backfires When You Axe Your Capacity to Produce
Your capacity to produce includes training and tools that would upgrade and expand the capabilities of your people. In fact, managers who boast about underspending a budget miss the point. The point is not whether the budget was underspent but whether it was well spent. Being able to manage money doesn't mean you're managing the business. And just like weight you lose while dieting, the excess fat won't stay off your organization unless and until you change your habits. It's shortsighted how managers cut a training budget that would make their people more competent at the same time they continue to advertise lavishly for more customers their untrained people will abuse. It's a cycle of stupidity. You can't cut your way to greatness — you must perform your way to greatness.

Up Your Business! Bullet	**Effective leaders are less concerned with the costs of building their capacity to produce and more concerned with the cost of neglecting it.**

Don't Just Optimize — Innovate!
As mentioned previously, *optimizing* is a tactic (cost cutting), while *innovating* is a strategy (developing an acceleration pool of upcom-

ing talent in your business, creating an owner loyalty program that would make it insane for your customers to buy elsewhere, implementing a unique marketing message, or establishing a proactive, year-round recruiting strategy). Innovating involves change and, regardless of how that word makes you cringe, there is no progress or competitive advantage without it. Let's talk about the strategy of positioning yourself more uniquely for a moment. I certainly don't trivialize the importance of advertising, but I'm amazed at the amount of money managers waste on it with so little strategic intent. Before you spend tens of thousands — hundreds of thousands in some cases — to spread your message each month, it'd be nice to have something worth saying: a value proposition that differentiates you from every other "lowest prices, biggest selection, and no-hassle buying experience" loudmouth in your field, and that communicates a message that changes the rules in your marketplace and earns you an unfair competitive advantage. It'd also be helpful to have well-trained people in place to serve and sell these customers once they arrive.

If your business is like most, some of the ad messages you've been running have been decaying for years. Perhaps you've fallen prey to the all-too-common practice of failing to renew yourself in the absence of a crisis. Quick — in three short sentences, what really makes your business measurably and noticeably different from your competition? More important, what would your customers, in overwhelming consensus, agree makes you different and better? If you don't have clear, convincing answers and don't feel your customers would either, you have serious work to do because today's easily bored customers are becoming increasingly promiscuous in their loyalties.

| Up Your Business! Bullet | **Optimization helps you maintain your business. Innovation grows it.** |

141

Don't Mistake the Scoreboard for the Game

As a speaker at numerous business meetings and conventions each year I see the intensity managers put into comparing their financial statements and benchmarking best practices to improve. These meetings provide an unmatched forum for support, accountability, and improving all aspects of a business. However, too often the participants confuse the scoreboard with the game. The financial numbers they work so hard to crunch are lagging indicators. More time and effort should be put into strategic reviews, not just financial reviews, because strategies — the *game* — determine what gets put on the scoreboard — the *numbers*. I'd like to see less time spent on best practices and more time spent on different practices. Rather than focusing hard on getting better (often at the wrong things), it would be more productive to talk about becoming different, standing out, and changing the rules in the marketplace in which you operate.

CREATE AN UNLEVEL PLAYING FIELD

Personally, I don't believe in a level playing field. I want it as unfairly angled to my advantage as possible. I don't want my fair share of a market, I want much more; I want it at my direct competitor's expense, and if I can put him out of business, so much the better. I don't believe in peacefully coexisting in a marketplace, I believe in dominating it. I want my competitor's best people and I want their customers. Perhaps it's politically incorrect to verbalize these thoughts. It's more polite and harmonious to talk about everyone getting along and getting "their fair share." (If you'll recall, this was the rationale behind Communism.) But my guess is that many who might be uncomfortable saying these things aloud feel them deeply inside. In fact, if you didn't have this drive and de-

142

sire you wouldn't have chosen a competitive business in which to invest your life. It's shameful to see so many hardworking managers and business owners tampering, cutting, and tweaking when they should be building, innovating, and swallowing up the incompetents who get in their way.

As you evaluate your strategies — or lack of strategies — it's time for a gut-check. Are you content to follow the herd, or will you get out front and leave footprints? Are you content to merrily coexist in your market, or are you committed to stepping up and dominating it? It doesn't matter whether you sell Suzukis or soap; what you do is less important than how you do it.

Up Your Business! Bullet	**If nothing changes then nothing changes. On the other hand, if change is not necessary then it's necessary not to change.**

In a tougher marketplace, those who are devoid of strategy and immersed in tactics will find the barbarians banging at the gate, and if you're not prepared they'll soon be eating off your best china. As more uncertain times loom, rest assured there's a bullet out there with your organization's name on it. The future is something you must deliberately create and not something you let happen to you. This means you'll need to shift from tactical to strategic thinking. There are two things to remember concerning strategy: If it's not different it's dead, and if you can't articulate it you sure can't execute it.

Keep in mind that true strategies, unlike tactics, are much more difficult to duplicate and imitate and often go undetected by competitors until it's too late. Think of tactics as means while strategies are ends. When implementing your strategy and executing the tactics it takes to succeed, don't confuse temporary tactical success with long-term strategic victories. Nor should you evaluate temporary tactical setbacks as a failure of your strategy. Tactics will win you battles but strategies win wars. For a glaring example of the difference, consider the Vietnam War. The United States won virtually every tactical battle but still lost the war because it had an ill-defined and flawed strategy. The Vietnamese had a simple but sound strategy: Keep killing the enemy while living to fight another day, and eventually you'll wear them out and they'll leave the country.

In your business, whenever you find yourself working longer and harder and moving faster but not getting the results, it's an indication you are locked in a tactical battle and must step back and evaluate whether you're hitting the right targets. This is why it's important that you evaluate your progress often and, if what you're doing is not getting results, that you change it. As Colin Powell said, "No battle plan survives first contact with the enemy."[20]

To keep your strategy vital it's essential that you conduct strategic reviews as well as financial reviews to determine the effectiveness of your strategy and evaluate needed adjustments for continued success. As General Patton explained, "One doesn't plan and then try to make circumstances fit those plans. One tries to make plans fit the circumstances. I think the difference between success and failure in high command depends upon the ability, or lack of it, to do just that."[21] While financial reviews are both common and important, they are the lagging indicators of what has already happened. Strategic reviews give you a chance to change the input that affects the financial numbers. If you spend too much time evaluating financial numbers and not enough time evaluating strategies, you'll be a great historian but a poor leader. Throughout the process of executing your strategy you should focus on recognizing tactical efforts but rewarding strategic success. There is also virtue in keeping your strategies simple. Socrates taught that the most likely solution to any problem had the least number of steps; and if you don't focus on simplicity you get complexity by default.

| Up Your Business! Bullet | **Lock like a laser on your goal but don't become attached to how you get there.** |

Many managers are poor at implementing strategy because they hate moving fast. They'd rather discuss than decide, prefer to study the race than ever join it, and stick their toes in but never take the plunge. They don't make a move until they're sure all lights are green and nothing has been overlooked. The left side of their brain is on steroids while they've put the right side on a starvation diet. The problem with this overly analytical approach is that at any given time there is an endless amount of information available, and the longer you discuss, contemplate, and study, the more your information grows stale and needs to be updated. While you embark on an unending fact-finding mission to gather more data to create the perfect plan, someone else is beating you to the punch. To paraphrase Patton, this is why a good plan executed now is better than a perfect plan implemented next week.

FOCUS ON YOUR STRENGTHS

Your most effective strategies should build on your strengths, the core business of your organization. To execute this it will be important to resist the temptation to devise sexy and daring strategies that cause you to stray too far from your core or to acquire or diversify into areas of noncore competence in pursuit of growth.

| Up Your Business! Bullet | **Don't confuse acquisition with growth.** |

Effective strategies develop the core business of an organization. In fact, most leaders underestimate how much there still is to gain from their core, so they go off on careless tangents. If you assume your core business is underperforming you'll be right most of the time. This doesn't mean you simply optimize your core but that you create new possibilities stemming from your core with creative innovations, value-added products or services, and complementary strategic alliances when appropriate.

UP YOUR BUSINESS! ACTION THOUGHTS

THE ROLE OF STRATEGY AND TACTICS

1. First devise your vision, since all other decisions are based upon it.
2. Create strategies that change the rules of the game in your marketplace. You must engage the right side of your brain to develop effective strategic plans.
3. Identify and hit multiple strategic centers of gravity simultaneously. This parallel approach will increase your chances of moving current systems in the desired direction and creating lasting change.
4. Remember that whenever you find yourself working longer and harder but not getting results it's an indication that you are locked in a tactical battle and must step back and evaluate whether you're hitting the right targets.
5. Involve employees at all levels in the strategic process, as people will support what they help create.
6. Identify and commit to fully developing the core competencies of your business before allocating precious resources to markets or areas where you don't have as strong a foundation; you'll spread your resources too thin.
7. Prepare for seismic shifts and create contingency plans to implement should they occur.

PLAN FOR SEISMIC SHIFTS

In his terrific book on strategy, *Winning in Fast Times* (Geo Group Press, 2001), John Warden explains how seismic shifts, which are unexpected occurrences that can drastically change your business landscape, should be factored into any strategic planning process.[22] The point is not to exhaust yourself trying to predict the future but to consider severe potentialities that have the ability to render your strategies impotent and your vision unreachable unless you have a plan of action should they occur. Examples of seismic shifts would be the following:

- A domestic terror attack
- A war on foreign soil
- An oil embargo or skyrocketing fuel prices
- A major competitor's moving into your marketplace
- A stock market crash

Obviously, the list could go on, but this is a scary enough start. How would these seismic shifts change the way you marketed or the amount you spent on advertising? How would they affect your inventory philosophy? What would you do to keep your employees focused, engaged, and motivated for the job at hand? How would your products or services be leveraged to provide solutions to customers facing these same perils? Penciling in a strategy in these areas will provide a substantial advantage and could be the difference between survival, success, and significance in your marketplace.

Up Your Business! Bullet	**Never play best-case scenarios: There is too little upside and a devastating downside.**

PITFALLS THAT DERAIL VISION, STRATEGY, AND TACTICS

Your best efforts to create vision, devise strategies, and execute tactics can go awry if you are not aware of a handful of pitfalls lurking in your business that can ambush you and steal your passion and momentum. While this list is not complete, heeding the items on it is a head start to avoiding trouble throughout the process.

1. *Your people will never buy into your vision until they've bought into you.* Don't be naive. Being the boss doesn't mean you gain automatic buy-in from your people. Leadership is earned, not assumed. Until people buy into you, they'll never be excited about where you're trying to take them. There are two aspects they must buy into: your character and your competence. One doesn't substitute for the other. In other words, people are asking themselves, "Can I trust you?" and "Do you know what you're doing?" Here's the catch to earning buy-in from followers: You have to do the selling. And you do so with your daily words and deeds.

2. *Not everyone will want to make the trip.* One of the toughest things for a high-achieving leader to grasp is the fact that not everyone wants to grow, stretch, change, and reach their potential. In fact, more people than you may realize just want to be left alone. There will be people you want to board your bus who will not. On the other hand, there will be some on the bus you'll need to get off. (And perhaps a couple you'll want to put under the bus.) As a leader, you've got to build a team of people who are ready, willing, and able. They must be three for three. After all, your job is not to smack people in the head with a bat and drag them around the bases.

148

3. *The vision must be clear, concise, and easy to communicate.* Don't conjure up a nine-page vision statement and expect people to be inspired. You should be able to articulate your vision in a few short sentences. This makes it easier to communicate and understand. Remember, it's hard to be aggressive when you're confused.

4. *Don't involve too many people in the vision process.* Effective leaders don't let followers reduce the vision to fit their comfort zone. Involving too many people in deciding the direction for the organization creates confusion and compromise. Defining the vision is the domain of the organization's leadership. You'll get everyone else involved and earn their buy-in and ownership as they help devise the strategy. Keep in mind that the world is filled with burn-outs, cop-outs, drop-outs, strike-outs, and wipe-outs who will try to talk you out of greatness if you let them.

5. *Enroll people in your vision one year at a time.* Five- and ten-year plans are great for the inner circle steering a business, but most employees have trouble seeing past the next pay period, much less ten years down the road. Thus, cast your vision to them in yearly increments. Turn it into the annual campaign. This is much more likely to engage them and keep them interested than a future picture that is so far removed it appears to be lost in space.

6. *Expect resistance.* Let's face reality: Setting a bold vision will scare the entitled, the comfortable, and the losers in your organization half to death. But that doesn't mean people won't give your vision the dreaded "kiss of yes." They'll nod their heads in agreement, tell you you're a genius, and go back to work and not change a thing. Be warned: Resistance oftentimes comes in code. In other words, people don't come right

out and say they don't want to stretch, grow, or change. Instead, they start saying and doing subtle things that undermine and sabotage your efforts. Learn to read between the lines and pick up on the "background noise" in your organization before it becomes an uncontrollable cancer that consumes your best-laid dreams and plans.

Don't Wait for the Perfect Plan to Begin Your Journey

Once you devise your vision and begin putting your strategy and tactics together, all the while factoring in a seismic shift or two, don't overburden yourself with the notion that you have to have every angle covered before you begin your journey. Devising and implementing strategy is a lot like climbing a mountain: You know you want to end up on top and can see the first few steps you must take on the trip, but you don't wait to have every zig and zag figured out before you leave base camp. Instead, you head off in the general direction of your goal, and you'll figure the rest out as you journey. The key is to get moving and to stop looking for reasons to delay, because you can rest assured you'll find them and immobilize yourself and your organization.

When Vision Is Not a Priority

While I'm a strong advocate of vision's organizational importance, there are situations when it is not a priority. They are when your company is fighting for survival, doesn't have enough of the right people, or is downsizing. In other words, if you're standing on a burning bridge, casting a compelling vision about how great it will be once you reach the other side isn't going to make much difference until you put out the fire and stop the damage. Stabilize your organization and stop the bleeding first. Otherwise, you'll never garner enough energy, focus, and resources to fight the fire and create, cast, and communicate a new vision.

Up Your Business! Action Thoughts

Pitfalls That Derail Vision, Strategy, and Tactics

1. Make yourself aware of the vision pitfalls listed and address them head-on. You've been warned—thus, you cannot claim to be surprised.
2. Get moving. There is no perfect time to begin the vision process for your organization, so you may as well begin. Stay aware and alert and you'll be able to alter and fine-tune the plan necessary to reach your goals. Remember: Stay focused on the goal but flexible in your approach.

Further Up Your Business

The Power of Visioneering

Business seminars, including my own, espouse the importance of having a corporate vision that unites your team behind a common cause and adds meaning to the workplace. One of the most prolific speakers I've ever heard teach on vision is pastor Andy Stanley, author of *Visioneering* (Multnomah, 1999). Following are a handful of my favorite gleanings from his lecture that will help shape your own understanding and appreciation of vision.

1. A few people end up somewhere on purpose. Those are the ones with vision.

151

2. Vision evokes emotion and shakes out apathy.

3. Having vision in the workplace is the difference between filling sandbags with dirt and building a dike to save a town. There's nothing glamorous or fulfilling about filling bags with dirt. But saving a city is another thing altogether. Building a dike gives meaning to the chore of filling sandbags with dirt. And so it is with vision.

4. Vision is a clear mental picture of what could be, fueled by the conviction that it should be.

5. Vision always stands in contrast to the world as it is. Vision demands change. It implies movement. But a vision requires someone to champion the cause.

6. The world is hard on vision. After all, a vision is about change. And change is not welcomed in most arenas of life.

7. Initially your vision will exceed your competency.

8. Visions are easy to criticize. In fact, visions attract criticism, and are difficult to defend against criticism. Visions often die at the hands of the critics. But nothing silences the critics like results.

9. Visions are *refined* — they don't change. Plans are *revised* — they rarely stay the same.

10. Generally speaking, people will not invest more in a vision than the one who originally cast the vision.

11. More often than not, it is the good things that have the greatest potential to distract you from the best things, the vision things.

12. Vision demands constant attention. Stay fully engaged. Just about the time you're sick and tired of talking about it is the time people start to realize that you mean business and that the vision is for real.

13. The best way to communicate the vision is to live it. Walk it before you talk it.
14. Lock like a laser onto your vision, but don't become attached to how you get there. Remain focused without losing flexibility.

A few final reminders on corporate vision: It must start with the leadership of an organization. Leaders are supposed to see farther, see more, and see sooner than followers. It is the leader's privilege and responsibility to define the future.

> "Just as no great painting was ever designed by committee, no outstanding vision has ever emerged from the herd." — Warren Bennis

In order to set a meaningful vision, leaders must be in tune with the aspirations and goals of their people. Leaders must take the vision from "me" to "we." They must engage their people and solicit their input on what it will take to reach the vision, because people will support what they help create. But the followers must weigh in before they buy in. All of the work involved with creating and communicating a compelling vision is worth the price, because vision-driven organizations feel differently. There is more purpose, more meaning, greater teamwork, and greater urgency because people feel they are part of a cause, a campaign. They no longer merely have "jobs."

CHAPTER 5

Look in the Mirror

Executing Your Leadership Twelve-Pack

Effective leaders are more self-aware than their less successful counterparts. They look in the mirror, assume responsibility for the success of their business, and focus on a handful of daily deliverables paramount to that success and execute them day in and day out. I term these deliverables your *Leadership Twelve-Pack*. As I present this daily priority to-do list for leaders, evaluate your proficiency and attention to these areas, as they will have a decided bearing on your success in fixing, building, or stretching your organization.

I had a conversation with a client recently who related how his general manager had fired three key people after the store had two consecutive bad months. The client was miffed because this was the same braggart who'd been taking the credit a few months back when business was rolling. My friend went on to mention that the general manager wasn't showing up on weekends and missed the last day of the month even though the store was struggling. He lamented that in recent months this guy had been acting more like he owned the place than like an employee there. The client took responsibility for letting things get so far off track. I suggested his general manager might be approaching his "sell by" date and recommended a course of action.

This encounter reminded me what's at stake when you choose a manager of your people. Careers will be made or broken based on this choice; the organization's reputation will be glorified or crucified because of this person, and whether good people stay or go elsewhere depends primarily on the environment created and reinforced by the leader. When you're the leader you have to come to grips with the fact that if you've been taking credit for the rain, you must shoulder the blame for the drought. Unfortunately, too many managers have a black belt in blame. By firing others, you take the focus off yourself and put it on all the "losers" who were booted out. Perhaps your people really were that bad and needed replacing, but ultimately, whom is that situation a reflection of? Great leaders take the heat and let their players take the bows.

| Up Your Business! Bullet | **Nothing gets measurably better in an organization until the leaders do. When you work on the leaders you're striking at the root. Everything else is merely hacking at the leaves.** |

UNDERSTAND YOUR LEADERSHIP ROLE

Good leaders know how to use both the window and the mirror. When things are going well they look out the window and credit the team. They determine what more they can do to support, reward, and motivate the people making it happen. When things turn sour, effective leaders look in the mirror and assume responsibility for results, and change their own course before they blame or alter the course of others. Poor leaders, on the other hand, use the window and mirror differently. When things are going badly they look out the window and blame the team. They complain that people aren't doing enough, aren't committed enough, and aren't good enough. But when business is rolling along they spend their time in front of the mirror taking bows and celebrating their genius. In leadership there are two words for this behavior: severe delusion. Real leaders accept responsibility for the health of their enterprise. They know that if they misdiagnose the causes of business problems they will mistreat them. They also know that leadership is earned and not assumed, that real leaders run for office every day. They sell themselves and their vision. They know they don't have a lifetime term and that there are two ways their people can fire them: by leaving and by not performing. Either way, the leader loses.

Up Your Business! Bullet	**Anyone who has to remind his people that he is the boss or that he is the leader isn't much of either.**

It's important to remember that having a leadership title doesn't make you a leader. What a foolish notion to think one's competency has been increased by virtue of a change in title. As a leader, you should also understand that it's your followers who decide whether you're the leader.

As a leader in your organization, your job is to go first. Leaders change, listen, and learn first. They trust first and connect with their followers rather than waiting for followers to connect with them. They understand that leadership is influence and relationships and that without both you cannot lead. As my friend John Maxwell noted, "He who thinketh he leadeth but hath no followers is simply out for a walk." A leader's job is to serve followers, not be served by them. Your job is to add value to your people. You are there for them; they're not there for you. Your team doesn't belong to you; you belong to your team. Any other conception of your role than this is a corrupt understanding of leadership.

Up Your Business! Bullet	**Leadership is performance, not position.**

As a leader you must commit yourself to a cause and not commit the cause to yourself. You must lead by personal example and not personal convenience. You must commit to a lifetime of learning and executing diligent daily disciplines whereby you do the right things day in and day out. As you study your Leadership Twelve-Pack in this chapter, look at it as a nonnegotiable commitment to a series of diligent daily disciplines through which you assume responsibility for living consistently. How you execute them and the time you spend on each will depend on your personal strengths, style, and organizational needs. Your calling is to take responsibility for making certain these disciplines are executed. There may be times when your situation dictates that your time be immersed in one or two disciplines to the temporary exclusion of others. Because of this, the ideal supplement to your own leadership is to build a team that carries the load of many twelve-pack tasks while you are engaged in others. To think you'll have time to execute all twelve every day is naive. The key objective is that they *are* executed; the "how" is your responsibility.

158

UP YOUR BUSINESS! ACTION THOUGHTS

UNDERSTAND YOUR LEADERSHIP ROLE

1. You are the primary architect of your organization's vitality. Accept responsibility.
2. When you want answers to problems in your business, look in the mirror before you look out the window.
3. Leaders are servants. They go first. They know that when they add value to others it comes back to them multiplied many times over.
4. Leadership is earned with your daily words and deeds, and the right to lead is lost in the same manner.
5. Your security is in an impressive team, not an impressive title.
6. Commit yourself to executing a handful of leadership deliverables through a series of diligent daily disciplines.

THE FIRST SIX-PACK

The first six-pack of responsibilities pertains to organizational clarity, resource allocation, and making a personal impact. They are listed in no ranked order of performance priority, as that will vary depending on each leader's individual situation, team, and organization. I can sum up in one word the key to identifying, working within, and sticking to the disciplines of executing your Leadership Twelve-Pack: awareness. As a leader, you must become more self-aware of where you're spending your time and with whom you're spending it, and commit to focusing on and adjusting your daily course so that the majority of your time is invested in this handful of daily deliverables that will most greatly determine your effectiveness as a leader.

1. ESTABLISH AND REINFORCE BEHAVIOR AND PERFORMANCE STANDARDS

People will try hard to hit a standard if they know what it is, but it's unfair to expect them to work longer and harder if their destination is covered in fog. In the culture of merit described in Chapter 2, accountability was a key component of creating a positive pressure to perform. But without clear performance and behavior expectations accountability is impossible. It's the leader's duty to define what is expected in both regards.

Core Values
Core values are not some Pollyanna happy hot-tub talk dreamt up by business schools to make your life as a leader more complicated. *Core values* are a code of conduct you are unwilling to compromise on in your organization. While I advocate diversity of thinking in a business, there must be complete agreement on and adherence to a common set of core values. Ideally, they will be memorable, few, and easy to articulate. They create a standard that positively influences the behavior of your people. They act as a North Star in guiding their interactions with customers and coworkers. Ideally, core values are discussed during the interview process. Share them with applicants and be very blunt. Tell applicants that this is the way you do business and that if they think they'd be a poor fit for these values they should let you know now, since those who come on board and don't live the values are not going to like their job — and you're not going to like them. You will also train on those values and communicate them endlessly in meetings and during performance reviews. Core values must be devised to fit your organizational needs. Some of the more effective core values I've helped clients develop are as follows:

- The good of the team comes before the good of any individual.
- The worst decision is to make no decision.
- We treat and reward people in the manner they earn and deserve.
- No one will be punished for making a decision or using good old common sense when taking care of a customer, even if it breaks our other rules.

Your own core values are up to you and your leadership team. Choose them carefully. The best way you can communicate their importance is to live them. The second-best way is to measure people against them. At employee review time, people should be held accountable to these behavior benchmarks. While at General Electric, Jack Welch developed a four-tier matrix system for evaluating employees.[23] It measured both performance and behavior standards. This clarity made evaluations easier and more consistent:

TYPE 1: Makes the numbers and lives the values. *Result:* The person goes onward and upward.

TYPE 2: Doesn't make the numbers or live the values. *Result:* The person is gone.

TYPE 3: Lives the values but misses the numbers. *Result:* Another chance or two, perhaps in a different position.

TYPE 4: Hits the numbers but doesn't live the values. *Result:* The person is gone.

Obviously, the first three groups are pretty easy calls. It's the type 4s that make you lose sleep because it's an unnatural act to remove someone making the numbers. But as a leader you are the steward of your culture and have an innate obligation to remove the type 4s. If you keep a skunk just because he makes the numbers you'll be seen as a sellout by the rest of the team. Try to turn the person around first, but know that in the long run a core-value violator costs you much more to keep than to remove. In fact, nothing reduces you to sellout status as surely as retaining or promoting skunks just because they make the numbers.

Up Your Business! Bullet	**If you don't clearly define what you stand for, you stand for nothing by default.**

Performance Expectations

There are two primary errors leaders make with performance expectations: They don't set enough of them, so people aren't sure what exactly is expected, and when they do establish them they set the bar too low. For instance, when you hire salespeople, do you let them know what their sales averages are expected to be after ninety days? Or how about the minimum number of phone calls they're supposed to make each day, how many outside prospects they're expected to contact, or the number of closing techniques they are expected to master? If you don't communicate performance expectations, how can you hold people accountable later for not reaching them? You can't. So you won't. And this is precisely why you keep some of the wrong people too long. Since there is no clear benchmark to hold them accountable to, you are reluctant to do so.

Second, when you do set performance expectations do you set them high enough? Expectations should not be designed to make people feel cozy and comfortable. They should stretch people. Some organizations have expected so little for so long they're in a rut and don't even know it.

Up Your Business! Bullet	**Low expectations presume incompetence. When you presume incompetence long enough, you unwittingly create it.**

162

Performance expectations should be set after careful thought, because once they are established you'll have to follow through with consequences when they're not reached. So make sure you can live with them. Just as with core values, when you set but fail to enforce performance standards they turn into a joke, and people will look at them as suggestions more than mandates. Many organizations develop minimum performance standards whereby an employee failing to sustain a predetermined production level over a sixty- or ninety-day period is put on probation or terminated. This is clearly explained up front and put in writing. If you set up minimum performance standards you will create clarity, focus, and urgency. There will be no gray area. People will know exactly where they stand and basically fire themselves if they fail to produce. I always recommend that minimum performance standards be set up as a negative guarantee, not a positive guarantee. In other words, if your minimum performance standard for a ninety-day period is eight sales, the fact that employees attain the eight doesn't mean they automatically keep their jobs. Factors like character, attitude, and customer care will also be factored in, and the employees know this. However, if they fail to hit the eight, they know exactly what the consequence is and are not surprised when it happens.

To execute this daily discipline as part of your twelve-pack will take constant communication, focus, and attention. Once you set standards, you must also stay flexible to amend or increase them as necessary over time. In addition, by rewarding those who are living the values and hitting the numbers at the same time you are confronting those who are not, you'll make the expectations real and they'll become a key component in defining your culture of merit. And this culture will dictate the behavior that determines your level of results.

Up Your Business! Action Thoughts

Establish and Reinforce Behavior and
Performance Standards

1. Have you created and communicated core values and performance expectations that create clarity for expected behavior and results? Are they credible? Are people measured against them at employee reviews?
2. Do you have minimum performance standards, and are they set up as a negative guarantee?
3. Do you and the other leaders in your organization model the right values, and do you hold top performers accountable when they don't live the values?

Up Your Business! Bullet	**When it comes to core values and performance expectations, you can talk your talk or walk your walk — but your walk is going to speak louder than your talk.**

2. Invest Time in High-Leverage Activities

Ultimately, it's not important that you get everything done at your job every day. Nor is it important that you get enough done. What is most important is that you get the *right* things done. Unfortunately, too many leaders do the wrong things well. They engage in tasks that are low return, that they're no good at, or that they shouldn't be doing at all and squander their most precious resource: time. The Pareto Principle, the 80–20 rule, states that 20 percent of your activities bring you 80 percent of your results. In other words, if you have a job description or a to-do list with ten things on it, two to three of those items will bring you substantial results. Not everything on that list has equal value or will bring equivalent return. Your job is to determine what your high-leverage activities are and commit to executing them as part of your Leadership Twelve-Pack, day in and day out. What the specific activities are depends on your position, strengths, and responsibilities, and they may change over time. But until you determine and commit to them you will continue to confuse activity with accomplishment. You may be busy all day and still not be effective. People who think they have ten priorities have no idea what their job is. They may have ten items on their to-do list, but they don't have ten priorities. If everything is important then nothing is important!

Up Your Business! Bullet	**It's not the hours or days you put in that make you effective, it's what you put in the hours and days. What good does it do to put in more hours and days if you're putting the wrong things in them to begin with?**

To help execute the Pareto Principle more effectively, schedule your high-leverage activities to make sure you get them done. Don't leave them to chance. As a sales manager, I attended a course that told me I'd get a high return from having one-on-one coaching sessions with my salespeople. I bought into this premise, but upon returning to my job I found that I never managed to find time to hold one-on-ones. It was frustrating to know where I would get a high return on my time but never do it. Finally, I began scheduling the sessions on the calendar as appointments. I journeyed a step further and scheduled them early in the day since I'm a morning person and am at my best at that time. I recommend you do the same and schedule your top-priority tasks. Perhaps you get a high return from training your people or recruiting new faces into your organization. Stop hoping to find time for them and commit to getting them done. When coaching managers on how to best utilize their time I am always amazed (but no longer surprised) when examining their list of priorities to rarely ever find thinking time scheduled. Few leaders ever block off time to lock the office door, take the phone off the hook, and consciously work on their problems and opportunities. They're so busy working *in* their business they don't take the time to step back and work *on* it. This is foolish, because you'll find that the more you step back and work on your business the easier it becomes to work in it.

| Up Your Business! Bullet | **You can't take a casual approach to your time. Casualness leads to casualties.** |

Motivational teacher Jim Rohn admonishes leaders not to spend major time or money on minor things and, just as important, not to spend minor time or money on the major ones.[24] Jim's words are great advice, but it takes discipline and awareness from the leader. You will get off track. You will find yourself immersed in the thick of things and not putting first things first. The key is to be more aware, to recognize when you've gotten off track and make a course correction by getting back to what matters.

Once you begin developing a more effective team as outlined in Chapter 3, you'll find it easier to work on your high-return tasks because you'll have more capable people around you helping to carry the load, protecting you from becoming immersed in the trivial, marginal, and menial. The leaders who are the worst time managers are the lone-ranger bosses who do far too much themselves because they never learn to get it done through others. Before you start adding things to your to-do list in a blundering attempt to become more effective, I recommend you do one thing first: Start a *stop-doing* list. Identify the low-return tasks you're not going to do anymore so you'll have more time freed up to do what counts. Once you make this trade-off and outsource, delegate, or stop doing the items on your stop-doing list, you'll be investing your time and energy where you get maximum impact and not letting activity fake you out. Once you begin your stop-doing list, you'll have time for the highest-paid activity in America: thinking time. As strange as it sounds, most people don't deliberately think. They operate out of instinct, or react, or make it up as they go along. Most people simply see a moving line and get in it. Sitting in a quiet room alone with your legal pad of problems and opportunities and thinking of appropriate action will pay bigger dividends than nearly any other activity on your to-do list.

For most leaders, working on their high-leverage activities also means working in their areas of greatest strength. It's essential you spend as much time in these gifted areas as possible and learn to delegate, train others to do, outsource, or simply stop doing altogether the things that take you out of your strengths. Too many leaders squander time working in weak areas. This hole-plugging approach to time management causes you to spend too much time on what doesn't work. Working in your areas of weakness causes you to play a perpetual game of catch-up. You gain self-esteem and momentum only when you work in your strong areas. You'll find that you can get by when you work on your weaknesses but you get great only as you work on your strengths.

I'll leave you with one final thought concerning time management and becoming a more effective leader. Some readers will think this sounds negative, while others will recognize its truth and feel a strange sense of relief. Here goes: You will never get all your work done. You will never get caught up. It won't happen. There is always an infinite amount of work that will be waiting in the wings. Come to grips with the fact that the only way you can expect to be more productive and happier at the same time is by doing the things that bring you the greatest return and create the highest impact.

Up Your Business! Bullet	**Some people immerse themselves in a whirl of activity to hide their limitations. You must do better.**

UP YOUR BUSINESS! ACTION THOUGHTS

INVEST TIME IN HIGH-LEVERAGE ACTIVITIES

1. What are your high-return activities? Are you spending enough time there?
2. Are your high-return activities scheduled?
3. What will you put on your stop-doing list?

Up Your Business! Bullet	**The more you are committed to the important the less you are chased by the urgent.**

3. INVEST TIME AND RESOURCES IN HIGH-LEVERAGE PEOPLE

The third component of your daily Leadership Twelve-Pack also takes heightened awareness because the natural tendency of leaders is to try to be everything to everyone. But just as you committed to investing in your high-leverage tasks in the prior section, you must become equally diligent and disciplined about investing more in your high-leverage people. Based on what we covered in Chapter 3 concerning the admonition not to treat unequals equally, you should already grasp the vitality of this discipline. From here on out your job is to discipline yourself to follow through and spend more time, money, energy, and resources leveraging your best people. You can apply Jim Rohn's advice in point 2 and apply it to people: Don't spend major time or money on minor producers. Don't spend minor time or money on the major producers.

Up Your Business! Action Thoughts

Invest Time and Resources in High-Leverage People

1. Who are your top performers?
2. What are you doing to give your best time, energy, and resources to these people?

Remember, if you find yourself spending excessive time motivating and tightly managing certain people, you have the wrong people. They will steal your time and resources away from the strengths of your organization, causing you to attempt to fix the unfixable while your best people's potential dies a slow death on a vine of neglect.

You can take this point to a higher and more effective degree by using the same "give your best to the best" mantra to your highest-return customers. Devise ways to identify, incentivize, reward, and serve them at higher levels. Since the cost of customer retention is miniscule compared to the expense of customer acquisition, giving your best to your best customers is great economics.

Up Your Business! Bullet	**When you work on the weaknesses of your organization you get by. When you work on the strengths you get great.**

4. BUILD YOUR PERSONAL CAPACITY TO PRODUCE

In the next chapter I'll discuss how failing to work on oneself is one of the six temptations of successful leaders. For now, suffice it to say that one of your daily disciplines is to make a concerted effort to increase your own capacity to produce. This means you read the books, listen to the tapes and CDs, and attend the courses that elevate your own personal growth. Some leaders get so busy doing that they stop learning. You can't afford this. But you must be aware that, since life isn't just going to come along and improve you, you must apply the same diligence to developing your mind as you use when devising a regimented workout program to develop your body.

Up Your Business! Bullet	**Getting better is a life's work. It's a daily thing, not a destination thing.**

Many leaders think they don't have time to read books or listen to audio programs in their field. They are wrong. The key is that you have to make trade-offs to get it done. If you commute to work, turn off the R-rated disc jockey and listen to a tape or CD on how to grow your business, improve your leadership, or get more done through others. Turn your drive time into improvement time. When at home, turn off the mindless television every once in a while, open a book, and study the life of a successful business or historical leader and determine how to apply their principles to your business. Zig Ziglar nailed it when he said that mindless television and radio was an income suppressant. Besides, if you don't have and model a personal growth program, how can you credibly tell others on your team they must change, risk, grow, and continue to learn? You can't. So you won't. And in the process you'll become a lid on your people. Start a library at home and at work filled with resources on how to manage, lead, motivate, think strategically, set goals, stay motivated, develop others, and manage your time. As a leader, it's up to you to create a learning culture. Besides, if your people are outlearning you, you're headed for trouble, because it is difficult if not impossible to lead people who have outgrown you.

Up Your Business! Bullet	**As long as you continue to learn you can continue to lead.**

It's also important to realize that time and experience in the business don't constitute personal growth. In fact, the wrong experiences can make you worse. Just because you show doesn't mean you grow. A personal growth program is a concentrated effort. You measure your progress just as you would on a diet, a workout program, or another project requiring discipline and accountability. It must be specific and simple: one book per month or one tape per month, for instance. Over time, you can take it up to new levels. The key is to make personal growth part of your daily discipline. It's like an apple a day. Eating seven on Saturday night doesn't have the same effect as consuming one every day. As you grow bigger on the inside you'll find you can grow your business bigger on the outside. Learning is energizing and motivating, and when you share what you learn with others you multiply your effectiveness. Personal growth for leaders is not an option. As John F. Kennedy was to say in a speech at the Dallas Trade Mart the day he was assassinated, "Leading and learning are indispensable to one another."

171

Up Your Business! Bullet

You must first grow personally and then advance materially. To get more than you've got you must become more than you are.

UP YOUR BUSINESS! ACTION THOUGHTS

BUILD YOUR PERSONAL CAPACITY TO PRODUCE

1. If you don't already have a deliberate, systematic personal growth plan, start one today. If you already have one, take it up to a higher level.
2. Start a library of resources related to management and leadership at home and at work. For recommendations on where to start, check out the "Dave Recommends" section of my web site at www.learntolead.com.

---

5. CREATE, CAST, AND COMMUNICATE ORGANIZATIONAL VISION AND FACILITATE STRATEGY

Since prior chapters have dealt intensely with creating vision and strategy, this daily discipline will focus on communicating the vision and evaluating and adjusting the strategy.

Communicating the Vision
Leaders bring vision to life by living it, modeling it, and talking about it every chance they get. This weaves it into the culture, keeps others engaged in the campaign, and reinforces credibility that the vision is real and not a whim or flavor of the month. Progress toward the vision should be discussed in each meeting, during one-on-one coaching sessions, and in memos and e-mails. Just about

172

the time you're sick of talking about it is when the rest of your employees start to get it. As mentioned before, keeping the vision concise and easy to communicate is essential since you'll be describing it often. The best things ever spoken or written were brief. The Lord's Prayer has 66 words in it. The Gettysburg Address has 286, and the Declaration of Independence, 1,332 (and that's pushing it!). On the other hand, the United States Department of Agriculture's regulation on the sale of cabbage has 26,911![25] Don't go there.

I once accompanied a small group that spent two hours discussing leadership at Ebenezer Baptist Church in Atlanta, Georgia, with Coretta Scott King and Bernice King, widow and daughter, respectively, of the late Dr. Martin Luther King Jr.[26] The Kings made special mention that one of Dr. King's gifts was his ability to turn every conversation back toward the vision of his movement. By doing so he kept the cause at the forefront of everyone's mind in spite of distractions and setbacks. You must find ways to emulate this skill in order to keep your vision in focus, alive, and potent.

Some leaders worry that they may overcommunicate their vision. Don't sweat this, because there is no such thing as overcommunicating. Most workers are inundated with so much information that they instinctively tune most of it out. Only as you repeat the vision endlessly will you break through the "here it comes again" defenses.

| Up Your Business! Bullet | **You must become a passionate lunatic in communicating your vision. If you're not excited about it, why should anyone else be?** |

Evaluate and Adjust the Strategy

Rigid strategies derail your efforts and waste time, energy, and resources. While you must remain focused like a laser on your vision, you must become very flexible in your strategy. In short, if something isn't working, change it. Part of your daily discipline is to read and respond to the results you're getting and determine if you are on the right track — and when you aren't, to alter your course. You must continually run through your mind the game film of how you're executing and how results are unfolding and be able to turn on a dime when necessary. Evaluating strategy also means you ask your team plenty of questions about what is working and what is not and pay heed to and act on the feedback you receive.

If you falter on the disciplines of communicating vision and evaluating and adjusting strategy, you'll find yourself presiding over a dead or dying future picture and acting as undertaker for decaying best-laid plans.

UP YOUR BUSINESS! ACTION THOUGHTS

CREATE, CAST, AND COMMUNICATE ORGANIZATIONAL VISION AND FACILITATE STRATEGY

1. What is your organization's vision?
2. What have you done today to communicate it?
3. If your people were asked to write the vision down on index cards without conferring, would their answers be the same?
4. Which elements of your strategy have you changed lately? Which will you have to change to improve results?

---

6. LEAD FROM THE FRONT AND POSITIVELY IMPACT OTHERS

Effective leaders show up. They climb out of the ivory tower and into the trenches. They lead from the front. In fact, you cannot effectively execute the aforementioned disciplines unless you stay engaged with your people. You can't create the right environment and positively impact people by remote control, memo, e-mail, or voice mail. Executing this discipline in your twelve-pack will separate you from those leaders who, over time, trade in "peoplework" for paperwork and lose their impact as leaders. As General Patton said, "You young lieutenants have to realize that your platoon is like a piece of spaghetti. You can't push it. You've got to get out front and lead it."[27]

Up Your Business! Bullet	**Leading from the rear — literally leading from your rear end — is a catalyst to leadership irrelevance. You cannot impact people as you polish a chair with your behind.**

Leading from the front and positively impacting others are accomplished by the following:

- *Committing to daily wander-arounds.* A wander-around is when you dislodge yourself from the administrative trap of your office and connect with your people. You are visible and accessible; you positively reinforce, ask questions, and listen to answers, hold one-on-ones, talk about and model the vision, confront poor performers, attend high-impact meetings, and train your people. Here's the catch: If you're having a bad day and your face shows it, stay in your office. Everyone has bad days. The key is to be self-aware enough to realize it and minimize the damage you do to morale, momentum, and the workplace environment. Wander-arounds are supposed to be constructive and empowering. You ruin their effect when you turn them into drive-by's. This brings us to the next point.

175

- *Control your attitude and emotions.* As a rule, leaders are expected to do a better job of controlling their emotions than followers. This comes with the territory. Realize that you are on display and everything you say will elevate or devastate, earn respect or lose it, enhance your presence or cheapen it. Thus, model the right attitude as you lead from the front. The Law of Leadership Modeling states that the positive things you do in excess, followers will emulate in moderation. But the negative things you do in moderation, they will emulate in excess.

  There is little more damaging or demoralizing than a leader with a lousy attitude: the continual critic, fault finder, whiner, gossip, or spreader of rumors. A manager in one of my seminars confided that he talked about his personal problems with his subordinates because it helped him build rapport. He declared that he wanted them to think of him as a normal person just like they were. I couldn't have been more stunned had I been treated well at a DMV office. I suggested to this whiner that he should not discuss his personal problems with underlings for a number of reasons. First, it would distract them. I asked what he thought it cost to take their eyes off their work and put them on his problems. Second, it would cheapen his presence and diminish his credibility as their leader. And third, they wouldn't care! They had their own problems! I told him that 90 percent of the people couldn't care less about his problems and the other 10 percent were glad he had them, so talking about them accomplished nothing. Remember the words of Winston Churchill: "If you can't laugh, smile. If you can't smile, grin. If you can't grin, stay out of the way until you can."[28] The Lion of Britain went on to observe that success in life is determined by one's ability to maintain enthusiasm in between failures.[29]

176

| Up Your Business! Bullet | When a leader's having a bad day no one should know about it. Suck it up and bear it, don't put it on your sleeve and wear it or share it. Because when you do, you can't calculate the havoc you wreak on morale and momentum, or the distractions you create. |

- *Be more self-aware and continually make adjustments.* There's that "awareness" word again. But good leaders are simply more aware of their actions than poor ones. Suffice it to say that everyone becomes more remote than they should be from time to time. They go from leader to administrator and spend more time presiding than impacting. The key is to be aware of when this happens and make an adjustment by getting back into the trenches. Failing to execute this discipline causes endless problems in your business. In fact, it's so important I'll cover it in greater depth in the next chapter as one of the six temptations of successful leaders and organizations.

I once had a manager tell me he avoided wander-arounds and engaging his people too often because he got tired of hearing all their gripes and the bad news they brought him. I told him that as a leader his job was to hear as much bad news as possible and to act on it. It certainly wasn't to avoid it or pretend like it didn't exist. In fact, the day your people stop bringing you problems is the day you stop leading them, because they think you either can't do anything about their issue or don't care enough to take action. Either way, you're done.

| Up Your Business! Bullet | The best way to get to the top is to get off your bottom. |

177

Up Your Business! Action Thoughts

Lead from the Front and Positively Impact Others

1. Commit to staying engaged in the trenches of your business by making peoplework a priority.
2. When you get off track—which you will from time to time— be aware enough to recognize it and make an adjustment to right your course.

The Second Six-Pack

The second six-pack of responsibilities relates to team building, people development, and upgrading your roster of players. As with the first six-pack, these are daily disciplines that require diligent attention. Remember the key words to execution: day in, day out.

7. Determine That People Are Developed at All Levels in the Organization

A major responsibility is to ensure that the people in your organization are growing. This is a daily discipline, not something you tend to once a year at an off-site training retreat. If your organization outgrows its people it will plateau. In fact, no organization can grow consistently faster than its ability to get enough people to implement that growth and still hope to become a great company.

Up Your Business! Bullet	**Grow your people and they'll grow your business.**

178

Ensuring that people are developed at all levels in your organization means you do the following:

- *Make certain that consistent and high-impact training meetings are conducted.* These meetings should include product knowledge, selling skills, and other competencies related to job performance.
- *Conclude training meetings with marching orders.* This ensures that skills and knowledge are internalized between formal training meetings. Marching orders can be a product of the week or a closing skill of the week that your people practice and refine, and are then tested on and held accountable for at the beginning of the next meeting. Managers must stop the "spray and pray" approach to training whereby they pontificate for an hour, conclude the meeting, and then next week start all over again with no accountability for learning what was covered previously.

An hour-a-week training meeting is barely enough to maintain people, much less get them better. Your people will get better at what they do in their daily routine between your formal weekly meetings. Take a salesperson, for instance. She will not get any better when in front of a customer. Whatever hand she's holding she'll have to play. She gets better in between customers, with her daily practice routine. This is when she puts her cards together and determines whether she holds four aces or has to fold and lose another deal the next time she's presenting a product to a prospect. Daily practice accomplishes something else of vital importance: It more directly invests your people in their own success. Once they put in the sweat and time of practice, it's tougher not to care or to mail in the month when it's not going well. They're less likely to quit on you when more of their own time and effort are at stake. As Vince Lombardi said, "The harder you work, the harder it is to surrender."[30]

| Up Your Business! Bullet | **The level of your practice determines the level of your play.** |

- *Attend, conduct, or help facilitate training meetings when appropriate.* One of your daily disciplines should be to lend your presence and talents to these meetings whenever possible. The message you send by showing up is "This is important," and it's more effective than a hundred speeches on the virtues of training.
- *Conduct one-on-ones with your key people and make sure other managers are doing the same.* Your people need these coaching sessions to give and receive feedback and to be challenged, held accountable, and reminded of vision, values, and expectations. At the risk of sounding like a broken record, one-on-ones are indispensable to growing your team and are too important to hold only when they're convenient. Schedule them.
- *Determine that you and the other managers have customized and are executing plans to personally develop the high-potentials on the team.* This should be done by identifying and closing skill gaps needed to contribute at higher levels. Your people with the most upward mobility deserve more of your time and attention through development initiatives.

| Up Your Business! Bullet | **The more you sweat in training, the less you bleed in battle.** |

180

```
UP YOUR BUSINESS! ACTION THOUGHTS

DETERMINE THAT PEOPLE ARE DEVELOPED
AT ALL LEVELS IN THE ORGANIZATION

1. Make training and development key components of your cul-
   ture by making certain that effective meetings are held con-
   sistently. Add punch to these meetings by personally attend-
   ing whenever possible.
2. Integrate marching orders into training meetings for appro-
   priate positions and make sure people are held accountable
   for results at the beginning of the next meeting.
3. Preach the power of practice and include it in your list of be-
   havioral expectations that people are evaluated on.
4. Consistently conduct one-on-one coaching sessions with your
   key people and make sure other managers do likewise.
5. Take a special interest in the development of your top people
   and accelerate their development.
```

8. TAKE AN ACTIVE ROLE IN RECRUITING, INTERVIEWING, AND HIRING

As outlined in Chapter 1, there is no better way a leader can spend time than in actively looking for great people to join the team. This means you make time to personally recruit and interview the people who hold the keys to building your organization. This must become a daily discipline, part of who you are and what you do, because proactivity is the key to finding great people. Leaders who wait until they're shorthanded to run ads, interview, and hire never bring on the best people. They become desperate, get clouded vision, and lower the bar so people can clear it and plug the holes.

I spoke with a manager recently who was complaining that the human resource personnel in charge of screening job applicants for his department continued to send him subpar candidates. He was playing the victim, and as I listened impatiently to his diatribe my disgust came to a boil. I told this sniveler that if it was his team, his paycheck, and his department he'd be well advised to go out and personally find people for his team rather than waiting for eagles to fall from the sky and onto his doorstep. In fact, if you're serious about building a great team you had better be prepared to go find the great players yourself.

I was reminded of the power of "eagle shopping" while visiting a major shopping center during the holiday season. This mall was filled with kiosks scattered throughout the aisles. Some of the kiosk vendors were slouched in their chairs working crossword puzzles or reading newspapers, others were talking loudly on their cell phones, a few were stuffing their face with pizzas and pretzels, and a rare, special one or two were actually working.

One young lady selling nail polish and accessories captured my attention. She was standing in the aisle, politely and assertively approaching shoppers as they passed her cart and offering a short demonstration. I watched as she was repeatedly rejected. She never lost her smile or broke her stride. Soon she made a sale. Within five minutes she made another. I bought a Diet Coke and pretzel of my own, sat at a nearby bench, and continued to watch this pro at work. Here she was, no supervisor present, surrounded by slugs at like kiosks waiting for something to happen. But she was making it happen. When my wife emerged from a shoe store, I purposely led her in the direction of the nail polish pro, and soon we were hearing the pitch I'd seen her give a dozen times. Within five minutes my spouse bought $50 worth of junk she didn't need, and I couldn't have been more pleased. I thought about all the managers in this city — even right there in that very mall — who cried about there being a shortage of talented people in their unique area and how they couldn't find good workers. What a cop-out! Great people are everywhere. You just have to want them badly enough to go look for them. And then you'd better have a compelling reason for them to join your team: the EVP that I discussed in Chapter 1. But they're worth the work it takes to get them, and finding them, interviewing them, and hiring them should be part of your daily disciplines as a leader.

Up Your Business! Bullet	**Your best employment prospects are not the unemployed. They are those already working and getting it done for someone else.**

UP YOUR BUSINESS! ACTION THOUGHTS

TAKE AN ACTIVE ROLE IN RECRUITING, INTERVIEWING, AND HIRING

1. You must make time to actively recruit and interview great people for your team. This is a priority.
2. Go eagle shopping and pass out the eagle calling cards described in Chapter 1. Go from being hunted to being the hunter.
3. Come to grips with the fact that the best, most talented people are working. There is always an exception to every rule, but you'll wear yourself out looking for the exception and sifting through dozens of turkeys in search of the elusive eagle.

| Up Your Business! Bullet | **Once you build a pipeline of talent you'll have the courage to hold nonperformers accountable more quickly. Until you do, you'll be held hostage.** |

9. CONFRONT, TURN AROUND, OR REMOVE POOR PERFORMERS

The ninth daily discipline in your Leadership Twelve-Pack is unpleasant. It's also one of the most important contributions you make to the organization and the rest of the team. By confronting, turning around, or removing poor performers you preserve your merit culture, reinforce company standards, and build your personal credibility. While it's acceptable to treat people in accordance with their potential for a while, eventually you must treat them in accordance with their performance. I've discussed poor performers and options for dealing with them throughout this book and have little to add in this section other than to urge you toward greater self-awareness of your daily responsibilities in exercising this discipline.

| Up Your Business! Bullet | **If you don't quickly confront, turn around, or remove poor performers, you endorse their debilitating behavior by default. You become a collaborator in their corporate debauchery.** |

Confronting poor performers and deficient performance should be done quickly, privately, and succinctly. Be professional, humane, and respectful. Correcting someone's performance is not a license to get personal, sarcastic, or caustic. Love the person; hate the performance. Understand the difference or you become an abuser of people. Think of confronting unacceptable behavior in

184

an employee much as you would in a child you loved. You care too much to see them flounder. You don't want to see them get hurt or do harm by continuing in their errant ways. At the same time, you don't want to destroy their self-esteem and render them vegetables for the rest of the day, week, or month. So you balance an iron hand with a velvet glove and proceed with compassionate firmness. You not only make them aware of the problem, you help them figure a way out. The whole idea behind confronting is to improve behavior and performance, not to humiliate.

UP YOUR BUSINESS! ACTION THOUGHTS

CONFRONT, TURN AROUND, OR REMOVE POOR PERFORMERS

1. Realize that to confront, turn around, or remove poor performers you'll need to spend enough time in the trenches to stay apprised of who is off track.
2. Confront quickly. Be direct but don't leave people there. Show them a way out.
3. When you must terminate an employee for performance shortfalls, he or she should have seen it coming. If possible, tie severance pay to an agreement not to sue.
4. Make certain your Human Resources Department understands that its role is to facilitate the removal of poor performers, not to block it.

When you confront, turn around, or remove poor performers you fulfill an important obligation to your team's momentum and morale. Others will respect you for your actions, and you'll lose their respect if you blink on this issue. The reason this is a daily discipline is that it takes constant attention to keep your people out of a gray area and focused on results, and to prevent them from straying too far off track. I can scarcely think of a poor situation that was improved by refusing to face it or by hesitating to meet it head on.

Up Your Business! Bullet	**Leadership is not a popularity contest. Seek improvement over being approved.**

10. ASSESS YOUR PEOPLE AND CONDUCT BRUTALLY HONEST PERFORMANCE REVIEWS

And make sure other managers are holding them with their direct reports as well. Your job is to force reality into every management position and department. Brutally honest performance reviews are a platform for accomplishing this task. They go above and beyond what a one-on-one coaching session entails. Performance reviews are more formal. Unlike in a one-on-one, you will do most of the talking. And while this is not a daily discipline per se, the feedback you observe on a daily basis will become a vital part of the review process. How often you conduct a performance review is up to you. I recommend one formal review per month. Obviously, you'll offer plenty of feedback between these monthly reviews to reinforce good behaviors and confront poor ones. But the formal review gives you an opportunity to formulate what you've seen in the past month into a bigger picture rather than daily bites. A formal monthly performance review affords you the chance to consistently force realism into every job function and every employee. They should include or cover the items discussed in the following sections.

Identify Both Strengths to Be Reinforced and Weaknesses to Be Addressed
These are equally important. The natural tendency of most managers is to take employees' strengths for granted and pick apart

186

their weaknesses. This is a severe error. It is impossible to motivate people by working only on their weaknesses. Your people can gain a sense of esteem and accomplishment only when working in areas of strength and having those strengths affirmed. Thus, you should spend disproportionate time affirming their strong points and encouraging them to spend more time in these gifted areas. This doesn't mean that you ignore weaknesses, but you must become more discerning about them. For instance, if an employee is weak in an area that isn't essential to his or her becoming great in that job, get the employee some help. Outsource the weakness or train someone else to do it. This will free the person up to spend more time at what he or she is best at and be more productive. However, there are four weaknesses that constitute a fatal flaw in most positions. A fatal flaw is a weakness in an area that makes it nearly impossible for people to approach their potential. These four weaknesses should be confronted and coached during the performance review, as they are key constraints to moving forward. The four weaknesses that must be brought to an employee's attention and worked on are discipline, attitude, character, and people skills.

Map Out Specific Plans to Move Forward
These will include behavior and results objectives that establish a basis for future accountability. Your job is to help the employee design a plan to move from where he or she is to the next desired level.

Hold People Accountable for Plans Developed at the Last Review
If you don't discuss progress or shortfalls based on the plans you established at past reviews, the evaluations turn into little more than a formality and will be devoid of impact. In fact, this should be among the first orders of business before moving on to new territory.

Be Brutally Honest

Be respectful but don't sugarcoat what you've got to say. If your employees have done a great job, tell them they're great. If they're failing, tell them they're failing. Create a culture of candor during these reviews so they know exactly where they stand and what they must do to move forward.

| Up Your Business! Bullet | **Formal performance reviews are not the time to trivialize, marginalize, or economize reality.** |

Put Your Main Points in Writing

Structure a review form that details the key points covered and the employee's commitments, and document progress or shortfalls. As much of this as possible should be prepared in advance.

As Part of the Review, Ask a Few Key Questions and Dig for Specific Answers

A few of my favorites are these:

- How did you end the month as compared to what you forecasted?
- What adjustments will you make next month to improve?
- How did you grow personally in the past month?
- What do you need from me to be more successful?

When you conduct them professionally and in the right spirit, good employees will positively anticipate these reviews. They'll look forward to kudos for the good works they've done, will seek out your advice on how to get better, and will be motivated by the clarity you provide as to where they stand. Predictably, the employees who dread these get-togethers will be those who missed their numbers, displayed poor behavior, or did not perform the tasks set out in the prior review and now have to bluff their way through the current one.

Consistent, organized, high-impact monthly performance reviews are among a leader's greatest tools to create clarity and establish accountability. You fail yourself and your team members if you merely throw your review outline together the night before your meeting. Take notes of key behavioral highlights and low points throughout the month. Give thought to the personal development of each person you're coaching, and focus like a laser on how you can help each person reach another level.

UP YOUR BUSINESS! ACTION THOUGHTS

ASSESS YOUR PEOPLE AND CONDUCT BRUTALLY HONEST PERFORMANCE REVIEWS

1. Formal performance reviews should be held monthly, but you should prepare for them all month.
2. If you wait longer than a month to hold formal reviews, your positive and constructive feedback will be watered down and lose its punch, since delayed consequences are not effective.
3. Throughout each review you should be brutally honest in your praise and critical coaching.
4. Formal reviews must be consistent to be credible.

If you or other leaders in your organization shun, dislike, or don't see the importance of these reviews, quite frankly, you have no idea what your real job is as a leader. There is little that brings a more significant return on your time than the personalized feedback and coaching presented in the employee performance evaluation. It takes work, resolve, and skill. If you ignore it you will never grow a team to its maximum potential, and you won't grow to yours. Nothing will teach you more about yourself or your people than the discipline of facilitating these reviews.

<table>
<tr><td>Up Your
Business! Bullet</td><td>**Simple, consistent, robust employee performance reviews are a defining component of your culture and a cornerstone of accountability. Make them happen!**</td></tr>
</table>

---

11. RATTLE THE STATUS QUO

The *status quo* is best described as Latin for "the mess we're in." It's the mind-set that declares that something must work because it's still around and that it's still around because it must work. Many leaders have become bound and gagged by tradition. This is why a key leadership daily discipline is to continually challenge the status quo in the workplace. This includes asking the right questions, making sure new voices are included in change and strategy conversations, taking and encouraging risks, and acting as a primary change catalyst. Following are four practices you can execute to help rattle the status quo in your organization:

Become a Questioning Machine, Not an Answering Machine
As you are working your way into a leadership position you are expected to come up with the right answers and are rewarded for doing so. But as you rise higher in leadership you are expected to ask more of the right questions. Effective leaders ask often and they ask the tough ones as well. They challenge current systems, philosophies, and practices. Two of their favorite questions are "Why?" and "What?" "Why are we still using this system? Why

not raise performance standards? Why is this person still on the payroll? Why aren't we dreaming like we used to? Why are we doing it that way? Why don't we try it this way? What would happen if we stopped this or started that? What if we changed our marketing message? What would be the impact of establishing minimum standards? What would it take to make it tougher for the average to join this company? What can I do better? What can I do to make you more successful? What do I do around here that breaks momentum? What should I do more of or less of, start doing, or stop doing altogether?"

Effective leaders ask pointed questions to challenge the status quo, to disturb the equilibrium, to stretch thinking, and to collapse comfort zones. But they don't stop there. They listen intently to the answers and take action quickly whenever appropriate. They create a culture where everyone knows sacred cows cannot find refuge.

| Up Your Business! Bullet | **Sacred cows make the best burgers.** |

Include New Voices in Change and Strategy Conversations
One of the biggest mistakes leaders make is limiting their interaction to a select group — their inner circle. Building and collaborating with an effective inner circle of trusted advisers is a key leadership responsibility. But if you don't include people from all levels in your change and strategy conversations you will disenfranchise 90 percent of the people in your business. When you think about it, you may have little to learn from your leadership team. Your positions are well documented, and you can finish one another's sentences. Thus, make it a practice to invite guests to your strategy

191

meetings — employees who have never before attended, people from all levels in your hierarchy. These are the people on the front lines, and they are often the first to identify trends, sniff out new competitors, or detect potential product or service problems.

<table>
<tr><td>Up Your
Business! Bullet</td><td>**The people on your periphery — in most cases the powerless — often have vital knowledge before the powerful.**</td></tr>
</table>

Who are the first people to hear customer complaints or questions about your product or service? The lowly clerks answering the customer service lines, of course. And those most likely to hear about how a new competitor is beating you or how your service compares with that of a competitor are your front-line salespeople. Bearing this in mind, when was the last time someone from either of these departments was invited to a strategy session or executive meeting? The thought of including new voices in change and strategy conversations will ruffle some executives who, while espousing openness to change, secretly hope for a more compliant organization over a vociferous one.

Take and Encourage Risks

When your people see you taking risks, trying new things, and attacking the status quo you give them license to do likewise. But when they see you frozen in a comfort zone and calcifying in a mold, they find reasons to play it safe and maintain. A good leader creates an environment where his or her people take shots and insists they keep taking them even when they miss. This is not permission to engage in reckless, bet-the-company craziness. I'm speaking of mature risk, where you do your homework, seek feedback from others, and if the upside looks worth it, decide to go for it.

192

| Up Your Business! Bullet | **The most successful people are not those who fail the least. They are those who are the least afraid to fail.** |

You will never gain a competitive edge by following the herd. The only way to get ahead is to take a risk. Otherwise, you play a perpetual game of catch-up and excel at optimization but never innovate. These are precursors to corporate irrelevance. If you play it safe you may never make a major blunder, but you'll never have a breakthrough, either. In fact, in most cases you're better off making a blunder, realizing you're on the wrong track, and righting your course than you are slowly killing your business with suffocating incrementalism.

| Up Your Business! Bullet | **It's better to try something, make a mistake, and shoot yourself in the foot than it is to sit still, do nothing, and have a competitor shoot you through the head.** |

UP YOUR BUSINESS! ACTION THOUGHTS

RATTLE THE STATUS QUO

1. How often do you ask the "what" and "why" questions, and do you ask the tough ones?
2. When you receive an answer, do you suspend judgment until you can think it through or discard it if it's not what you were looking for?
3. When is the last time you included new voices in your strategy meetings and when discussing change initiatives? Whom will you invite to the next one?

---

12. CONTAIN COSTS

Cost cutting is normally a knee-jerk reaction to a bad month, quarter, or year. As mentioned previously, while cost cutting is important, you cannot shrink your way to greatness. However, great companies never stop looking for ways to cut costs, contain costs, and better leverage their dollars. This is why developing a cost discipline mind-set rounds out your Leadership Twelve-Pack. It does you little good to innovate and create top-line growth if you spend more than you take in to get it. The easiest money to bring to your bottom line is reduced costs. In fact, to build a business that sustains greatness over the long haul, cost discipline must become a guiding precept, a core competency. Since the results of cutting costs can be disastrous when executed with reckless abandon, following are three guidelines to intelligent cost cutting and containment.

Up Your Business! Bullet	**While you can't shrink your way to greatness, you can spend your way to obscurity.**

Reminder: Don't Ax Your Capacity to Produce!
As noted in Chapter 4, cutting your capacity to produce backfires on your cost containment efforts. Cutting your capacity to produce covers a multitude of sins: scaling back on the frequency or quality of both initial and ongoing employee training; shortcutting the interview or predictive testing process and hiring recklessly as a result; cutting your line staff back so drastically that the people still on the payroll become overwhelmed and lose all motivation and effectiveness; going too far in reducing management staff so that your leaders have no time to develop people and merely maintain them by default; reducing revenue-generating jobs in sales as

part of wholesale; making across-the-board cutbacks — and the list goes on.

Up Your Business! Bullet	**When you cut your capacity to produce, a drop in production will soon follow. The two have a natural cause-and-effect response to one another.**

Cost Cut by Department, Not across the Board

Focus each department on cutting the 20 percent of activities that create 80 percent of costs and you will spawn dozens — even hundreds — of cost-saving ideas throughout your organization. This also ensures that the right things are being cut, since managers can customize the cuts to best fit their departmental situations. This is more effective than when the out-of-touch corporate gurus mandate across-the-board cuts in specific areas without any regard to the unique needs of a business unit.

Tie Cost Cutting to Your Strategy

If you just start blasting away at expenses without any strategic consideration, you may fix some problems but you'll also create many more. For instance, if you run a sales operation and your cost strategy is to cut advertising expenses, you had better consider tying the following applications into your strategy:

- How can you train your sales team to do a more efficient job with the traffic they have, since they will be seeing less of it? This may include polishing up presentation skills, closing techniques, and proficiency at overcoming objections.
- What can you do to retain the customers you already have and entice them to make additional purchases? Since the cost of

195

customer retention is miniscule compared to the cost of customer acquisition, how do you plan on keeping what you have and ensuring a flow of future sales that will help compensate for the lack of fresh traffic that advertising cuts create?

- What systems do you have in place, or will you need to fine-tune, for prospect follow-up so that if a customer leaves without purchasing your product or service, you increase your odds of bringing him or her back through diligent and organized follow-up? Since you will be seeing fewer customers, you will need to maximize every opportunity, and you'll need a plan to do so.
- What training will you need to start or intensify as part of your strategy for executing these three points? Who will conduct the training, how often, and when?

UP YOUR BUSINESS! ACTION THOUGHTS

CONTAIN COSTS

1. What costs have gotten out of hand that you need to contain or cut immediately?
2. How will you instill a cost-discipline mind-set into your culture?
3. Have you tied previous cost reductions to your growth strategy? If not, what was the result?
4. Have you unwittingly cut your capacity to produce? If so, how will you reverse your mistake?

Just about the time you think you've trimmed all the fat from an operation, you can rest assured there's probably one more layer to go. This is why cost containment must be a daily mind-set — not something you react to after a budget review or a red-ink month. If you are aware of and thinking in terms of cost containment on a daily basis, you will infect others with the same attribute.

UP YOUR BUSINESS! ACTION THOUGHTS

THE TWELVE-PACK AT A GLANCE

1. Establish and reinforce performance and behavior standards.
2. Invest time in high-leverage activities.
3. Invest time and resources in high-leverage people.
4. Build your personal capacity to produce.
5. Create, cast, and communicate organizational vision and facilitate strategy.
6. Lead from the front and positively impact others.
7. Determine that people are developed at all levels in the organization.
8. Take an active role in recruiting, interviewing, and hiring.
9. Confront, turn around, or remove poor performers.
10. Assess your people and conduct brutally honest performance reviews.
11. Rattle the status quo.
12. Contain costs.

I mentioned at the start of this chapter that executing your Leadership Twelve-Pack can be summed up in one word: awareness. I want to close the chapter with the same thought in order to reinforce this awareness in you. You are going to get off track in your daily disciplines, but that's not the point. The point is that, by being more aware of what your job as a leader really is and where you'll gain maximum return, you'll be less likely to stay off track, and you'll make a faster adjustment and get on with the business of leading effectively.

FURTHER UP YOUR BUSINESS

UNDERSTAND THE FOUR RULES OF RUTS

There is little question that after you identify the key tasks in your Leadership Twelve-Pack and begin to execute them consistently you will fall off track from time to time as you try to implement them. In fact, since we are all fallible human beings, this is to be expected. The key to limiting the damage that comes with getting off track, however, is to realize it quickly and make an immediate adjustment to right your course. This chapter is designed to make you more aware of your potentially highest-return activities so that when you do start to major in minor things you can straighten out in a hurry. The danger with not realizing that you're off track and staying adrift is that you start to create a rut for yourself. Ruts are very misunderstood in business and in life. Because of this, you will benefit by considering the following passages to gain a greater perspective on these devastating and demoralizing business traps so you can avoid them or extricate yourself quickly when you find yourself trapped in one.

1. *The First Rule of Ruts:* Realize when you find yourself in a rut that it's not the result of something you did last night. Rather, it's the result of a series of bad decisions, failed disciplines, and repeated errors in judgment over time that are just now manifesting themselves. For instance, somewhere along the line you may have gotten away from the following practices:

   a. *Consistently training your people.* You found reasons to cancel the meeting rather than making it a priority and holding it without excuse. This weakens discipline and allows your team's

198

sharp edges to become dulled and diminished. Some managers have the same aversion to conducting effective, consistent, and credible training meetings that Superman does to Kryptonite. If you think your job is just to close deals and develop inventories, budgets, and forecasts, you don't have a clue what leadership is about.

b. *Holding people accountable.* Rather than confronting and correcting poor performance you opted to live with it, since at the time comfortable inaction was more convenient. By turning a blind eye to defunct performance and/or deficient behaviors you tacitly reinforced the wrong thing, and as a result you're reaping a harvest of mediocrity sown by your own neglect.

c. *Making necessary decisions and changes.* Rather than continuously rattling the status quo and innovating your way to new and higher levels to maintain your momentum, you pledged allegiance to the status quo.

The bad news is that when you abandon these listed activities and other disciplines in your Leadership Twelve-Pack, the negative results don't show up overnight. In fact, you'd be much better off if the instant you got off track you were cursed with a Goodyear Blimp–sized boil on your backside that didn't go away until you took action. But since that doesn't happen it's easy to keep doing the wrong things until they become a devastating habit.

2. *The Second Rule of Ruts:* When you find yourself in a rut, stop digging — and start climbing! In other words, stop doing the stupid things that put you in the rut in the first place and get back to the disciplines necessary to build and sustain results. If you stay in your rut it can turn into a grave. In fact, the only difference between a rut and a grave is the depth, width, and amount of time you're in it. Make no mistake: The results you're getting are the results you

should be getting, and if you want different results you must change what you do.

3. *The Third Rule of Ruts:* The seeds of your next rut are often sown during the good times. When are you most likely to abandon training, holding people accountable, and making needed changes and decisions and to become isolated in your office spending more time with paperwork than peoplework? When business is good! It's during the good times that training just doesn't seem as necessary, holding people accountable doesn't appear as urgent, and building a fence around what you have is more attractive than changing it; and it's when you're likely to believe you've paid your dues in the trenches and can now retire to the friendly confines of your office to impersonate a real leader. The keys to combating the tendency to let up when things are rolling are acute awareness and fierce discipline. Since you now know that this is when you're most vulnerable to letting up, you must make the extra effort to pull yourself and your team through the natural tendency to see success as a permission slip to crawl into a hammock and take a nap.

4. *The Fourth Rule of Ruts:* Personal ruts normally precede corporate ruts. The speed of the leader is the speed of the pack, and that can be bad news when the boss gets lazy, rusty, or just plain complacent. On a recent cruise vacation I was reminded that human beings are not at their best when life is too safe. For seven glorious days I had no appointments, no pressure to perform, no place I had to be, and nothing that I had to do. The result? I gained seven pounds in seven days. If I had taken the two-week cruise I'd have gotten fat enough to run for sheriff when I returned home. The lesson? The good times can put you to sleep, personally as well as organizationally, but a personal rut normally precedes a corporate decline. That's exactly why more is expected from leaders than from followers: There is so much more at stake when a leader lets up, loses

focus, or goes stale. This is the price of leadership, and there's no sense whining about it. It simply comes with your position.

I want to reiterate two keys that will help you avoid ruts: awareness and discipline. Once you become more aware of the pitfalls of ruts and of when you're most vulnerable to sowing the seeds for them, you'll be less likely to aid and abet their emergence. And as you develop the discipline to do the right things every day, not just the days when it's convenient, easy, cheap, or popular, you can bulletproof your business and yourself against future declines. It doesn't take brilliance but it does take tenacity.

CHAPTER 6

Survive Success

How to Overcome the Six Temptations of Successful Organizations

THE ENEMY OF GREAT IS GOOD

The enemy of great is good. The primary reason so few leaders or organizations ever become great is that they get good and they stop. They stop growing, learning, risking, and changing. They use their track records or prior successes as evidence they've arrived. Believing their own headlines, the leaders in these successful organizations are ready to write it down, build the manual, and document the formula. This mentality shifts their business from a growth to a maintenance mind-set, and trades in innovation for optimization.

Up Your Business! Bullet	Neither you nor your business ever "arrives." You're constantly in the process of becoming better or worse.

203

Perhaps you've seen — or been — a leader who reached the top of a mountain and opted to build a vacation home there rather than look for a higher mountain. Maybe you've even caught a case of acrophobia (fear of heights). In other words, you reached a certain point of success and decided it felt pretty good there. And you knew that if you were going to leave that comfortable spot you'd have to change something, risk something, learn something, or stretch something. So even though you never came right out and articulated it, you unconsciously decided to stay put and build a fence around what you had rather than continue to climb. If you've done this or are doing so now, you're not alone. The world's business chronicles are littered with now-mediocre leaders and businesses that failed to renew themselves in the absence of a crisis — that failed to survive success and became victims of it instead.

Up Your Business! Bullet	**Yesterday's peacock is tomorrow's feather duster.**

Occasionally, managers will boast to me about how easily their business is coasting and clicking along. I remind them that they shouldn't be coasting. After all, what is the only direction you can coast? Downhill, of course. Let this be a warning sign for your business as well. If it ever feels too smooth, too easy, too much like a coast, it's a wake-up call that you haven't bitten off enough, that you're playing it safe and have regressed from growth to maintenance mode. Business should always feel challenging because the next level is always uphill. You have to climb to the next level. You don't slide or coast there.

Here are the brutal facts about success: It can make you arrogant, it can make you complacent, it can close your mind and turn you into a know-it-all. The best way I know to survive success is to

204

realize it's not the point and should never be the ultimate objective of enterprise. The objective of business is to strive to reach its fullest potential. I define *full potential* as focusing on seeing how far you can go, how good you can get, and how many people you can bring with you. Reality dictates that you will most likely never reach your full potential. But it's the journey that keeps you humble, hungry, and focused. It's what you become in the process that helps you and your organization make the leap from good to great.

Following are six temptations of successful organizations. These six stumbling blocks prevent you from making the leap from good to great. The key again is awareness. The more you are aware of these six temptations, the more likely you are to take action to overcome them.

Up Your Business! Bullet	**Use your success as a stepping stone, not a pedestal.**

TEMPTATION 1: LEADERS OF SUCCESSFUL ORGANIZATIONS STOP WORKING ON THEMSELVES

Why? The leaders of successful organizations often think they've got it all figured out. So they continue to work hard on their jobs but stop working on themselves. They use their experience and track records as license to never read another book or attend another course in their fields. They point to their acclaim and accomplishments and decide to take the skills they learned once upon a time and run the rest of their careers with them. They develop an intelligence arrogance that creates a disabling ignorance. This ignorance disables them, their people, and, as a result, their businesses. Quite frankly, I can't think of two more debilitating traits in a leader than ignorance and arrogance. I suppose I can tolerate some arrogance if someone is capable, but dumb and arrogant is a little much! Many good people in businesses today suffer working under one of these know-it-alls. My definition of a *know-it-all* is anyone who has stopped actively seeking out ways to improve their business and themselves. For the record, being a know-it-all has nothing to do with the amount of time someone has been on the job or in a specific field. I know leaders who have decades of experience yet continue to learn, change, grow, and stretch. On the other hand, I've seen managers come into a job and in sixty days become know-it-alls! You can't tell or teach them anything. Thus, being a know-it-all has nothing to do with tenure and everything to do with attitude. To overcome this temptation you must continue to work on yourself as a daily discipline, just as was outlined in point 4 of your Leadership Twelve-Pack.

Invariably, while I'm conducting a leadership workshop, an attendee will ask my opinion as to when I think business will pick up and get better. Another will complain about how tough things are: how he or she is faced with inventory challenges, customer heat, employee turnover, and pressure to hit quotas. My answer to these questions and concerns is always the same. I inform my class that the business will get better when they themselves get better, and that they will get better when they go to work on themselves. As Jim Rohn says, "Don't wish it were easier, wish you were better. Don't wish for fewer problems, wish for more skills. Don't wish for smaller challenges, wish for more wisdom."[31] I would add that the only way to get better, develop skills, and increase wisdom is to commit to personal growth.

Here's the ultimate penalty an organization pays when its leaders stop working on themselves: When leaders stop growing they start to plateau. And when leaders plateau, they plateau everyone underneath them. The leader becomes a lid on his or her people.

Up Your Business! Bullet	**Growing people grow people. But when you don't grow, you plateau. It's just a matter of time. Once this happens you plateau everyone working for you.**

If there is a sector of your business that's stopped growing, look first and foremost at the leader. Chances are that the person leading the flatlined sector stopped growing, risking, learning, or changing long ago.

Continuing to work on yourself changes the way you see yourself, and how you see yourself is reflected in your performance. Thus, the more you grow, the higher your self-esteem. As your self-esteem elevates you become more willing to change and risk. And the more you risk and change, the more likely you are to attain breakthroughs and avoid complacency or the ruts that accompany it. Another benefit you'll discover is that as you learn more about your job and become better at it, you'll become more passionate about what you do. Passion is the fuel of great leadership. But it's tough to get excited about something at which you're only marginally proficient. You've probably never woken up in the morning and exclaimed, "All right! Today I get to do something I suck at!"

I received a letter from a reader who asked, "How much should I learn? How much is enough? How high should I try to grow?" My answer was that you learn all you can, that enough is all you can do, and that you try to grow as high as possible. After all, a tree doesn't grow to half its size and declare, "I guess this will do." The day a tree stops growing is the day it dies. Wouldn't this make for an interesting incentive for people? People in business are always looking for an edge, and the great news is that we live in a society where it's easy to earn one. When you consider that in our society only 3 percent of the population own a library card, that a mere 3 percent have a deliberate plan for personal growth, and that twice that number — 6 percent — believe Elvis is still alive, just how tough should it be to gain an edge and rise above the crowd?

| Up Your Business! Bullet | **As a leader you should learn like you'll live forever and live like you'll die tomorrow. Either way, you're covered.** |

As we close out creating awareness about Temptation 1, ask yourself whether you've created a learning culture in your business. Do you have a library in the workplace filled with learning resources and, more important, do people use them? Which resources have you bought and placed in the hands of your people? Which resources do they see you learning from? And most important, are *you* growing? If not, how can you take your people on a trip you've never been on? Weak leaders are travel agents; great ones are tour guides. It's important to note that having years of experience doesn't mean you're growing. Time and experience can make you worse off if you're repeating the same errors and doing the same dumb things. The fact that you show doesn't mean you grow. The action steps in this section will help prioritize personal growth throughout your business. This culture component will change your people's attitudes toward changing, risking, stretching, and learning. It is a key to sustaining your success and helping you and your business make the leap from good to great.

| Up Your Business! Bullet | **Effective leaders maintain a learning posture throughout their lives.** |

UP YOUR BUSINESS! ACTION THOUGHTS

LEADERS OF SUCCESSFUL ORGANIZATIONS STOP WORKING ON THEMSELVES

1. What will you do to create awareness of the importance of self-improvement and overcome the temptation to stop working on yourself, and how will you instill it in your business culture?
2. What does your library look like at work? Do you need to start one?
3. Which resources have you purchased for key team members lately?
4. What conferences to improve your skills are you registered for this year? Which do you have your people registered for?

TEMPTATION 2: LEADERS OF SUCCESSFUL ORGANIZATIONS STOP THINKING BIG

Why? When a team gets on a roll, some leaders get spooked and start to play it safe. They stop playing to win and instead play not to lose. Where they once thought big and new, they now think incrementally. In fact, you see this same mentality on the football field. A team jumps out to a twenty-one-point lead and what happens? They start to run the ball every down and play "prevent defense." Before long, the momentum shifts. And no one broke the leading team's momentum — they broke their own.

Up Your Business! Bullet	**When things are on a roll, don't sit on the ball. Run up the score!**

209

In business as in sports, some teams just can't seem to get out of their own way. To appreciate the need to continue thinking big and playing to win you must understand the power of momentum. Momentum is the great exaggerator. It's a leader's best friend. When you have it you look better than you are, and when you lack it you look worse than you are. But once you have it you want to leverage it for as long as you can. Never break your own momentum by resting, reflecting, or celebrating too long, because momentum is much easier to steer than to start.

Up Your Business! Bullet	**Don't let the pat on your back turn into a massage.**

Eventually, your momentum will diminish. That's the time to rest, reflect, and regroup — not while you're on a roll. When you have momentum rest should be a necessity, not an objective. In Chapter 4, I reminded you that if you built the foundation of the right people in the right places doing the right things you earned the right to think big and go for stretch goals. The more challenging mind-set to develop is to continue thinking big even after you've done great things and human nature tells you to let up a bit and enjoy the fruits of your success. But to sustain success in your business and strive to reach your highest potential you must stay in attack mode. Here are four strategies to keep you in an attack mind-set:

- *When you're doing well, go shopping.* One of the best ways to stretch your thinking and disturb the comfort of routine is to visit companies that are doing better than yours is. Study their success and benchmark your results against theirs. This is of-

ten a great lesson in humility and creates the urgency and resolve to get moving again.

- *Stir up an inspirational dissatisfaction.* An inspirational dissatisfaction does not mean you are never pleased or satisfied. It's
not a license to beat yourself (or your people) up. Instead, it's
a creative awareness that you can do better, that you can do
more to work harder on yourself and invest exhaustively in
your team. This state of mind unfreezes your comfort zone
and prompts you to keep stretching.

- *Develop a daily dose of paranoia.* There's a difference between a
daily dose and an overdose of paranoia. An overdose makes
you and everyone around you miserable. A daily dose is that
inner rustling — a pebble in the shoe — that creates just enough
discomfort to keep you continually alert and engaged. In fact,
the best leaders act as though someone is out to get them, like
they're on the verge of losing every customer every day.

- *Continue to set goals that stretch your team.* Since I covered this
extensively in Chapter 4 I'll use this space to remind you that
if you can reach your goals with a business-as-usual approach
it's an indication that your goals are too small. A goal is effective only when it forces change, big decisions, and bold action — a.k.a. discomfort.

Up Your Business! Bullet	**A leader who thinks small infects the team with the same inept orthodoxy.**

WHEN NOT TO SET STRETCH GOALS

Big thinking should be rooted in legitimate optimism, not wishful
thinking. The difference between the two is that legitimate opti-

mism is built on a foundation of preparing for it. You have the people and the plan to execute successfully. I know many managers who think they're optimistic and have high hopes it'll all work out, but they have neither the personnel nor the strategy to succeed. These leaders are the kings of wishful thinking.

Thinking big and setting stretch forecasts can be frustrating when the following conditions exist:

- You don't have enough of the right people.
- You have a decaying product or strategy.
- You are downsizing.
- You are fighting for survival.

If you're in one of these situations you must first stop the bleeding, build a foundation, and get into a rhythm or predictable pattern. Otherwise, stretch goals are a joke. In fact, businesses suffering under these afflictions while striving to reach stretch goals live in a perpetual state of barely contained panic and frustration.

Overcoming Temptation 2 takes plenty of awareness and a focused mind-set. Unsuccessful leaders focus their thinking on survival. Average leaders focus theirs on maintenance. And successful leaders focus their thinking on continual progress. If you're a manager who concentrates more time on holding your own than on moving forward and have gone from careful to fearful, from free enterprise to afraid enterprise, you've got to seize the offensive. To quote Patton, "I don't want to get any messages saying that 'We are holding our position.' We're not holding anything! Let the Hun do that. We are advancing constantly and we're not interested in holding on to anything."[32]

Up Your Business! Bullet	**Advance as conditions permit, and if conditions don't permit, create them.**

UP YOUR BUSINESS! ACTION THOUGHTS

LEADERS OF SUCCESSFUL ORGANIZATIONS STOP THINKING BIG

1. Is your business in attack mode? Do you have a plan and the people to execute it successfully?
2. What have you done in the past that broke your momentum, and what will you do differently the next time?
3. Does your culture support and reward stretching? If not, how will you weave that support into your environment?
4. What business or industry that is outperforming yours can you shop to glean ideas and inspiration?
5. How can you develop an inspirational dissatisfaction and daily dose of paranoia that will keep you and your team alert and engaged?

TEMPTATION 3: LEADERS OF SUCCESSFUL ORGANIZATIONS STOP LEADING FROM THE FRONT

Why? When a business is getting results and steamrolling along, it can feel like everything's tidy and under control. Thus, the leaders hit the remote control button and leave the trenches for their offices, where they preside and administer but no longer lead.

Up Your Business! Bullet	**If it feels like everything's safe and under control it means you're just not going fast enough.**

Quite frankly, many managers prefer paperwork to people-work because they don't have to get as involved with the messy human conditions of motivation, accountability, problem solving,

213

relationship building, or influencing. They perch in their ivory towers and get dazed by data and numbers and lose touch with their number one asset: their people. The inexcusable part of this behavior is that these leaders should recognize that it was the peoplework that brought them the success they're enjoying in the first place. It was the training, the one-on-ones, the holding people accountable, the countless conversations about vision and values, the mentoring of high-potentials, and the engaging in recruiting and hiring that made them successful — and, incredibly, they forget what got them there. Leading from the rear doesn't happen overnight. It's normally a gradual regression. But once a manager's office becomes a comfort zone it's tougher to dislodge that manager from it. If you're a leader who has fallen into this trap, you're not alone. In fact, we are all susceptible to disconnecting from our people. The key, again, is awareness. Become more aware of when it's happening to you so you can make an adjustment and get back to what made you great in the first place.

Up Your Business! Bullet	**Don't sit in your office and try to turn the numbers around. Get out front and turn the people around, and the people will turn the numbers around.**

Before you overreact and surge to the front with the same grace as Kirstie Alley assaulting a buffet line, keep the following in perspective.

WHAT LEADING FROM THE FRONT DOES NOT MEAN

1. *Micromanaging.* Leading from the front does not mean you butt in or become overinvolved in activities you know little

about; that you nitpick, breathe down necks, terrorize, intimidate, or otherwise smother your people. If you're going to commit these sins, stay in your office.

2. *Making every decision.* Remember, you cannot grow people if you do all their thinking for them. While you're at the front, teach people to think for themselves rather than making all the decisions yourself.

3. *Abandoning administrative responsibilities.* You can't afford to spend so much time in the trenches that you ignore the important administrative duties you must perform. Overleading and undermanaging is just as dangerous as overmanaging and underleading.

WHAT LEADING FROM THE FRONT DOES MEAN

Biographer Robert Allen once remarked about General Patton that "In dominating, he did not domineer. Patton always led his men. He did not rule them."[33] Here are eleven criteria for effectively leading — not ruling — from the front.

1. *You attend meetings where your presence makes a positive difference.* As discussed in Chapter 3, when you lend your presence to meetings you heighten their credibility and intensity.

2. *You stay involved with the recruiting and hiring process.* This function is too important to delegate completely. Top leaders take recruiting and hiring personally.

3. *You conduct one-on-one coaching sessions with your high-potentials.* These are your best opportunities to listen to, coach, challenge, and develop your best people. They are not an option.

4. *You take the time to connect with and build relationships with your people.* You are running for office every day, selling yourself

and your vision. You can't build relationships or gain influence by memo or with mere incidental contact. You must get up close to people to have an impact. Remember, they won't buy into your vision until they've bought into you.

5. *You make yourself available for questions, ideas, and problems.* Being open to feedback and ideas, helping solve problems, and hearing bad news are all part of your job and are great opportunities to impact your people and shape your culture.

6. *You give fast positive reinforcement and confront poor performance just as quickly.* Since delayed consequences — both positive and negative — are ineffective, you must be in the trenches to be effective in this area. When you don't quickly reinforce good behavior you extinguish it, and when you don't confront poor behavior you endorse it.

7. *You study the effects of your strategy and make fast adjustments when necessary.* Rigid strategies are a death wish. But you can't gain feedback on what is or isn't working by roosting in your office chair pondering charts. To be a nimble leader and organization you have got to get in the thick of things.

8. *You communicate vision and values.* There is no such thing as overcommunication. You bring your vision and values to life by talking about them, getting feedback on them, and most important, visibly modeling them. You can't do this from your hierarchy horse.

9. *You contribute to training meetings when appropriate.* When you roll up your sleeves and personally invest yourself in the growth and development of your people you trump a thousand speeches on the same subject.

10. *You engage yourself in brutally honest performance evaluations.* You can't keep people out of a gray area if you don't interact with them honestly and consistently. Your people must know

where they stand and where you stand at all times and in no uncertain terms.

11. *You ensure that all disciplines in your Leadership Twelve-Pack are executed.* These daily disciplines require you to show up and execute day in and day out. By committing yourself to your twelve-pack you are assured of staying in the trenches and making a consistent impact.

When speaking of General John Fremont, prior to firing him, Abraham Lincoln observed: "His cardinal mistake is that he isolates himself and allows nobody to see him and by which he does not know what is going on in the very matter he's dealing with."[34] Sound like someone you know? I find it fits a majority of managers I observe in the workplace today. If you are serious about creating a culture of merit in your business you must become more aware of the danger of this temptation and its tendency to infect you and your other leaders with the "we have arrived so let's coast" mentality. Incidentally, Lincoln was a leader who exemplified leading from the front. During the Civil War, rather than hiding away in the White House he visited several generals at battlefields: McClellan at Antietam, Hooker at Chancellorsville, and Burnside at Fredericksburg.[35] He personally came under sniper fire at Fort Stevens, near Silver Spring, Maryland, when he appeared atop the Fort's parapet to personally survey the Confederate troops closing in on Washington, D.C.[36] Because he stayed engaged he was able to make the decisions that led to eventual victory.

Up Your Business! Bullet	**You cannot build or reinforce a healthy culture if you are disconnected from it.**

Failing to lead from the front is the cause of another major management dereliction of duty: failing to make fast decisions. Some leaders paralyze their organizations because they cannot or will not make decisions.

The reason most cannot make the call is they don't know enough about what is going on to do so. And the reason they don't know what's going on is that they're not engaged at the front lines of their business. Thus, they study the race but never join it. They discuss but never decide. They stick their toes in but never take the plunge. The good people around these leaders become frustrated because they know what must be done.

Technology executive Andy Grove observed, "Most companies don't die because they are wrong. They die because they fail to commit themselves. They fritter away their momentum and valuable resources while trying to make a decision."[37] He went on to say, "I can't help but wonder why leaders are so hesitant to lead. I guess it takes a lot of conviction and trusting your gut to get ahead of your peers, staff and employees while they're still squabbling about what path to take and set an unhesitating, unequivocal course whose rightness or wrongness may not be known for weeks, months or years." It's the leaders who productively spend time at their front lines who are in the best position to make solid decisions and overcome the debilitating hesitancy that wreaks havoc on morale, momentum, and results. They are also the leaders more likely to sustain their momentum and increase their success because they've devoted themselves to the disciplines that made them great in the first place.

| Up Your Business! Bullet | There are three types of leaders: those who make it happen; those who watch it happen; and those who, at the end of the day, scratch their heads, stare out the window, and wonder, "What happened?" |

218

Up Your Business! Action Thoughts

Leaders of Successful Organizations
Stop Leading from the Front

1. Do you spend enough time in the trenches of your organization?
2. When you are at the front, do you do what's productive or do you micromanage?
3. While at the front, which of the productive activities listed do you need to execute more often?
4. Do you have other leaders in your business who are leading from their rear ends? How will you redirect their energies?
5. Can you honestly say you go to work each day to be a catalyst and make it happen, or have you been more of an administrator?

Temptation 4: Leaders of Successful Organizations Stop Developing Others

Why? Successful leaders look at their results, stare in the mirror, pound their chests, and convince themselves it's all because of them. They don't want to rock the boat by delegating, sharing power, pushing decision making down, or developing an inner circle. They adopt the Lone Ranger mind-set toward leading, wherein they assume more and more responsibility rather than developing a team to share the load. As these leaders become obsessed with their self-importance they start working eighty-hour workweeks and become martyrs to the cause. Before long, they run out of personal capacity and plateau, and when they do

219

they take the business down with them. As Jack Welch remarked, "If you've been in your position for a year or more and must work eighty-hour workweeks you're doing something terribly wrong. Put down a list of twenty things you're doing that make you work that schedule and ten of them have to be total nonsense."[38]

What's frustrating to these lone wolves is that they look like heroes for a while because it's common for leaders to grow their organizations — temporarily — strictly on their own backs by bringing personal energy, great work ethic, and new attitude to the job. They gain the attention of their bosses and are acclaimed as the new messiahs. But, out of nowhere, they hit a ceiling. They're working just as hard as they used to but not getting the same results. What happened? They ran out of personal capacity. They took it as far as they could on the strength of their own will, energy, and effort. In order to get to a higher level, a leader must broaden his or her capacity by developing a team to help carry the load. Only after this is done can one move to a higher level.

Up Your Business! Bullet	If you can't learn to get it done through others you'll eventually fizzle and burn out. It's just a matter of time.

There are three categories of people that pull eighty-hour workweeks:

1. Leaders absolutely passionate about their businesses who put in grueling hours for the sheer joy and thrill of it — because they want to, not because they have to.

220

2. Leaders taking over new positions or operations who make up-front investments of extra effort to right a course or build a foundation in a business.
3. Leaders who have been established in their positions and operations for over a year and who routinely work eighty-hour weeks because they have to in order to get the job done.

While eighty-hour workweeks eventually take a physical, mental, and emotional toll on all three groups, I will focus on the third group. If you're in this group, you may not like what I have to say, but it needs to be said. The fact is that you're so busy making a living, you're not making a life. In fact, early on in my management career, I was just like you. I'd pride myself on how many hours I worked. I bragged that nothing moved until I said so, liked having everyone so dependent on me they couldn't think for themselves, did all the talking, had all the answers, and made all the decisions. Result: I failed to build a team, plateaued my organization, became a lid on my people, and personally burned out. To put it mildly, neither work nor life outside of work was much fun. I have found three primary reasons people like my former self fall into the group of those who work eighty-hour weeks because it's the only way the job gets done. Let's take these reasons one at a time:

1. *You think you're indispensable.* If, after our addressing this matter in Chapter 3, you still think you are indispensable I have two words for you here: GET REAL! You're not that good. Until you shift from tyrant to team you can list yourself as the number one liability on your balance sheet. People who think they are indispensable are burdened by excess pride. Effective team builders are humble. In fact, you can't build a team until you are humble because personal pride will inflate your

221

self-worth and you'll expect others to add value to you rather than assuming a servant leader's role and adding value to them.

2. *You are personally insecure.* As an insecure leader you hoard power. You get your value by doing everything yourself and are afraid that if you delegate you'll diminish your own importance. You think if someone else succeeds and looks good, you will look bad as a result. You look at people development as competitive rather than cooperative.

3. *You think your people aren't any good.* Two more words for you here: WAKE UP! If your people aren't any good, whose fault do you think that is? (Hint: Is there a mirror handy?) If you feel you have to work eighty-hour weeks because your people aren't good enough to get the job done by themselves, you are confessing your own leadership sins. After all, my guess is that you are responsible for hiring, training, and motivating these "losers," so if they aren't what they should be, guess who gets the blame. Remember, a fish rots at the head.

Up Your Business! Bullet	**One of the key transitions an effective leader must make is focusing less on what he or she can accomplish personally and focusing more on what can be done through others.**

Incidentally, if your family, health, or emotional well-being has become or is close to becoming a casualty of your unwillingness to grow up as a leader and build a team to help free you from your eighty-hour weekly sentence, you're headed for a personal train wreck. It's just a matter of time. And just so you know, if you're no good at home, eventually you'll be no good at work either. You can't be a better leader than you are a person. Thus, I suggest you get serious about building a sustainable future by investing in your team. Build a bench, because when you commit to developing people the day will come when you can clip some pretty nice coupons. You'll be able to make a great living as well as a great life.

If you're serious about building a sustainable, successful organization you must build a team. No company can grow revenues consistently faster than its ability to get enough of the right people to implement that growth and still become a great company. If your growth rate in revenues consistently outpaces your growth rate in people you cannot build a great company.

Throughout *Up Your Business!* I've presented strategies for training, coaching, and mentoring your team. There is nothing I can do to enhance them at this point. My objective is to create awareness of this temptation so you don't become a victim of it. Don't allow yourself or other leaders in your organization to become deluded and seduced by the results you're getting. The question is, *how* are you getting them? Are you getting them by putting in eighty-hour weeks and carrying the load yourself? Are you getting them by driving your people like a herd of cattle, kissing up and kicking down in the process? Or are you getting them because you've built a capable team that multiplies your effectiveness and is capable of augmenting and sustaining future increases? The answer to how you or your managers are getting results says more about the future of your organization — and your own success — than any fancy forecast or prospectus conjured up at some off-site team-building love-in.

A remark John Maxwell made at a conference best sums up why you must be serious and committed to building a team. He said, "Leaders don't act alone. They have followers. They have to, because they have a cause that's bigger than they are — they need others to pull it off."[39]

Up Your Business! Bullet	**One is too small a number for greatness. One of the greatest leadership lessons of all time is that you can't do it alone.**

> ## UP YOUR BUSINESS! ACTION THOUGHTS
>
> ### LEADERS OF SUCCESSFUL ORGANIZATIONS STOP DEVELOPING OTHERS
>
> 1. Do you or your other managers work eighty-hour weeks because it's the only way the job will get done?
> 2. What is your organization's specific and deliberate plan to develop people at all levels in your organization? How can you improve your plan?
> 3. Who is your right arm, the person who covers your back when you're not on the job? If you don't have one, who could you develop to become one?
> 4. Who in your organization can you claim to have deliberately brought to a higher skill level than they were at a year ago? What will you do to bring them to even higher levels in the coming year?

Up Your Business! Bullet	**Effective leaders are never lonely at the top because they bring people with them. If you're lonely at the top it's because you've put yourself on a pedestal.**

TEMPTATION 5: LEADERS OF SUCCESSFUL ORGANIZATIONS STOP HOLDING OTHERS ACCOUNTABLE

Why? Since results are satisfactory and there's no immediate crisis, why should they rock the boat by getting in people's face and applying pressure to perform? After all, the rationale goes, not everyone can be a superstar, so why run people off by being a hard case? Live and let live.

Up Your Business! Bullet	**If you don't make waves you'll drown. If you don't mess with your success someone else will.**

I learn volumes about what's on a manager's mind and the issues managers struggle with by virtue of the questions I'm asked at seminars and via e-mail and letters. Without a doubt, one of the most significant struggles leaders face worldwide is the unpleasant task of holding people accountable. I've found three key reasons this is true:

- Clear performance expectations were never established in the first place, so leaders are reluctant to hold people accountable for not executing them. After all, how can you say to me, "Anderson, you're not cutting it" when you never defined what "cutting it" is in the first place? You can't. So you won't. And so the cycle of poor performance continues unchecked. As discussed in Chapter 3, when you don't confront deficient behavior, in effect you reinforce it and can expect to see more of it.

Up Your Business! Bullet	**Accountability is impossible without clear expectations.**

225

- Since the leader has built no pipeline of talent as outlined in Chapter 1, he or she is afraid to confront poor behavior because there's no one to replace the employees if they leave. Thus, these leaders live and let live and shrink their standards down to the employees' level rather than stretching employees up to their standards.

Up Your Business! Bullet	The inconvenience of proactively building a pipeline of talent pales in comparison to the inconvenience and embarrassment of being held hostage by employees so mediocre you wouldn't rehire them if given the opportunity.

- Leaders have become conditioned by society's perverse "don't offend anyone" mind-set and are more concerned about political correctness than their obligation to the rest of the organization and everyone in it. The result of this behavior is a culture of entitlement, and, as outlined in Chapter 2, it will paralyze a performance-based environment.

Up Your Business! Bullet	Trying not to hurt someone's feelings or make them mad runs a distant second to doing what's best for the organization.

You cannot fix, build, or stretch your organization unless everyone at all levels is held accountable for results. Holding people accountable is a key component of creating the positive pressure to perform necessary to stretch, change, and grow your business over the long haul. Following are a combination of thoughts and phrases designed to round out your accountability mind-set. They are direct and pull no punches. Once you work these thoughts into your psyche and vocabulary, holding people accountable will be easier.

FIFTEEN TENETS OF ACCOUNTABILITY

1. Holding people accountable is nothing to apologize for. In fact, you owe this to your people. Failing to stretch them and bring out their best is something to apologize for.

Up Your Business! Bullet	**Care enough about your people to confront them when they fall short of the behavior and performance you know they're capable of delivering.**

2. A leadership obligation is to keep your people out of the gray areas. They must know exactly where they stand and exactly where you stand.
3. When holding people accountable, don't let them focus on why something shouldn't be happening. Deal with what is. People must face reality and see life as it is, not simply as they'd like it to be.
4. Holding people accountable means you shake them out of denial. Denial leads to inertia.
5. Your obligation as a coach is to get your people to look at their own lives and at their own performance and decide whether the results they're getting are what they really want or just safer and easier than what they really want. Challenge your people to pay the price for the prize and not to settle too early or too cheaply.
6. Teach your people that they must accept responsibility for their work and their lives. When they choose the behavior,

they choose the consequences for that behavior. They are not victims. Remember that whenever people complain they do so to deflect responsibility away from themselves and onto the cold, cruel world. Hold up the mirror and make them look into it.

| Up Your Business! Bullet | **When people choose to come in late, project a lousy attitude, and persist in not getting their work done, they choose the lousy paycheck that comes along with that.** |

---

7. Don't allow people to sweep problems and shortcomings under the rug. Push them to the forefront and deal with them.
8. Teach people that failure is not an accident. Either they set themselves up for it or they don't.

| Up Your Business! Bullet | **Failures become failures long before anyone realizes that they are failures. Somewhere along the line they start making poor decisions, repeating the same errors in judgment, and failing to develop necessary disciplines. One day it shows up.** |

---

9. Teach people they are accountable for their own lives. If they don't accept accountability, they will misdiagnose and mistreat every problem they have. The inability of most people to do this has turned therapy, psychology, and psychiatry into a booming growth industry.
10. Teach people that life is often unfair. And while they cannot choose what happens to them, they can choose their responses.

11. When holding people accountable, remember: People do what works. They are not going to continue to do things that bring them personal pain. At some level they're getting a payoff or they wouldn't be doing it. Thus, to change their behavior, attach a consequence to it.

> **Up Your Business! Bullet**
>
> **If people come in late, fail to perform to standard, and project negativity to others without any consequence for their actions, they're simply doing what works for them. Until there are consequences, they'll continue doing these things.**

12. You can't change what you don't acknowledge. If you don't get them to see themselves as the real problem, they'll continue to misdiagnose what's really wrong and place the blame elsewhere.

13. Life rewards action — not experience, knowledge, or wisdom. It even rewards wrong action, because if you take initiative and are paying attention to results, you'll realize it's not working and will be able to adjust and move on to something that brings results. What life doesn't reward is sitting still.

> **Up Your Business! Bullet**
>
> **Some people need to put some verbs in their life . . . verbs other than *sit, wait,* and *eat.***

14. Ultimately, people must understand they are measured by results, not best efforts or good intentions.

15. Excuses must be uncovered and exposed. While they are a natural tendency, they are the DNA of underachievers.

| Up Your Business! Bullet | **The best day of your life is when you give up excuses and start making results.** |

As a longtime student of leaders and leadership principles, I labored to find the ultimate example of a leader who effectively leveraged accountability to successfully build and sustain success in an organization. I wanted to use this person's principles as a case study in one of my workshops. The leader I chose was Vince Lombardi, legendary coach of the Green Bay Packers. Regardless of whether you know a football from a footrest, you can learn from Lombardi's principles.

| Up Your Business! Bullet | **Success leaves clues.** |

First, I'll present background facts about Coach Lombardi; then I'll relate how he used his principles to turn around a losing team and then sustain and extend success once he attained it.

Background Facts about Coach Vince Lombardi

- After years of cutting his teeth at collegiate levels and as an assistant in the pros, Vince Lombardi finally got his first shot at head coach with the Green Bay Packers. He only coached ten years in the pros as a head coach before dying of cancer, yet he left the game a legend.[40]
- He never had a losing season. To appreciate this fact you must realize that the team he took over had a record of 1-10-1 (wins-losses-ties) the year before his arrival.[41]
- During his professional head coaching career, he coached only 146 games, winning 105, losing 35, and tying 6.[42]

230

- His postseason record was 9-1,[43] which included victory in five of seven championships.[44] The ability of his team to sustain excellence under the pressure of playoffs and championship games is unmatched in professional sports.
- There was no free agency when Lombardi coached. You had to win with the players you had. Again, to fully understand his ability to turn around existing players it helps to understand that in the three years before his arrival as head coach the Packers were 4-8 in 1956, 3-9 in 1957, and 1-10-1 in 1958.[45] Thus, it's safe to say he inherited a team devoid of momentum and in a downward spiral. Incidentally, if you have ever believed that coaching doesn't make all the difference in people development, consider that thirteen of the players Lombardi inherited from the 1-10-1 team went on to become All Pros under Lombardi's leadership.[46]

Keys to Lombardi's Unparalleled Success

- When you played for Lombardi, you knew the expectation. Lombardi created perhaps the most famous mission statement in the world: "Winning isn't everything. It's the only thing."[47] In fact, the first day of training camp he made his expectations very clear: "There are trains, planes and buses leaving out of Green Bay every day and if you don't perform for me you'll find yourself on one of them."[48] While some managers may think this was harsh, I find it very fair. People understood exactly what was expected.
  Self-checkup: Do your people know exactly what is expected? Is your mission as clearly defined as Lombardi's?
- When you played for Lombardi, you knew exactly where he stood and where you stood. There was no gray area. Lom-

bardi was a straight shooter. He spoke from the heart in terms so plain as to be impossible to misunderstand.

Self-checkup: Can you say without wavering that your people know exactly where they stand and where you stand on performance issues?

- Lombardi used clear expectations and accountability to turn around a losing team and sustain winning teams. This is perhaps the most challenging of all organizational endeavors. It's normally easier to turn around a losing team than it is to keep winning once you do. He did both.

  Self-checkup: Regardless of which of these situations you are currently in, are you executing the disciplines necessary to turn your ability to create results into a marathon rather than a sprint?

- Lombardi's teams were brilliant in the basics. They kept it simple. Under Lombardi, the Packers had eight plays they ran to near perfection. The opposition knew what was coming much of the time but was unable to stop it because of the Packers' execution. Lombardi understood that it's hard to be aggressive when you're confused.

  Self-checkup: Is your team brilliant in the basics? Are you committed to the training necessary to achieve this state as outlined in Chapter 3?

- Lombardi treated every player as a unique individual. He customized his approach to fit each person and avoided the assembly-line management style that treats each person like another head in a herd of cattle. He was fond of saying, "My job is to find forty different ways to move forty different men." Lombardi knew that Bart Starr hated being yelled at in public, so he didn't. He confronted him privately.[49] On the other hand, he

232

knew that Lee Roy Caffey responded to a harsher, more direct approach — and Lombardi was happy to oblige.[50] Max McGee, the star receiver, abhorred blocking drills, so Lombardi found a way around them for him — as long as he performed well.[51] *Self-checkup:* Do you know what moves your people? Are you treating them as unique individuals?

- Lombardi stayed focused on his mission and didn't succumb to distractions. He kept such a ferocious focus on the discipline of practice that he refused to cancel practice at key times, such as during the Cuban Missile Crisis and during historic space launches, when assistants and players alike suggested postponement or cancellation.[52]

Self-checkup: Are you merely *interested* in building great people and a great organization, or are you truly committed to it?

| Up Your Business! Bullet | *Accountability* is not a bad word. It's something you owe to your people. Letting your team wallow in mediocrity and pretending they're not losing when they are is a betrayal of your leadership position. |

To overcome Temptation 5, you are going to have to get serious about setting clear expectations, offering fast feedback on performance, and installing consequences for failing to get the job done. If these are tasks you are uncomfortable with or don't see the value in, you should excuse yourself from a leadership position because effective leadership is not possible without them. The fact is that if you're a good leader, you're going to tick people off from time to time. Not by being a jerk or abusive, but by expecting the best, confronting slack behavior and performance, and being brutally honest in your interactions with others.

Up Your
Business! Bullet **If you're not ticking people off from time to time you're not pushing the envelope.**

In fact, if you have a group of smiling and comfortable under-achievers lounging around your workplace who are going through the motions and feeling no pressure to perform, you have serious work to do! Many leaders find themselves in this precise situation because, quite frankly, it's easier to be a bad leader. Bad leaders think everyone wants to stretch, grow, and reach their fullest potential. They believe everyone is beautiful and if you give enough hugs and pep talks people will do whatever it takes to get the job done. You should be able to compete head to head with these Alices in Wonderland because in today's bare-knuckle marketplace they make easy and appetizing prey.

If you still don't feel the urgency to hold people accountable in good times or bad, or if you feel that imposing consequences for failing to perform is a harsh way to manage, I'll take one last stab at convincing you with my all-time favorite story of accountability. If you attended Sunday school or vacation Bible school as a youngster I'm sure you will recall this story, although when you heard it back then you may not have seen it in the perspective I'll present it from.

The Parable of the Talents
In the New Testament, Jesus told the parable of the talents.[53] (In ancient times, a talent was a measure of money.) To paraphrase, the story went something like this: A businessman was preparing to leave town for an extended period of time and met with three of his workers to delegate tasks before his departure. He gave them talents to invest while he was gone, with the understanding that they'd be held accountable for results upon his return. The businessman

allocated the talents in proportion to his workers' abilities, giving five to the best worker, two to another, and one to the third.

When he returned to the scene, the businessman gathered the three together as promised to give an accounting of what they had done with the money during his absence. He met first with the person to whom he had given five talents, and the worker reported that he had worked hard, invested the money, and turned the five into ten. The businessman was very pleased and told the employee that since he had done such a great job with what he had been given, he'd give him even more responsibility in the future. He then met with the worker to whom he had given two talents, and this worker reported that he had worked hard and invested the money wisely and was pleased to report he had doubled the two into four talents. Again, the businessman was appreciative and promised this worker that since he'd also done well with what he was entrusted, he could expect more responsibility in the future. At last, he called in the employee to whom he had left the one talent. He could barely maintain his cool when this weak link explained that because he was afraid of losing the money, he'd buried it in the ground to preserve it and returned the one talent to his boss. Well, the businessman lost it. He told the others to take the useless, worthless servant and throw him out! Then (and this is my favorite part of the story) he instructed that the one talent be taken from the person who did nothing with it and be given to the man who had ten with the explanation that those who did well with what they were given would receive more, and those who didn't use even what little bit they had would have it taken from them. There are three primary lessons in this story I find useful for application in business:

1. *The funds were initially distributed according to prior performance, not equally across the board.* This would offend the politically

correct sensibilities of some managers today who rationalize, "If I do this for one of my people, I have to do it for all of them."

2. *The amounts returned on the successful investments doubled: from five to ten and from two to four.* I believe this is symbolic of our tendency not to expect enough and to settle too early, too cheaply, too often.

3. *Jesus, who told the story, didn't chastise the businessman for being tough and holding the sluggard accountable.* Instead, He was hard on the nonperformer for not using what he was given and failing to get the job done.

UP YOUR BUSINESS! ACTION THOUGHTS

LEADERS OF SUCCESSFUL ORGANIZATIONS STOP HOLDING OTHERS ACCOUNTABLE

1. Are you willing to hold people accountable, even when there is no visible crisis and business is going well?
2. Do you keep your people out of gray areas?
3. Have you clearly established performance and behavioral expectations so you have a benchmark for accountability?
4. Do you care enough about your people to confront them with brutally honest feedback when they are off track?

Up Your Business! Bullet	**If you can't tell it like it is, stay out of business and go into politics.**

Temptation 6: Everyone in Successful Organizations Begins to Abandon the Basics

Why? Since the natural tendency when you're doing well is to let up, people start getting away from the disciplines and decisions that made them successful in the first place. Each chapter of this book has outlined basic disciplines necessary to fix, build, or stretch your organization. From hiring proactively and intelligently to exercising your Leadership Twelve-Pack and in every chapter in between, basic principles have been presented and explained. Since there is little I can add to these strategies at this juncture, my goal is to heighten your awareness of this temptation. Often you'll hear a coach explain that his slumping team must "get back to basics." The fact that they lost focus on them in the first place is the culprit. Don't let this happen to you, and if it does, quickly correct your course before your rut turns into a grave. In fact, there are two prime occasions when your people are most susceptible to abandoning the basics:

- *When you're on a roll.* Oftentimes you can't survive your own success and start to get sloppy, take shortcuts, and discard the hard work and sound decisions that brought you success initially.

Up Your Business! Bullet	Embrace and execute the basics when things are going well. Don't wait for the bottom to fall out. If you are continually getting "back to the basics," give yourself a swift kick for abandoning them in the first place. Develop the discipline to make the basics the rule, not the exception.

237

- *When you're in a rut.* When the bottom falls out, before you return to the basics, you're likely to press longer and harder — often at the wrong things — trying to right your course. Or you may veer even farther off track by chasing fads and whims in the search for a quick-fix return to success. At any time or place you must be aware that when you, as a leader, abandon the basics it accelerates the downward spiral and creates exponential damage to momentum and results.

Up Your Business! Bullet	**When a leader abandons the basics it gives followers license to do likewise. Each day, with every action, you are either modeling a devotion to the basics or modeling abuse of them.**

Following are three final thoughts on overcoming Temptation 6:

1. *Sweat the small stuff.* Contrary to prevailing pundit wisdom, I highly suggest you sweat the "small stuff" in your business. As a leader, you should sweat the basics, the other five temptations, the execution of your Leadership Twelve-Pack, and breaches of core values and character compromises of any kind.

2. *Weave the mantra "Become brilliant in the basics" into your culture.* As a leader you should embrace the mantra to become brilliant in the basics, and there are four key words to doing so: day in, day out. You have to press the issue on good and bad days alike. J. W. Marriott remarked, "The most important thing is to serve hot food hot and cold food cold."[54] This seemingly simple quotation is profound. Marriott was, of course, referring to the importance of becoming brilliant in the basics. You might also ask yourself what good it does for you to

invest time, money, and energy into building a business if your people don't know how to handle an incoming phone call, set an appointment, ask for a referral, overcome an objection, close a deal, interview properly, motivate their staffs, conduct a one-on-one, or turn around a poor performer.

3. *Understand that when you abandon the basics you plant the seeds of broken momentum.* When you abandon the basics you lose your momentum and must exert several times the energy and effort to regain it. As Patton advised, "Never yield ground. It is cheaper to hold what you have than to retake what you lost."[55] Unless you want to waste countless resources regaining lost ground and expend time and energy plugging holes instead of climbing to new heights, you must develop a savage devotion to the basics. Awareness begins with the leadership of your organization and becomes embedded in your culture when you personally execute those basics and publicly reward those doing the same.

Up Your Business! Bullet	**The more you prepare the less you repair. You are preparing for something today — the question is, for what?**

Up Your Business! Bullet	**You don't have to do anything extraordinary to build a great business. You just have to do the ordinary things extraordinarily well.**

As we complete the chapter on the six temptations of successful organizations, I recommend you print and laminate them, then post them in your conference room or anywhere else you can to heighten awareness of them. For your convenience, I've grouped them together as the last box in this chapter.

UP YOUR BUSINESS! ACTION THOUGHTS

EVERYONE IN SUCCESSFUL ORGANIZATIONS BEGINS TO ABANDON THE BASICS

1. The key to sticking to the basics is being more aware of the discipline necessary to execute fast corrections when you veer off track.
2. Be particularly aware of abandoning the basics both when you are on a roll and when you are in a rut.
3. Sweat the small stuff, especially the key deliverables that spell trouble when abused.
4. Embrace the mantra "Become brilliant in the basics" and weave it into your psyche and corporate culture.
5. The key to becoming brilliant in the basics is embodied in the four words "day in, day out."
6. Remember that it is easier to keep momentum and hold the ground you have than to have to regain it after it has been lost.

UP YOUR BUSINESS! ACTION THOUGHTS

THE SIX TEMPTATIONS OF SUCCESSFUL ORGANIZATIONS

1. The leaders of successful organizations stop working on themselves.
2. The leaders of successful organizations stop thinking big.
3. The leaders of successful organizations stop leading from the front.
4. The leaders of successful organizations stop developing others.
5. The leaders of successful organizations stop holding others accountable.
6. Everyone in successful organizations begins to abandon the basics.

FURTHER UP YOUR BUSINESS

YOU MAY BE MORE COMPLACENT THAN YOU THINK!

Next to *loyalty*, which is oftentimes misdefined as "tenure," *complacency* is one of the least understood words in a leader's business vocabulary. The general assumption is that someone complacent is also lazy, bored, or just plain indifferent. However, the true definition of complacency may startle you: As you read it, you'll realize that you've been in the state of complacency more often than you'd like to admit. Oxford Dictionary defines complacency as "calmly content or smugly self-satisfied." Haven't you worked hard in the past to reach a certain degree of success and, after achieving it, discovered that you became so calmly content and smugly self-satisfied that while you still worked long hours and days, you no longer changed anything, held people accountable, made big decisions, or took risks? Yes, as strange as it sounds, you can still work seventy to eighty hours per week and become complacent; you're so busy maintaining and protecting what you have that you fail to continue growing your organization.

This is exactly why I go out of my way in speeches, seminars, tele-seminars, and books to warn successful people against the dangers of complacency. It is the successful people and organizations that become prone to defending the status quo, become calmly content and smugly self-satisfied, and begin to sow the seeds of eventual destruction for their enterprise. After all, if you're failing, drowning, or struggling to survive, it's safe to say that you're most likely not calmly content or smugly self-satisfied. In fact, it may have been the fact that you were once in a state of complacency and did nothing to remedy the situation that resulted in your current attempt to hold your head above water.

Think about it: When are you most likely to hold people accountable, to train, to make changes and big decisions, or to try something new — when you're doing really well, or after the bottom falls out? Normally, it's the latter that gives us the wake-up call to get back to solid business basics. This is why it is essential that leaders become more aware of the drift toward complacency and face the truth about when that drift normally begins: while they're at the top of their game. The slide toward complacency has been defined as the incremental descent into poor decision making. In other words, you don't become complacent overnight; it happens over time. It starts with the decision to cancel the training meeting or hire the less-than-stellar job candidate and then gets worse when you let someone talk you into keeping a nonperformer rather than holding him accountable. The plunge picks up speed when you begin hearing phrases at meetings like "let's not mess with our success," "if it's still around it must work, and it must work because it's still around," "if it ain't broke, don't fix it," and the pervasive "let's just keep doing what we've been doing . . . after all, we are number one in our area."

As stated in Chapter 4, when you find yourself in a rut, it's not the result of something you did last night. Instead, it's evidence of a series of bad decisions, failed disciplines, and repeated errors in judgment over time that are just now manifesting themselves. An even better strategy would be to continue to play to win and "fix the roof while the sun is shining," while you're doing well, so the descent into poor judgment never happens in the first place.

CHAPTER 7

Build Long-Term Vitality

Steps for Execution and Follow-Through

This is one of the most important chapters in the book. Because if you don't follow through and execute the disciplines provided, your traverse through the previous pages will have been no more than an intellectual exercise. Too often, attendees at my workshops say that they will take the strategies learned and gradually phase them into their businesses. They're afraid of moving too fast, trying too much at once, and becoming overwhelmed. However, the greater danger is in not doing enough. If you don't move quickly and substantially, your efforts will fizzle and resolve will wane. Why? If too much time passes before you take meaningful action you'll get used to the status quo and learn to live with it. It's like discovering a dead body in your living room. When you first see it you're alarmed and offended. But as you get busy with your routine it seems to fit. Soon, you cover it up, walk around it, and step over it and lose the urgency to remove it. You learn to live with it.

GET OFF YOUR DEAD HORSE

Dakota tribal wisdom declares that when the horse you're riding on dies, dismount. Oftentimes the dead horse is an impotent strategy, an ineffective leader, or a poor process. For some of you, it's time to dismount. Of course, there are other strategies you can choose, and many leaders will choose these routes first because they seem less painful. You can change riders. Go ahead and put a new rider on a dead horse and see how far he gets. Or you can appoint a focus group within your business to study dead horses. If you prefer, you can benchmark how other companies ride dead horses. You might even declare it cheaper to feed a dead horse and decide to stay with it. Or you can harness several dead horses together and see how far they get you. But when all is said and done, you're still going to have to get off the horse. You're going to have to innovate, not just optimize; think strategically, not just tactically; and start playing to win again, rather than playing not to lose. If the need for change is obvious and you know it will ultimately benefit the organization, why do so few change efforts succeed? As much as you may want to deny it, it's the leader who screws it up. And if you'll permit me to be direct, I'll explain why and offer remedies.

THE NAKED EMPEROR RIDES AGAIN

The reason I'll explain it to you is because no one in your organization wants to. After all, you hold their future in your hands. Thus, you continue to stride through your organization like the naked emperor as onlookers nod in affirmation, all the while their inner selves wanting to scream, "You're the problem! You're out of touch! Stop saying you're open to change when everyone knows you're its natural assassin! You talk like a leader but act like an anchor! Let me out of the box! Let me innovate! I want to make a difference! Shut up and listen for a change!"

The fact is that no one cares more about a business than the boss, but it is equally true that no one does more to hold it back, break momentum, undermine change, and keep good people down. You're too close to the problem to realize it's you, and no one working for you wants to come out and say it. So I'll help them out: Your team has met the enemy and it is you. Perhaps you'd make changes if you grasped that you were the problem, but because most of your team gives your mandates the "kiss of yes" you figure you're on the right track and they're behind you. Not quite. Recall when they did bring you feedback only to have it fire-hosed, belittled, trivialized, or done in by delay? Your team is frustrated and intimidated more than they are motivated, and they don't know what to do about it. They want to do better. They want to make progressive change. Here are five reasons you unwittingly prevent them from doing so:

1. As a leader you have the most emotional equity in the status quo because you were the chief architect of where the organization is today. Thus, you have the most to defend and be defensive about. *Remedy:* Develop the discipline to detach yourself from current strategies and suspend judgment while others give input on what should be done. Challenge your assumptions of what made you successful in the past and let everyone else challenge them as well. The best reformers the world has ever known started with themselves. As Tolstoy said, "Everyone thinks of changing the world, but no one thinks of changing himself."

Up Your Business! Bullet	**If everyone is thinking alike then someone isn't thinking.**

2. Time and experience can work against you since you have the most to unlearn in changing times. The tendency is to continue using an old map to find new lands. *Remedy:* Know that time and experience can be helpful when optimizing but can be a hindrance when innovating, since your thinking is locked in a box. Be willing to forget much of what used to work and embrace new strategies and tactics.

Up Your Business! Bullet	**Make yourself as perfectly attuned to the timeless as to the ever-changing.**

3. You're too close to the action to see the big picture. You've gotten so immersed in routine that you're an unwitting prisoner of out-of-date beliefs and strategies. *Remedy:* Question the relevancy of industry dogmas concerning standards, metrics, and strategies that were accepted in the past and become open to new thinking. Ditch tradition and sentimentalism whenever necessary to move forward. Clearly, not all accepted industry standards are impotent. After all, there's a difference between dogma (the earth is flat) and laws of physics (things go up rather than down).

Up Your Business! Bullet	**Most of what industry insiders and experts claim is God-given is actually man-made.**

4. If your tendency in the past has been to fire-hose ideas and views that conflict with yours, know it will take much more effort to encourage others to contribute. *Remedy:* When debating an issue, reserve your opinion for last and others will feel freer to speak honestly. Start your meeting by saying,

"Here is the issue we face. Here are the potential options for resolving it. What do you all think?" Remind everyone that every idea is a good idea until you find the best idea, and that good ideas become great ones when they are challenged. Then shut up and let them go at it. Keep things on track, make sure everyone is heard, play devil's advocate without taking a specific stance to ensure that all sides of an issue are heard and examined. After you're comfortable this has been accomplished, take the feedback you've heard, use it to refine your thinking, and then speak your piece. Let them know that even at this stage you want your people to shoot holes in what you're suggesting. After the decision has been made, however, the debate ends and everyone must get on the same page and support what's been decided. During these discussions everyone has an equal voice but not an equal vote. You still make the call, but by gaining more input from others, you'll improve your own perspective and earn buy-in to your decision.

Up Your Business! Bullet	**Effective business is neither democracy nor dictatorship. Strike a balance.**

5. Top leaders get to the point where they can learn little from one another. Think about it: The inner circle at your enterprise has been talking at each other for years. Your positions are well known and you can finish one another's sentences. If you never include new people from varied levels and departments in your strategic planning you will disenfranchise 95 percent of your employees. *Remedy:* Include new voices in strategy and innovation conversations, or your chances of coming up with a rule-breaking strategy or product are nil. This is

tough for many managers because they secretly long for a more compliant organization rather than a more vociferous one. Some organizations boast of their workforce's diverse ethnic and gender makeup. But this sort of diversity misses the point. Diversity in thinking is what changes organizations.

| Up Your Business! Bullet | **What do you gain by having an ethnic makeup that mimics the United Nations if no one thinks differently or for themselves?** |

It's important to humble yourself as a leader and acknowledge that being boss doesn't mean you have to do all the talking or have all the answers. Instead, your task is to surround yourself with people who do. If your people feel like they are working in a box with strict boundaries and simply carrying out your orders they will never have breakthroughs.

As popular as it is for leaders to believe that change starts at the top and that they are their organizations' primary change champion, it's simply not true. I used to believe leaders liked change more than followers but have found that this is the case only if the change is their idea. The lesson: Be more self-aware. Be aware of the stultifying effect your ego-driven beliefs can inflict on others' passions. Be aware of your tendency to project antiquated business models into a more complex marketplace. Be aware that you use your history to solve everyone else's problems and fire-hose new ideas as they are presented, and of the natural inclination to defend what you have created. And be very aware of the cost to your organization every time these offenses break momentum, sap morale, or cause a shining star to leave for an opportunity to grow, be heard, and have an impact elsewhere.

UP YOUR BUSINESS! ACTION THOUGHTS

DEAD HORSES AND NAKED EMPERORS

1. Which dead horses that you're riding must you dismount: the wrong people, strategy, product, or process?
2. Are you willing to face that you may be a "naked emperor" and the chief obstacle to change in your department or organization?
3. Do you fire-hose ideas brought to you by others? How many meaningful ideas or strategies have you solicited, received, or implemented other than your own?
4. Have you built a team of diverse thinkers? Does your environment insist on different points of view, welcome the challenging of ideas, and have the robust and candid dialogue necessary to attain breakthroughs?

FOUR REASONS CHANGE FAILS

Needless to say, the reason change doesn't happen in organizations goes far beyond the five points presented earlier. While they are a good start, there are broader issues that you must be aware of. For starters, here's a scenario that may sound familiar.

You travel across the country to spend thousands of dollars and many days of your life at seminars and conventions, returning with a sheaf full of notes and good intentions. You're excited about what you learned and you're going to make some changes. After some second-guessing, you water down your action plan considerably before presenting it to your team. You announce the new edicts and start people moving in the right direction just in time to get hit with the latest crisis. Soon your new master plan has turned into credenza-ware and the latest flavor of the month has gone sour — again — and your course workbook and action plan have also become credenza-ware. Why doesn't change stick? Why can't highly paid, professional people take an idea that clearly makes sense, implement it, and see it through?

1. *No guiding coalition.* You must get the influencers in your organization behind the change before making a wholesale announcement to the entire team. Your inner circle will be the key to cascading your message to the rank and file, modeling the new change, selling others on its benefits, and snuffing out resistance as it surfaces.

Up Your Business! Bullet	**You can't do it alone. Your guiding coalition is the key to implementing change more quickly and giving it the credibility necessary for it to stick.**

---

2. *No sense of urgency.* No change has a chance without your first creating a sense of urgency. Thus, the reasons for the change must be clearly articulated, a positive pressure to perform imposed, and accountability for the desired changes upheld. This means you quickly and publicly affirm desired behaviors, both verbally and tangibly. And just as quickly, you correct and redirect actions that undermine the change. People often go into denial when change is implemented, secretly hoping it will fade away. Thus, it's important to maintain pressure to perform long enough that everyone knows the change is not an experiment and that you mean business.

Sagging urgency is the number one enemy to sustaining your change efforts.

> | | |
> |---|---|
> | **Up Your Business! Bullet** | **To ensure urgency and the pressure to perform necessary to implement change, the new objective must be clearly defined, fast feedback given on performance, and accountability for results established.** |

3. *Lack of buy-in.* While determining direction is a leader's prerogative, a fatal flaw is failing to include others in the strategy for reaching it. Let people know the objective, why it's important, and what's in it for them, but solicit their input on how to make it happen. People will support what they help create. Including them in the strategic process helps gain commitment over compliance. As stated previously, top management's job isn't to conjure up strategies. It's to build an organization capable of continuously generating new business concepts and invigorating old ones. Its contribution is to design the context rather than inventing all the content.

> | | |
> |---|---|
> | **Up Your Business! Bullet** | **You can't just command change any more than you can order a great performance. You have to plan it, encourage it, nurture it, and focus on it. Too often, when change brings grief rather than growth it's because the transition was bad.** |

4. *Failure to do enough.* Contrary to the myth that changing too much at once destroys your efforts, the opposite is often true. Not doing enough quickly enough to change your business

causes your efforts to fizzle and you to lose resolve. Organizational inertia will overcome you. When you return from a meeting armed with your action plan for change, chances are that if you don't begin the implementation process within forty-eight hours and don't complete the priorities on the list within sixty days they will never get done. Instead, you'll get used to the way things are, learn to live with the status quo, and drift back toward stasis.

Every change initiative needs early momentum. Go after low-hanging fruit first to gain short-term wins and necessary credibility. These short-term wins validate your efforts and help bring the stragglers along.

Up Your Business! Bullet	**Nothing silences cynics like success.**

Winning fast, early, and often snowballs your momentum and helps make the change stick. Then you'll have the credibility to consolidate your wins and leverage your progress to tackle even bigger change. And to make a significant difference, you will have to go after the major changes. Otherwise, as Gary Hamel says, it's like putting a belly-button ring on granny. It'll cause a stir and grab attention, but what granny needs is a liver transplant, not a navel ornament.[56]

Managers should become more self-aware, swap rhetoric for reality, and grasp that they tend to soak flames of change more than stoke them. While it's important to acknowledge what made you successful in the past, becoming sentimental and enamored with tradition can devolve you from leader to laggard and render you irrelevant as you preside over dead or dying objectives and strategies.

Up Your Business! Action Thoughts

Four Reasons Change Fails

1. Who makes up the guiding coalition you'll need to get on board to move change forward in your organization? How will you enroll them in your change vision?
2. How can you create a sense of urgency that grabs people's attention and motivates them to move forward with the needed changes? How will you sustain the urgency once you create it?
3. To earn buy-in, what will you do to involve people at all levels in creating the strategies necessary to bring about the change?
4. What priorities can you attack that will make a meaningful difference and ensure your efforts don't fizzle? What will you do to keep people focused on continual progress so the change is entrenched in your culture and the status quo has less chance to reestablish itself?

THIRTEEN STEPS TO OVERCOME "FLAVOR-OF-THE-MONTH" SYNDROME

Now that you have a better idea of why change doesn't happen, or stick, and possess remedies to beat the odds of its derailing, I'll formalize much of what I've presented in a thirteen-point plan to help

253

you overcome the latest flavor of the month in your business and entrench change into your culture.

| Up Your Business! Bullet | **The passage of time cools passions and good intentions. Lack of follow-through and execution drains passion, diminishes credibility, and entrenches resistance to future change efforts.** |

---

1. *Turn up the heat.* You can't get change out of the blocks or make it stick without urgency. The reasons for change must be explained: where you were, where you are, where you are going, and why it is important. You can't just command people to change. They must understand the "why."

| Up Your Business! Bullet | **Raising awareness unfreezes the status quo.** |

---

2. *Create a guiding coalition.* As failing to create a guiding coalition is one of the four key reasons change fails, this is not an option. Until you gain the buy-in of influencers who will passionately move the change forward at all levels in your organization, you're setting yourself up for failure and perhaps sabotage.
3. *People must understand what is in it for them.* Whether it is the opportunity to grow, earn more money, or save the company and their jobs, reasons must precede mandates.

| Up Your Business! Bullet | **Take the vision from *me* to *we*.** |

---

4. *Paint a clear vision of where you're headed but let everyone know it may take multiple strategies to get there.* Let people know up

front that you will lock like a laser on the goal but must remain flexible in your approach. This takes the sting out of changes or adjustments you may need to make later.

5. *Involve people in the strategy.* Your vision is nonnegotiable, but you must involve others in how to reach it. This gives you great ideas and gives them a vital sense of ownership. Remember, people support what they help create. Thus, their involvement ensures commitment to your change efforts over compliance with it. In fact, one of the most effective meetings you can conduct is to tell your team: "Here's where we are. There's where we need to go, and this is why it's important. Here's what's in it for you if we pull it off. Now, tell me what we need to do to get there." Then facilitate the ideas you get without fire-hosing. Pay particular attention to the most powerless voices in your organization, those closest to the periphery, because they will have a better idea of what's really going on than those who roost in the ivory tower.

   Some leaders declare that strategy should be the domain of the elite few at the top. After all, if the game plan is well known, competitors can benefit from this knowledge. But unless your competitors can execute your strategy, knowing what it is will do them little good. On the other hand, if your employees don't know what it is they sure can't execute it, so involving others in the strategy and communicating throughout the organization is a chance you have no choice but to take.

| Up Your Business! Bullet | You can't create lasting change by yourself, even if you're the CEO. You don't have enough energy and there aren't enough hours in the day. You must involve others, or change is dead. |

---

6. *Identify the new behaviors necessary to implement the change, and positively reinforce those new behaviors quickly and often.* This is essential when you are trying to create new behavior and habits. In fact, when trying to anchor new behaviors in your culture, you can count on having to reinforce them four to five times more often than you think is necessary.

7. *Communicate the message incessantly and through various media.* Stick with your program because just about the time you are sick of saying it is when your people begin to get it.

| Up Your Business! Bullet | **One of the best ways you can communicate change is by living it. Make decisions congruent with your new direction and walk your talk day in and day out.** |

---

8. *Clarify specific expectations for improvement for each department and each person.* Leave no doubt what you expect. Follow up with feedback and accountability. You will need to communicate more clearly and more often so people know you mean business. Good people will try hard to hit a new standard if they know what it is and know they will be held accountable for results.

| Up Your Business! Bullet | **People do what they're held accountable for.** |

---

9. *Attach positive consequences for getting the job done and negative consequences for repeated shortfalls.* Clarify them up front and follow through quickly in either case. You cannot change behavior without changing the consequences for that behavior.

You will need to pay more attention to performance, hold reviews with fast feedback more often, and follow through quickly with both the positive and the negative consequences.

10. *Maintain a positive pressure to perform.* Whenever the bar is raised or change is implemented many people will give it lip service, hoping it will fade away. You must stick to your guns and maintain pressure to perform long enough that everyone knows the good old days are over and that you mean business. Too much anxiety is detrimental to performance, but so is too little. Find that optimal level and sustain it. It takes constant attention and is art, not science, which is exactly why change requires strong leadership. If you heighten pressure to perform and then let up and allow the status quo to reestablish itself you're in serious trouble, since regaining your lost momentum will take several times the effort. Thus, it's important not to declare victory too soon, as a let-up will ensue. As pointed out previously in the last section, "Four Reasons Change Fails," you must steer momentum when you're doing well so you keep moving toward the next objective, continue to overwhelm the current system, and make change stick.

| Up Your Business! Bullet | **Pressure to perform has three components: clearly defined expectations, fast feedback on performance, and strong accountability for results.** |

---

11. *Honestly relate your progress and shortfalls related to the change program openly and one on one.* Keep people tuned in to what is going on. At the company luncheon or in the company newsletter, say, "Two people were promoted, one retired,

and one was fired for poor performance." If you don't provide strong and honest communication your people will create their own information to discuss.

Up Your Business! Bullet	**When you don't mention what is really on people's minds, their focus automatically latches onto what isn't being said.**

---

12. *Demand written goals and strategic plans from each performer, focusing on high-leverage tasks.* Then hold people accountable for
results and keep them moving toward achievement. Where
you begin on your action plan will depend on your individual situation. The important thing is to start. With each victory you gain momentum. Remind people that where they
and their department are is not as important as where they
are headed, and that it will take consistent and successful
execution of the plan to succeed.

13. *Focus on the middle 60 percent.* In every change effort, it is essential to get the influencers — the top 20 percent — on
board first. In most cases, this is the easy part. Your top
people should be tuned in to what needs to be done and
won't need much convincing. Keep in mind that the bottom
20 percent in most organizations is nearly incorrigible.
Thus, very clearly spell out exactly what will be done and
the effort required to pull it off. By avoiding sugarcoating
and happy talk you force the bottom performers to face reality and flush them out more quickly. Once you unearth
their resentment and unwillingness to change, these feelings are easier to deal with. As long as you let the discontent
stay underground you're susceptible to sabotage. Since the
top 20 percent doesn't need much convincing and the bot-

tom can't be convinced, your focus should be on the middle 60 percent. This is where your change efforts are made or broken.

If you're stuck somewhere in the middle of your organization and have a boss who will not get behind a change program, you may be tempted to work around that boss. Don't even think about it, because it will never work. Your job is to go back to step one and find ways to create enough urgency so that the boss clearly sees the problem and gets behind the change effort. You need to find a way to set that person's hair on fire. You may need to get out of the box to get your point across, but the effort will be worth it.

A general sales manager I consulted with was trying to convince the owner that their company needed to change their hiring procedures. Turnover in the sales force had reached unacceptable proportions. The manager wanted to change interviewing procedures. He also felt the predictive competency tests they used missed the mark. The problem was that the owner had a sentimental attachment to the old systems. He pointed out several top people the current system had brought in over the years and declared that there would always be a degree of turnover in any business, so there was no need to change a good thing. The sales manager then had the office manager pull all the W-2's from salespeople who had left the company, either voluntarily or involuntarily, over the past twelve months. To their amazement, there were over 300! They then proceeded to have a like number of metal company name tags made up, each with the name of a departed employee. At their next meeting, the manager carried a bulging pillowcase into the conference room, noisily dumped the 300-plus name tags on the polished conference table, and announced that he'd like to discuss again how to remedy the company's 300 or more personnel failures over the past year. The owner's jaw dropped as he stared at the metal mass grave of failed hires. The point was made. Urgency was created. The boss was on board. The manager moved forward quickly with new interview and testing initiatives.

ENTRENCHED CULTURE

Throughout the process, understand that the greatest challenge to bringing about change is the entrenched culture in your organization. The wrong culture can take you from leader to laggard and create an exhausting struggle to remain relevant. There are patterns of behavior that have been accepted, punished, repeated, and reinforced that make up where you are today, for better or for worse. To overcome the negative impact of these forces you must follow these thirteen steps diligently, and remain consistent and patient. The payoff of transformed culture and improved performance is worth the effort. As much as you may try, you cannot fix, build, or stretch your organization strictly by optimizing. It will take innovation. Change. And to sustain long-term vitality in your business it's imperative that you continue to disturb the equilibrium in your organization.

| Up Your Business! Bullet | **Sustaining intensity, momentum, and progress is one of a leader's greatest challenges.** |

RATTLE THE STATUS QUO

If you'll recall, rattling the status quo was one of the daily disciplines presented in Chapter 5, "Executing Your Leadership

Twelve-Pack." In the life of any organization, merely maintaining or tweaking the status quo precedes decline. In fact, when a business is in a maintenance mode it is less responsive to market changes, lurking competitors, and customer defections. In this state, it is at maximum risk. No person or business is at its best when life is too safe. This is why leaders must stay in attack mode. You must continually change the conversations in your business, evoke fresh ideas, challenge the current process, amplify survival threats, and foster disequilibrium. To get bigger and bolder answers, ask bigger and bolder questions.

You must also be aware that the longer your business is in its comfortable maintenance mode, the less able it is to rally itself in the face of new challenges or to seize new opportunities. The result is a performance rut or plateau that is the beginning of the end of your enterprise.

Even once your business is in attack mode and is filled with intensity and innovation, inattention and inaction will allow the status quo to reestablish itself. Remember, this is nature's course — to drift backward, not forward — which is precisely why taking your business to new levels requires consistent innovation and attention. These components must become ingrained in your mind-set and culture. You may be able to power your way to better results with an occasional adrenaline rush but you'll never sustain success without ongoing intensity, pressure to perform, and innovation. Don't be seduced by the idea that simply doing more of what you're already doing faster and harder will disturb the equilibrium in your organization. The only way you can drive out complacency, collapse comfort zones, and exchange optimization for innovation is when behaviors are changed. If you'll recall, culture will dictate behavior, and to create the right culture you'll need the right people —

which takes us back to where we began our journey in Chapter 1, "Always Remember, It's the People, Stupid!"

THERE IS NO PERFECT TIME

If you're waiting for the perfect time to implement change it will never happen. Depending on what changes you implement, timing is important, but there is no perfect time. If you're waiting for your people to be ready to change, you're dreaming. Most people will never be ready for change. Your job is to get them ready. If they were ready they wouldn't need you or the other leaders in your organization. And don't kid yourself into thinking change won't be awkward. If it's not awkward, it's not change.

We've come full circle, and it's time to look in the mirror again and evaluate what you must personally do to lead your organization up the peak that stands before it. Rest assured you will not ascend to a higher peak by climbing still higher on the peak you're on. It will take a change of direction. You must develop a daily dose of paranoia that someone's out to get you. You must be the catalyst. You must step up and continually ask what can be done to raise the bar, to change the course, to hold others more accountable, to create more focus, to stretch, cajole, and harass. Most important, you must heighten awareness that equilibrium/stability is an enemy and that, although it is natural to drift there, it can only be overcome by deliberate and constant action. Raise the bar so goals cannot be achieved with business as usual. Change the culture and you change behaviors. Change behaviors and you change results. But change quickly and consistently. There is nothing to gain by delay. In fact, the longer you procrastinate the less likely it is you'll ever do anything. As George Cecil observed, "On the plains of hesitation bleach the bones of countless millions who, at the dawn of

262

victory, sat down to wait, and waiting, died."[57] I'll leave you with the words of wisdom concerning procrastination from my friend Zig Ziglar, who nailed it when he said, "Mister, if you're going to have to swallow a frog, you don't want to stare at that sucker too long!" Get busy and good luck! Aim high, dig deep, and you'll finish strong!

Up Your Business! Bullet	**Great companies are always worried.[58] When your memories are greater than your dreams your days are numbered.[59]**

UP YOUR BUSINESS! ACTION THOUGHTS

THIRTEEN STEPS TO OVERCOME "FLAVOR-OF-THE-MONTH" SYNDROME

1. How will you teach the thirteen steps to your team and incorporate them into your change efforts?
2. Are you willing to accept that without the right people, all your strategies and efforts to execute those strategies are for naught?
3. What sectors of your corporate culture will be most resistant to change? How will you overcome the power of this entrenched culture?
4. What will you do over time to consistently stir up the equilibrium in your organization? How can you teach and encourage others to do the same in their areas of responsibility?
5. What centers of gravity will you attack first so your change efforts gain momentum, and what can you do to begin these efforts quickly? When, precisely, will you begin?

FURTHER UP YOUR BUSINESS

DIAGNOSE BEFORE YOU PRESCRIBE!

We've covered a lot of ground in these seven chapters. Before we conclude the book with Chapter 8, it is appropriate that you re-group and ask yourself some pointed questions that will help you determine the health of your organization and what is required to elevate its efficacy to an even higher plain. Some of these are issues we've tackled directly throughout this book and others will raise new questions for you. Read through them in an effort to properly diagnose your current state before moving any further to prescribe solutions.

1. Do you move far enough, fast enough? Regard this Jack Welch confession and learn from it: "I've made my share of mistakes — plenty of them — but my biggest mistake by far was not moving faster. Pulling off an old Band-Aid one hair at a time hurts a lot more than a sudden yank. Of course you want to avoid breaking things or stretching the organization too far — but generally, human nature holds you back. You want to be liked, to be thought of as reasonable. So you don't move as fast as you should. Besides hurting more, it costs you competitiveness."

2. Is your organization flat enough that you can move fast enough? Since information theory tells us that every relay doubles the noise and cuts the message in half, do you have a nimble organization with as few layers as possible involved in decision making — especially with regard to taking care of customer problems?

3. Whether you lead by example is not the right question — do you and your managers lead by the *right* example? For instance, do you tell your receptionist that if so-and-so calls she should tell him you're not in? If so, you're asking the receptionist to lie for you. Do you think that is fair? Too many leaders today habitually and unthinkingly lie in their dealings with customers, vendors, and fellow employees and ask others to lie for them — and then act confused and alarmed when they find that their people do the same thing. Lead by personal example, not personal convenience. This quotation from St. Francis is the best I've ever read on leading by example: "Preach the gospel at all times. If necessary, use words."

4. Since even the largest of enterprises — other than monopolies or the government — rarely have more than 30 percent share of any market and thus have many more noncustomers than they have customers, do you know who your noncustomers are and why they are noncustomers? These people normally comprise at least 70 percent of any market area and cannot be ignored or forgotten about.

5. Do you know when to ask and when to order? To paraphrase Peter Drucker, when a ship is going down the captain doesn't call a meeting, he gives an order. And if the ship is to be saved, everyone must obey the order, know where to go and how to carry it out without participation or argument.

6. Since the cost of customer retention is miniscule compared to the cost of customer acquisition, how much of your advertising budget is designated to retaining current customers?

7. Do you mistake motion for action? Putting a new body in

charge of a failing department is a good start, but the action the new manager takes — or fails to take — will portend more about future results than simply moving people around.

8. What performance metrics or employee behaviors have you deemed nonnegotiable in your business? While it is beneficial to leave many decisions up to the creativity and discretion of your managers, you must designate a handful of key tasks as "my way or the highway" in order to maintain your culture, standards, and corporate identity.

9. Do you carry the club of consequences? Peter the Great — all 6'7" of him — used to carry a club to smack his key people in the head when they moved too slowly in their efforts to help him transform eighteenth-century Russia into a more modern society. You needn't go to such extremes, but you are obligated to establish meaningful consequences for failure to execute the nonnegotiable premises of operations discussed in point 8. Consequences are the "or else" of your business: "execute these behaviors or else"; "hit these numbers or else." There comes a time when begging, pleading, and sweet-talking runs its course and you must bring out the "or else." What is yours and where does it apply?

10. Does your organization have a balance of good entrepreneurship and strong management? An entrepreneur who does not learn to manage will not last long. A manager who does not learn to innovate will not last long either. Don't miss the point here: Management and entrepreneurship are not incompatible; rather, they are different dimensions of the same task.

11. Do you and your leaders spend more time creating change or reacting to it? When is the last time your organization did something for the first time?

12. Do you spend more time pursuing and measuring customer satisfaction or customer loyalty? Do your people even know the difference?

13. Have you found a way to make your key people equity partners in your enterprise? What Aristotle said around 2,400 years ago still holds true today: "Observation shows that men pay most attention to what they own and neglect what is not their own. The sense of possession is natural and brings duty and obligation."

14. Do you really know your people? You must know them to move them and to effectively evaluate them. Read what Thomas Merton wrote nearly fifty years ago: "If you want to identify me, ask me not where I live, or what I like to eat, or how I comb my hair, but ask me what I think I am living for, in detail, and ask me what I think is keeping me from living fully the thing I want to live for. Between these two answers you can determine the identity of any person. The better answer he has, the more of a person he is." Do you ask your people the right questions so you are able to know them, move them, and effectively evaluate them?

15. Do you have too many chiefs for a single "Indian"? One person in an organization should have one "master." There is wisdom to the old Roman law that a slave who has three masters is a free man.

16. Do you invest enough time and resources in your personal strengths and those of your enterprise, or are you spread so thin you excel at little or nothing and spend the majority of your time fixing things and plugging holes?

17. Where do you and your managers spend more time: developing your golf swing or developing your leadership skills?

18. Is your organization saturated with gossip and politics?

There is one key reason this happens: Communication in both your formal meetings and one-on-ones is too selective and one-sided. As a result, people do not feel free to express their opinions or ideas publicly and thus have no choice but to do so in private — behind the boss's back.

19. What did you do yesterday to ensure that today is a masterpiece? What will you do today that ensures tomorrow is one?

20. Which of the previous nineteen questions bothers you the most? Realize that whichever it is probably has the most to teach you.

CHAPTER 8

Close the Gap between Knowing and Doing

Develop the Commitment to Do What Is Easier Said Than Done

After I gave a two-hour leadership presentation, an attendee commented that "what you say is a lot easier said than done." Naturally, I've heard this many times previously, but the defensive tone of his voice made me realize that his assertion was designed to demean, belittle, or minimize the potential effectiveness of what I was suggesting. I then realized that if this intelligent, successful businessperson could be so far off track as to assume that because a task is "easier said than done" its importance is somehow diminished, others like him might believe the same. In fact, these same words may have popped into your mind as you read the strategies in the preceding seven chapters. It would be tragic for you to discard or disregard principles that could transform your business simply because they sound too obvious or ordinary. To create some perspective concerning the absolute necessity of something being "easier said than done" in order to be usable and valuable, consider the follow-

269

ing: If something is not easier said than done, it's not likely to require the discipline, persistence, change, and growth necessary to positively impact your business. Thus, its value is doubtful at best. For instance, the act of showing up at work each day is easily said *and* done, and as a result the vast majority of employees are able to pull this off. It requires minimal effort and a rudimentary level of commitment.

On the other hand, holding people accountable while you're at work is easier said than done. It requires that you set clear expectations, offer fast and honest feedback on performance, and submit yourself to the unpleasant task of inflicting consequences on those failing to deliver the required results. Because it is easier said than done, few managers do this well. But those who develop the discipline and persistence to hold others accountable acquire a significant advantage over the leadership lightweights who fail in this regard. The art of holding others accountable is of immense value in business precisely because it is "easier said than done."

Tolerating poor performers in an organization is an extremely common practice. It is easier on a leader in the short term than having to fire them, replace them, and train new employees. Because of this, bonding with morons, misfits, and moochers is a pervasive practice in most businesses. It is so easily said and done that you see it in the vast majority of organizations.

In contrast, installing minimum performance standards and firing morons, misfits, and moochers when they fail to hit them is easier said than done. First, you have to create, communicate, and put in writing a meaningful standard. Second, you have to follow through and terminate the people who fail to hit the mark. Third, you must become a more proactive recruiter so that you have a pipeline of people in the works to upgrade your roster and replace the dearly departed. Combined, these tasks are a lot of work. They create pain, discomfort, and discipline. These things are certainly easier said than done, but because they are their value is immense, and the return on your time in this regard would be substantial.

You can probably think of many other tasks in business and in life that are easier said than done and that bring an immense return precisely because they are: quitting smoking, eating healthier, exercising twenty minutes per day, loving your enemies, listening to or reading ten minutes of inspirational material in the morning, investing ten minutes in planning tomorrow before you go home tonight, holding one sixty-minute training meeting per week, making three prospecting calls per day — the list could go on for pages. The tasks listed are valuable because they require discipline, persistence, change, and growth. They are basic tasks that are within reach. You can get your hands around them and begin implementing them without fancy formulas or rocket-science calculus. And it is the fact that they are doable, simple, and within reach that exponentially multiplies their power. It should encourage you that you don't have to do anything extraordinary to change the complexion of your business or your life. But at the same time you should realize that what is basic is not necessarily easy, because you will need to do the ordinary things extraordinarily well and do them day in and day out.

So the next time a book, a teacher, a preacher, or a speaker suggests something that sounds "easier said than done," it should get your attention and pump you up with possibilities. The fact that you don't need academic formulas or complex equations to improve your business ought to uplift you, encourage you, and motivate you. Besides, would you rather they suggest something that intimidates you with its complexity, dazzles you with its degree of difficulty, or demoralizes you with its demands? Of course not! The fact that they are usually telling you something that you already know is beside the point. Knowing is not normally the problem. *Doing* is the problem, and the more you are nudged, cajoled, harassed, and reminded that you should be doing what you know the more likely you are to actually do it. Without a doubt, the biggest gap in business and life is the gap between knowing and doing. Take losing weight, for instance. I'm always amused by the number of books, courses, and highly paid gurus that turn huge profits by telling people how to lose weight. However, knowing is not the problem when it comes to losing weight. Most people know darned well what they must do in order to shed the pounds. It's the doing it that's a bit inconvenient! To get anywhere in business or in life you've got to work at closing this pervasive gap, and there are two keys to pulling this off: decisions and discipline. Decisions get you started, and discipline helps you finish. Think of it as goal setting and goal getting.

I'm not ashamed to admit that I've made a small fortune over the years telling people what they already know through books, speeches, and seminars. People in my profession create value by presenting common knowledge in a way that makes sense, that encourages action, and that strips away excuses for inaction while it inspires, motivates, or irritates — whatever it takes to move the listener into motion. I want to thank you for paying the twenty-five or so bucks you dished out for this book so that I could tell you what you mostly knew in the first place. But my hope is that the words in these pages have acted as a catalyst to move you toward what you knew you should have been doing all along.

Would you like to reach the next performance level in your business over the next ninety days? Then sit down with your management team and pinpoint the five highest-impact tasks from this book that will most significantly elevate your team's performance, and then commit to executing them on a day-in and day-out basis, without fail and regardless of the cost. This one discipline will be the catalyst to an incredible climb for your business during the next quarter. "Easier said than done" you say? You had better hope so.

Are You Interested in or Truly Committed to Taking Your Business to the Next Level?

This question is not rhetorical. Before you answer in haste, give some thought to the following story.

In a *Wall Street Journal* interview I was asked my opinion of the difference between good companies and those that hit the big time, the elite. I responded that I believed the gap separating the two could be explained by the difference between interest and commitment. When asked to elaborate I explained that good companies are interested in getting to the next level. They talk big about training their people, improving their hiring practices, setting higher standards, holding others more accountable, and creating the painful change necessary for sustainable growth. But because these companies are merely *interested* in these things they do them only when they're convenient — on the good days, when it is easy, cheap, popular, and convenient.

"Interested" business leaders talk the talk but don't walk the walk necessary to substantially improve their operations. Frankly, many of these folks are fortunate to be working in industries and countries strong enough that they can make money in spite of themselves. I've spent far too many frustrating hours in front of these types of audiences, who hire me to teach their team and who talk big while I'm in the room but never follow through on their commitments to elevate their organizations after I'm gone.

In comparison, there is no greater return for a speaker than to spend time with those truly committed to getting better, and every once in a while I get lucky enough to speak before a great group that quickly diminishes the memory of pretenders I've encountered from Podunk to Palm Springs. Committed companies are filled with leaders that train consistently, hire slower, fire faster, set higher standards, tighten up accountability, and change before they have to — day in, day out, without excuse and regardless of the cost. In other words, they are willing to pay the price necessary to rise above the crowd of average masses in their field and join the ranks of the elite. For leaders like this who are truly committed to getting better and building a better people I'll occasionally fly halfway around the world and work for free — and pay my own expenses for the privilege. In fact, I do so three weeks per year on mission trips, and my most recent class taught me more about the true meaning of commitment than any other.

As many of my friends are aware, I volunteer three weeks per year to train leaders in hostile parts of the world through author John Maxwell's nonprofit organization, EQUIP. My territories are Moscow and Iran. EQUIP teams up a business leader and a church leader and sends them to an area six times in a three-year period to teach a multiphase leadership course to Christian pastors. I've taught hundreds of leaders in Moscow in recent years, and in 2005 I trained a group of 100 Persian leaders from Iran. However, we couldn't conduct the training in Iran or we would have been arrested, since pastors attending our meeting could have been accused of learning techniques to evangelize, which is prohibited by Iranian law. Thus, we held the conference in a different country. The Iranian pastors in my class left Tehran and other Iranian cities to attend this conference knowing full well they could be detained, questioned, and possibly arrested upon their return to Iran for doing so. But they came anyway.

It was a grueling week of nearly all-day teaching. When the Q&A session started after a presentation, it would go on for two or three hours. I've never met people anywhere in the world so hungry to learn about leadership and get better at what they did, or more committed to building their organizations. When I returned home to Los Angeles I got an e-mail from the conference coordinator confirming that, indeed, some of the attendees had already been arrested and others detained for attending our conference. This somber realization taught me a greater lesson about commitment than any book, speaker, or course: Commitment means that you are willing to grow personally and organizationally regardless of the cost. And it's those last four words that stop most leaders in their tracks and relegate them to pitiable windbags and wimps who routinely talk right and then walk left.

Perhaps this explains why I stress the importance of personal growth so much in Chapter 6, "Survive Success: How to Overcome the Six Temptations of Successful Organizations." After seeing firsthand the commitment of these leaders to improve themselves I've become quite intolerant of spoiled whiners in the Western world who won't walk across the street and into a library to check out a book that is free in order to improve their state in life. The very people who tell me they don't have time to read books or attend seminars are the same folks who can tell you who is left on *Survivor*, who got voted off of *American Idol*, and what type of bugs were eaten on *Fear Factor*; who can recite all the highlights from the ball game the night before; and who have time to smoke cartons of cigarettes and drink cases of beer. They have time to kill themselves and amuse themselves but no time to improve themselves. And then they have the gall to declare themselves as committed to growing their organization. Impostors! Pretenders! Pathetic!

Incidentally, paying the price to grow personally and organizationally isn't a onetime payment. It is an installment plan with a starting point but no finish line. Commitment shows up more in your actions than in your words. In fact, when you are truly committed you won't have to tell a soul; they'll quickly figure it out by watching you. Following are just some of the ways commitment shows up in an organization. Many of these I've discussed in this book, but that's not the point. The point is whether you are doing them.

1. You hold your weekly training meeting even when you're shorthanded, even when it isn't convenient, even when it's the last week of the month.
2. You don't hire the questionable candidate even when you lack coverage, even when you'll have to personally work more hours to pick up the slack.
3. You hold accountable the superstar who abuses your values. You don't sell out the rest of your team or culture for the sake of "the numbers."
4. You find a reason why you can attend the off-site training course rather than looking for reasons at the last minute to explain why it's inconvenient.
5. You continue to plant seeds with employment prospects you meet and recruit for the future growth of your business even when you seem all filled up at the moment.
6. You shun tradition and sentimentalism and fire the long-term manager who has stopped performing and is stifling the growth of your people.
7. You have the courage to set and enforce performance and behavioral standards even when you know holding others accountable for these benchmarks will never be easy, cheap, popular, or convenient.

8. You turn off the television or foul-mouthed disc jockey often enough to read at least one book per month in your field so that you can upgrade your own skill capacity and bring something new and fresh to the table for the benefit of those who call you their leader.

9. You get out of your office and go help make the deal even when you're busy with paperwork, preoccupied with personal problems, or just plain exhausted.

10. You get your managers together at least once per month to train them on being better leaders, not just to go over budgets, forecasts, and marketing. This includes those who think they know it all and are constipated by a been-there-done-that attitude.

To better determine the price you or an employee has been unwilling to pay for greater results, ask this question whenever someone falls short of delivering what they promised: "What weren't you willing to do to make it happen?" You ask this question not to beat them up but to get them to look in the mirror and determine what they weren't prepared to sacrifice to get results. When employees fall short of their potential there is a price they were unwilling to pay to reach it, and your job as a leader is to help uncover it. In fact, you'd be well advised to ask yourself this question whenever you fall short of what you aspire to. It's a not-so-gentle reminder that in order to continue to grow you'll need to continually make sacrifices. You can rest assured that you will stop growing personally and organizationally whenever the price gets too high, when you're no longer willing to devote yourself to the diligent daily disciplines necessary for growth. My guess is that some of you are stuck at this point right now and need to step it up and work harder for the prize you're chasing. I suggest you start right away, because you can pay now and play later, or you can play now and pay later, but either way you will pay. The problem with waiting to pay is that, since time is money, the price will be higher later — because you'll be paying with interest. This being said, haven't you droned on long enough about getting better? Isn't it time to put up or shut up, to let your walk speak louder than your talk? If the answer is "yes" you needn't say a thing. Just get moving.

Notes

CHAPTER 1

1. Jim Collins, *Good to Great* (New York: Harper Collins, 2001), 25.
2. Ibid., 45.
3. Ibid.
4. Ibid.
5. Ibid., 25.
6. Lou Adler, *Hire with Your Head* (Hoboken, NJ: John Wiley & Sons, 1998), 252. Used by permission of John Wiley & Sons.
7. Author interview with Myles Dolan in East Hanover, New Jersey, 23 October 2002.
8. Herb Greenberg, Harold Weinstein, and Patrick Sweeney, *How to Hire and Develop Your Next Top Performer* (New York: McGraw Hill, 2001), 241.
9. Ibid., 9.
10. Jon Katzenbach, *Peak Performance* (Boston: Harvard Business Press, 2000), 222.
11. Four Seasons Hotel, Chicago, 8–10 April 2002.

CHAPTER 2

12. Judith Bardwich, *Danger in the Comfort Zone* (New York: AMACOM, 1995), 11.

CHAPTER 3

13. John C. Maxwell, *The 21 Irrefutable Laws of Leadership* (Nashville, TN: Thomas Nelson, 1998), 109.
14. Donald T. Phillips, *Lincoln on Leadership* (New York: Warner Books, 1992), 131.
15. Ibid., 114.
16. Al Kaltman, *Cigars, Whiskey & Winning: Leadership Lessons from General Ulysses S. Grant* (Paramus, NJ: Prentice Hall, 1998), 8.
17. Oren Harari, *Leadership Secrets of Colin Powell* (New York: McGraw Hill, 2002), 172.

CHAPTER 4

18. Robert Slater, *Jack Welch and the G.E. Way* (New York: McGraw Hill, 1999), 166.
19. John A. Warden III and Leland Russell, *Winning in Fast Time* (Newport Beach, CA: Geo Group Press, 2001), 44.
20. Oren Harari, *Executive Excellence Magazine: Powell Leadership Principles* (Venice, FL: Mill Pond, 2002), 3.

21. Alan Axelrod, *Patton on Leadership* (Paramus, NJ: Prentice Hall, 1999), 126.
22. Warden and Russell, *Winning in Fast Time*, 55.

CHAPTER 5

23. Slater, *Jack Welch and the G.E. Way*, 38.
24. Jim Rohn, *The Treasury of Quotes* (Deerfield Beach, FL: Health Communications, 1996), 98.
25. Roger Dow and Susan Cook, *Turned On* (New York: Harper Collins, 1996), 96.
26. Author visit with John Maxwell, Atlanta, Georgia, 3 October 2002.
27. Axelrod, *Patton on Leadership*, 33.
28. Steven Hayward, *Churchill on Leadership* (Rocklin, CA: Prima, 1997), 115.
29. Ibid., 29.
30. Gary George, *Winning Is a Habit* (New York: Harper Collins, 1997), 33.

CHAPTER 6

31. Rohn, *Treasury of Quotes*, 91.
32. Axelrod, *Patton on Leadership*, 65.
33. Ibid., 34.
34. Phillips, *Lincoln on Leadership*, 13.
35. Ibid., 70, 126–127.
36. Ibid., 134.
37. Andrew Grove, *Only the Paranoid Survive* (New York: Doubleday, 1996), 152.
38. Chicago, 8–10 April.
39. Vince Lombardi Jr., *What It Takes to Be #1* (New York: McGraw Hill, 2001), 3.
40. Ibid., 146.
41. Ibid., 3.
42. Ibid.
43. Ibid., 201.
44. Ibid., 146.
45. Ibid., 236.
46. Ibid., 137.
47. Ibid., 231.
48. Ibid., 209.
49. George, *Winning Is a Habit*, 78.
50. Lombardi, *What It Takes to Be #1*, 210.
51. Ibid., 137.
52. Ibid.
53. John C. Maxwell, *The Maxwell Leadership Bible* (Nashville, TN: Thomas Nelson, 2002), 1186. Based on Matthew 25:14–30.
54. Dow and Cook, *Turned On*, 35.
55. Brian Tracy, *Victory* (New York: AMACOM, 2002), 221.

CHAPTER 7

56. Gary Hamel, *Leading the Revolution*, rev. ed. (New York: Penguin Group, 2002), 250.
57. Tracy, *Victory*, 280.
58. Michael Hammer, *The Agenda* (New York: Crown, 2001), 261.
59. Ibid., 263.

Bibliography

Adler, Lou. *Hire with Your Head*. Hoboken, NJ: John Wiley & Sons, 1998.

Axelrod, Alan. *Patton on Leadership*. Paramus, NJ: Prentice Hall, 1999.

Bardwich, Judith. *Danger in the Comfort Zone*. New York: AMACOM, 1995.

Collins, Jim. *Good to Great*. New York: Harper Collins, 2001.

Dow, Roger, and Susan Cook. *Turned On*. New York: Harper Collins, 1996.

George, Gary. *Winning Is a Habit*. New York: Harper Collins, 1997.

Greenberg, Herbert, Harold Weinstein, and Patrick Sweeney. *How to Hire and Develop Your Next Top Performer*. New York: McGraw Hill, 2001.

Grove, Andrew. *Only the Paranoid Survive*. New York: Doubleday, 1996.

Hamel, Gary. *Leading the Revolution*. Rev. ed. New York: Penguin Group, 2002.

Hammer, Michael. *The Agenda*. New York: Crown Publishing, 2001.

Harari, Oren. Executive Excellence Magazine. Venice, FL: Mill Pond Press, 2002.

———. *Leadership Secrets of Colin Powell*. New York: McGraw Hill, 2002.

Hayward, Steven F. *Churchill on Leadership*. Rocklin, CA: Prima, 1997.

Kaltman, Al. *Cigars, Whiskey & Winning: Leadership Lessons from General Ulysses S. Grant*. Paramus, NJ: Prentice Hall, 1998.

Katzenbach, Jon. *Peak Performance*. Boston: Harvard Business Press, 2000.

Lewis, C. S. *Mere Christianity*. New York: Harper Collins, 1952.

Lombardi, Vince, Jr. *What It Takes to Be #1*. New York: McGraw Hill, 2001.

Maxwell, John. C. *The 21 Irrefutable Laws of Leadership*. Nashville, TN: Thomas Nelson, 1998.

———. *The Maxwell Leadership Bible*. Nashville, TN: Thomas Nelson, 2002.

Peoples, David. *Presentations Plus*. Hoboken, NJ: John Wiley & Sons, 1992.

BIBLIOGRAPHY

Phillips, Donald T. *Lincoln on Leadership*. New York: Warner, 1992.

Rohn, Jim. *The Treasury of Quotes*. Deerfield Beach, FL: Health Communications, Inc., 1996.

Slater, Robert. *Jack Welch and the G.E. Way*. New York: McGraw Hill, 1999.

Stanley, Andy. *Visioneering*. Sisters, OR: Multnomah, 1999.

Tracy, Brian. *Victory*. New York: AMACOM, 2002.

Index

Index

poor performance and, 35–36

presentation skills (*see* Leadership, and presentation skills)

See also Coaching; Job descriptions; Mentoring

Transfers, poor performance and, 36. *See also* Performance; Reinforcement

Twain, Mark, 84

United States Department of Agriculture (USDA), 173

Values, core. *See* Core values

Vietnam War, 144

Wander-arounds, 175–177

Warden, John, 147

Web sites. *See* Job applicants, finding

Welch, Jack, 44–45, 131–132, 161, 220, 264

Welfare, government. *See* Entitlement, culture of

Winning in Fast Times (Warden), 147

Ziglar, Zig, 170–171, 263

Acknowledgments

Many thanks to my wife, Rhonda, who runs our business, covers my back, and keeps it all together as I jet around the world acting like I have a real job. Thanks also to the outstanding support staff and work partners in our California, Texas, and Virginia offices. You're my very own dream team.

The idea for the revised edition of *Up Your Business!* was not my own. Thanks to editor Matt Holt for suggesting we take a good thing and make it even better.

About the Author

Dave Anderson is president of LearnToLead, an international sales and leadership training organization. Dave has authored six books, including the Wiley titles *If You Don't Make Waves You'll Drown* and *How to Deal with Difficult Customers.* He gives over 100 seminars and keynote speeches internationally each year and writes leadership columns for two national magazines. His web site, www.learntolead .com, has tens of thousands of subscribers in forty countries who enjoy an archive of over 400 free training articles. To inquire about having Dave speak to your group contact his office in Agoura Hills, California, at 800-519-8224 or 818-735-9503 (international). Dave is a member of the National Speakers Association.